engaging resistance

Creating Partnerships for Change in Sexual Offender Treatment

D1086877

Charles A. Flinton, PhD
Robert Scholz, MA

Contents

Preface

In social settings, a sexual offender treatment provider is often asked, "Why do you work with sexual offenders?" This question is usually asked with a mixture of novelty, apprehension, and dismay and is often followed by, "You don't have to tell me if you don't want to." I have concluded this postscript is meant to protect me from exposing some horrible fact about myself (which must exist if I choose to work with sexual offenders). In addition, it protects the questioner from facing the dark reality that sexual offenders really do exist. They are not simply characters in a sensationalized news story about inhuman monsters that troll the streets searching for prey. The fascination and repulsion matrix that stimulates one's interest in sexual offenders often reflects ambivalence toward an in-depth exploration of the causes of sexual abuse and its interventions. While sexual offending makes great fodder for headline news as something that happens "out there," most people do not want to acknowledge how close the issue is to their own lives. Consequently, it is much easier for people to isolate the sexual offender and view him not as a part of society, but as an anomaly to the human race. Few realize just how frequently sexual offenses occur and how many sexual offenders there are.

As of December 31, 2003, the California Department of Justice reported 99,470 sexual offenders registered in California; 69,438 living in the community and 16,771 incarcerated[1] (Attorney General of the State of California, 2004). According to the California Current Population Survey (2005) approximately 12.7 million adult males live in California, indicating that approximately one of every 147 adult males living in California is a registered sexual offender.

---

[1] 1,969 registrants were deported and 11,292 live out of state.

Another interesting statistic is that 19 of every 20 rapists are never convicted (www.RAIN.org), and as most of us know, all types of sexual offenses go undetected. Therefore, the actual number of sexual offenses is much higher than statistics indicate. Nevertheless, society resists the truth that sexual offenders are not "out there" but rather living next door to us, riding the bus with us, and driving it.

Little doubt remains regarding societal reluctance to take a hard, reality-based look at the causes of sexual offending and particularly prevention strategies. This book is not intended to take on the complex dynamics that feed public denial. Instead, it is intended to help those who work with offenders (therapists, probation/parole officers, lawyers, and judges) consider and change the manner in which society, the criminal justice system, treatment providers, and the offender create obstacles to effective, sustainable intervention. Throughout this book those individuals who work with offenders will be referred to as "change agents."

The best way to reduce the likelihood that an offender will reoffend is to address the issue of recidivism in a systemic fashion. The roots of sound sexual offender treatment can be traced to fundamental behaviorism, and interventions are most successful when they immediately follow the behavior that is targeted for change. Unfortunately, many offenders do not have the opportunity to enter a therapeutic environment until years after their offense. Instead, they are often caught up in a punishment model that emphasizes external restraint without acknowledging the additional need for personal change. Our position is that therapeutic change does not necessarily have to wait for the structured environment of a treatment program. The first person who has contact with an offender can be empowered to make appropriate interventions that can encourage change. In most cases, this is an attorney or judge who can direct offenders to the appropriate treatment resources. Too frequently, however, offender change and insight are overshadowed by the game of "he said/she said" or other legal maneuvering that further distances the offender from truth, accountability, and change. In the context of uncovering obstacles to offender change, we will explore the differences between a "punishment-focused" approach and a "containment/management-focused" approach.

In psychotherapeutic language, obstacles to change are traditionally referred to as "resistance." Resistance is generally viewed as a defense, a protective reaction to a threat that is intended to ward off negative feelings such as vulnerability, anxiety, shame, and guilt. Freud (1953) defined resistance as "whatever interrupts the process of analytic work." In later years, he and others (Strean, 1985) began to acknowledge that resistance is not something that simply creates obstacles to therapeutic change, but is an essential element of the change process. The ability to tolerate negative emotions, while maintaining conscious awareness of one's thoughts and control of one's urges, will facilitate insight and, ideally, long-term behavior change.

More than most therapeutic populations, sexual offenders are viewed as resistant to accountability and change. Psychologists see this acted out most commonly during the course of psychotherapy. We are acutely aware that most offenders enter treatment because they are mandated to do so and would never choose to be there if given the option. As a result, most treatment providers at some point encounter overt obstacles to treatment, such as missed appointments, verbal insults, silence, etc. Resistance, acted out in these explicit forms, often facilitates therapist frustration and the determination that the offender cannot be treated. However, resistance is not always this obvious. Sometimes topics that invoke negative emotions are avoided through politeness, lying, or a penchant for superficial discussion during therapy. In some cases, an offender's resistance will clearly preclude him from benefiting from treatment. However, understanding all of the factors that contribute to resistance can, in fact, shift the tide from impasse to transformation.

The task of the treatment provider is to identify how an offender "resists" awareness, accountability, and change through resisting the therapeutic process. For others in the criminal justice system, an offender's lack of cooperation might be viewed and dealt with in different ways. Yet, some of the ways in which an offender is handled by society, the criminal justice system, and many treatment providers only intensify rigidity and push offenders into entrenched positions where behavior change, accountability, and victim awareness are never attained. Consequently, the goal of managing offender behavior is undermined by a stern intent to punish. As a result, what they resist persists.

In order to overcome resistance, each part of the system needs to examine the offender and his resistance. This process also requires an inquiry into the ways that society, the criminal justice system, the treatment provider, and the offender increase resistance, and what each person who has contact with the offender needs to do to maximize change and increase the likelihood that the offender will not victimize others.

Society and the Criminal Justice System

Both the criminal justice system and society as a whole treat sexual offenders differently from offenders of other serious violent crimes (e.g., domestic violence). Sexual offenders are treated differently because of the general public's beliefs about sex and sexual crime. Many decisions regarding how sexual offenders should be managed in the criminal justice system are driven by society's increasing attentiveness to sex crimes, recidivism, victim impact, and assumptions about the causes of sexual offending (Berliner, 1998). This may be problematic because, as some authors have suggested, there is societal confusion regarding recidivism and severity (Grubin & Wingate, 1996). For example, in response to the public's concern regarding perceived dangerousness, many states have created legislation to limit where offenders live and how the community is notified regarding their whereabouts. Much of this legislation targets all sexual offenders, not necessarily those at the greatest risk of reoffending. In addition, despite public perception that all sexual offenders represent a high recidivism risk, the fact is that sexual offenders reoffend at the relatively low level of 13.4% (Hanson & Bussiére, 1998).

This is not to say that a sexual offense is not appalling or shocking; however, the intensity of such shock often contributes to a myopic perception that society does not produce sexual offenders but rather offenders are sole actors, beyond the influence of society. This phenomenon is explained by attribution theory, which tells us that people are far more likely to attribute negative behaviors, such as criminal activity, to the person rather than the environment. This tendency to underestimate the role of situational factors in the explanation of the behavior of others is called the "fundamental attribution error" (Ross, 1977). It is a key concept in understanding how people gauge offenders and make judgments about the root causes of antisocial behavior and future recidivism. In other words, people tend to seek out and recall information that confirms existing stereotypes more readily than they give attention to other available evidence.

Research has shown that very diverse groups of people hold stereotypical beliefs about criminals, partly because offenders are easily stereotyped as a socially unacceptable out-group (Roberts & White, 1986). Sexual offenders are no exception to this rule. In fact, the judgments that such offenders receive may be an extreme form of stereotypical thinking. It has long been assumed that our beliefs about crime and its causes will affect our decisions about how criminals should be treated (Cullen, Clark, Cullen, & Mathers, 1985). Stereotypical thinking, or an over-reliance on preconceived notions about the motives or characteristics of criminal perpetrators, affects our encounters with others (Filkins, 1997; Stalans, 1993). For example, the effect of criminal stereotypes on our informational and decision-making processes has been demonstrated in studies of verdicts and sentencing decisions of mock juries. These inquiries have demonstrated that public support for various criminal justice policies are informed by misperceptions that criminal behavior is stable and due to actor disposition (Bodenhausen, 1988). People who attribute crime to causes in the environment tend to favor rehabilitation while those who look toward individual causes tend to support punishment more readily. This dichotomy of attitudes has held up among samples of law students, criminology students, and probation officers (Cullen et al.). In conclusion, societal preconception and stereotypes are often used to inform and influence criminal justice decisions. At various points throughout this book, we will examine the role of preconceptions and stereotypes as well as consequences and the need to educate the public in regard to offender management, containment, and change.

Few studies accurately explore and identify the attitudes among police, psychologists, probation officers, correctional officers, etc.

in regard to sexual offenders (Lea, Auburn, & Kibblewhite, 1999). After surveying various professionals, Lea et al. found that professional attitudes lie somewhere on a continuum from highly positive to highly negative, with most expressing attitudes on both sides of the continuum. Predetermined and rigid beliefs regarding sexual offenders are usually at odds with known factors that contribute to recidivism. For example, Hanson and Slater (1993) found that significantly harsher sentences are meted out to offenders who claim, "I can do what I want; the law is wrong" in contrast to those who attribute their behavior to delusional beliefs or their own childhood abuse. Although it seems intuitive that an offender's ability to demonstrate some psychological insight may mean that he is at lower risk for recidivism, the research does not identify this factor as related to actual recidivism.

Our work with offenders also informs us that within the prison environment, both prison staff and prisoners can develop many negative attitudes toward this population. Few would argue that sexual offenders are marginalized and given "outcast" status more than any other type of inmate. As a consequence, many offenders feel forced to conceal their offense history for fear of physical and social retribution. Sexual offenders are at particular risk of being subjected to extortion, beating, rape, humiliation, and even killing (Polermo, 2005). Ireland (2004) found that next to a general ability to defend oneself, the characteristic of being convicted of a specific offense (e.g., sexual offending) predisposed prison inmates to being the target of bullying.

Many offenders express, in different ways, that a system that repeatedly brutalizes them decreases their willingness to acknowledge accountability. An individual at risk of losing his life in the process of being accountable is likely to lash out and resist anyone who encourages accountability. In later chapters, we will discuss the consequences of this system and then explore how the risk potential if sexual offenders is influenced by system policy and practices.

Probation/Parole Officers, Treatment Providers, and Other Agents of Change

Though not a popularly accepted notion in the sexual offender treatment and management community, some experienced and highly trained forensic professionals hold views of sexual offenders that are inaccurate and unnecessarily negative. Some professionals respond to sexual offenders differently from how they respond to other types of criminal offenders and make efforts to keep them at a distance. As a consequence sexual offenders are often viewed only through a nomothetical lens that ignores individual needs or differences. In a survey of prison staff, Weekes, Pelletier, and Beaudette (1995) found that staff tended to fall into one of two camps (those who held positive views of offenders and those who did not). Prison officers who were not involved in sexual offender treatment tended to hold significantly more negative attitudes toward sexual offenders than prison officers who were involved in sexual offender treatment. Those with negative attitudes maintained that sexual offenders were more dangerous, harmful, violent, tense, immoral, unpredictable, mysterious, unchangeable, aggressive, weak, irrational, and afraid than other types of offenders. In addition, sexual offenders who committed crimes against children were considered as more immoral and mentally ill than those who committed crimes against women. Sexual offenders were also judged to be more immoral and mentally ill than other types of offenders. Only a small number (20.7%) of this group believed that sexual offenders were able to benefit from treatment.

Many factors can potentially influence our thoughts, feelings, and perceptions of sexual offenders. Personal experience, stress, work environment, social influences, and the media are just a few examples. Craig (2005) stressed the importance of adequate training in order to minimize negative and false attitudes toward sexual offenders. Weekes et al. (1995) found that older, more experienced correctional officers working with sexual offenders reported significantly more job stress than younger, less experienced officers in similar placements. Job burnout and stress are of particular concern for change agents working with sexual offenders (Shelby, Stoddard, & Taylor, 2001; English, 2005), and evaluating the impact that these types of experiences have on change agent attitudes is important for each person taking on the task of working with this population.

The importance of such an evaluation is crucial to sexual offender work. Gabor (1994) observed, "Factually incorrect and rigid views of criminals, if held by many, can lead us seriously astray in our attempts both to understand crime and to control it." Clearly, as much attention needs to be given to the change agent as to the offender. There is a need for accountability within the change agent system. We offer suggestions aimed toward facilitating ongoing self-assessment that can direct educational efforts to develop accurate pictures of criminal behavior that can, in turn, inform crime control strategies. Any educational effort should include an acknowledgment that some of the offender's resistance to participate in sexual offender treatment is facilitated by the change agent's own attitudes and beliefs about the offender. This is consistent with Blanchard's (1998) perspective that there are no resistant offenders, but rather therapists who do not know how to connect. Although Blanchard's statement may be somewhat extreme, it does counter the often-implied false perception that resistance only exists within the offender, and it challenges us to examine the who, what, when, and where of resistance. We assert that resistance occurs in a context and is a product of many factors. Therefore, it must be examined in order to make treatment pertinent to a number of dynamics that affect the change process.

Granted, working with perpetrators of sexual violence is exceptionally stressful and demanding, both personally and professionally. The stress of working in an environment that is sometimes judged to be unproductive and useless by outsiders, as well as by many in the criminal justice sector, can affect the behavior of even the most experienced and best-trained professionals (Edmunds, 1988; McGowan, 2003). How we handle our own work-related challenges and stress can inadvertently fuel the shame-based dynamic of the sexual offender and increase the rate of sexual recidivism, rather than decrease it. We strongly insist that sexual offender change agents be well informed in regard to specific sexual offender characteristics without losing sight of the role that they have in changing, and sometimes entrenching, offenders in those characteristics. Further on we will focus on identifying how offenders change, based on Prochaska, DiClemente, and Norcross' Trans-theoretical Model of Change (1992).

Taken in total, the research discussed shows that how we, as professionals, act and think can and does make a difference. If we choose to frame offenders in pejorative ways, then such perceptions may become self-fulfilling prophecies. In other words, we can create the very resistance that we do not want to deal with if we send negative meta-communications to our offenders. Unfortunately, negative societal perceptions of sexual offenders can lead to a "get tough" attitude, resulting in the widely held but erroneous belief that punishment reduces recidivism. In addition, a culture has been created that leads to an "us versus them" mentality and adversarial relationships. In contrast, if collaborative relationships with offenders can be developed, change agents may be more willing and able to investigate how different professional stances influence outcome and how resistance may be more effectively addressed at varying stages in the change process. Such collaboration will likely increase motivation to change on the offender's part. This is important because change is best elicited from individuals rather than being imposed upon them.

Viewing sexual offenders from a punishment-and-control perspective precludes looking at other dimensions of sexual violence (e.g., desire for healthy sexuality and relationships built on respect and caring; shame-based aspects of powerlessness; men's fears of each other; atonement and the desire for restorative justice). Some professionals also fail to acknowledge the complexity of the offender's social and psychological lives. Jenkins (1998) illustrated a more comprehensive perspective when he stated, "Most of the men I see are not wanting relationships in which they abuse those whom they love. I believe that their preferred ways of being and relating are respectful and equitable, despite their disrespectful practices" (p. 120). The tendency to think in dichotomous ways affects the very constructs of our thinking and the ways in which we act.

The Offender

The focus of this book is to look at all aspects of the change process and its obstacles. Understandably, most of the literature on offender treatment has focused on the offender and not the system as a whole. The shift toward an evaluation of the change agent is crucial as long as the problems that are found among change agents are not interpreted as blaming them for the failures of some offenders. Our contention is that many of the obstacles that impede successful treatment, which were once perceived as the "offender's problem," can be overcome by changing the change agents. This is not to say that the psychological make-up of some offenders might inhibit effective treatment and reflect problems that are frankly untreatable. For example, offenders with severe mental disorders will pose unique challenges for under-equipped facilities. Similarly, offenders who pose a risk to staff safety should be excluded from treatment where security measures are inadequate.

Debate also continues regarding the efficacy of treatment for individuals with psychopathic traits. Many view these offenders as untreatable because their emotional detachment prevents them from establishing a strong, genuine alliance with a therapist. Other psychopathic traits, such as a tendency to be manipulative, a propensity for lying, and eschewing all manner of responsibility precludes treatment (Henry, Strupp, Schacht, & Gaston, 1994). However, our own experience, as well as the literature of Marshall, Thornton, Marshall, Fernandez, and Mann (2001), Skeem, Monahan, and Mulvey (2002), and Dolan and Coid (1993), indicate that treatment may be appropriate for even the most difficult offenders if effective plans have been developed and the offender has been thoroughly evaluated. In any event, each program should take steps to evaluate their policies in regard to accepting individuals into their programs who do not accept responsibility, pose a safety risk, or are simply noncompliant with treatment. Without proper evaluation, many offenders are too quickly deemed untreatable because they appear hostile or uncooperative. We will review the psychological characteristics of offenders and assist in distinguishing between those characteristics that might exclude an offender from treatment and those characteristics that appear problematic but could also be framed as resistance that is amenable to treatment. This book will also address some of the personality disorders that we commonly see, along with the features that contribute to resistance.

Aside from the offenders with overt personality disorders, many offenders enter treatment with an assortment of schematic thoughts, beliefs, or coping strategies that increase resistance. Offenders commonly believe treatment is not effective or is not focused on broader life issues, or treatment may remind them of the stigma of being labeled a sexual offender or of the loss of status with peers. Offenders may also have competing theories of change (e.g., psychotherapy does not work, but they have willpower, or will rely on God, etc.). Although there is sparse empirical support, many sexual offenders appear to hold central beliefs (or cognitive distortions) that contribute to both their offending and their ability to participate in a process of change. Such beliefs include sexual entitlement, control, self-blame, externalized blame, suspiciousness, worthlessness, and shame (Bumby, 1996; Ward, Keenan, & Hudson, 2000).

Many offenders struggle with feelings related to the loss of personal choice and control. They feel pressured into admitting their offense. Even if they are willing to disclose on some level, they refuse to cooperate because they feel forced to disclose. If an offender feels powerless, he is less likely to be truthful and benefit from the program. It is important to remind oneself that these manifestations of resistance are defensive coping styles that keep the offender stuck in denial and non-participation, and prevent him from moving forward in treatment.

Moving Forward

A multi-dimensional theoretical model that assesses the factors that increase resistance among society, professionals, and offenders is crucial if the ultimate goal is to reduce recidivism and possibly prevent sexual abuse. Our hope is that this book may better equip forensic professionals to evaluate the offenders with whom they work as well as engage in effective self-evaluation, which may include the following questions:

■ At which stage of change is this individual?

How am I matching my interventions to this specific stage of change?

Do I confront my offenders in a way that teaches, or am I reinforcing old stereotypical beliefs that offenders have about others?

How do I know if my beliefs about sexual offenders are accurate?

What are my stumbling blocks to doing the work?

Am I positively contributing to an environment where offenders can change?

Do I need to change my approach to working with sexual offenders?

Most sexual offenders, like all human beings, need attachments. If we are resistant to developing positive relationships with offenders, and are unwilling to make room for them to be positive, prosocial people, we will play a role in keeping them entrenched in resistance, and ultimately stuck in a cycle of offending. Additionally, we must be willing to develop and maintain our partnerships with other change agents in order to enhance our ability to instill long-term changes in offender behavior. This book discusses existing partnerships for change, highlights various models, and provides recommendations to facilitate collaboration with other professionals and those representing the victim's perspective. Efforts must also be made to incorporate those most likely to assist and maintain change, such as family members and the community at large. In order to create and maintain an agency of change that is collaborative and proactive, paradigms that promote growth and communication must be developed. Organizations that consistently evaluate and adapt effective strategies promote offender and systemic change.

In the ensuing chapters, the authors will review the process of change enhancement that moves an individual along a continuum from external control to self-determinism. Transforming resistance in offenders will be discussed. Programmatic interventions as well as ways to change the change agent will be identified.

"I did it," says my memory. "I cannot have done it," says my pride and remains adamant. Finally, my memory complies.
–Fredrick Nietzsche, Beyond Good and Evil

The Challenges of Working with Resistant Sexual Offenders

Most of us who have intentionally taken on the task of changing, or modifying, an aspect of our behavior can attest to the challenges involved. From changing a tendency for lateness, to being less reactive to a spouse or significant other, to overcoming a severe addiction, change is often a long and difficult process. Sometimes the rewards to change are obvious, and at other times they are not. Even if the rewards are obvious, we still may rigorously resist change. Predictability and familiarity seem to offer comforts that newness and change do not. For some, simply acknowledging the need for change can be painful, so much so that most of us employ complex mechanisms, such as cognitive dissonance and other cognitive distortions, either to justify our not changing or to dispute our need to change. This was well illustrated in a study by Milam, Sussman, Ritt-Olsen, and Clyde (2000), who found that young smokers believed that statements directed toward them regarding the health risks of smoking were either exaggerated or did not apply to them.

Some of the tactics that we use to ward off change, or the awareness of the need to change, are conscious and others are unconscious. Even during those times that we acknowledge the need to change a problematic behavior, the amount of effort that we are willing to expend is determined by a sometimes irrational formula that weighs the costs against the benefits of changing. If the rewards seem worth it to us, we are likely to endure more anxiety and pain in order to achieve the desired goal.

As agents of change, most of us know that the often-intense or-deal of changing an aspect of ourselves can pale in comparison to the tribulations we experience when we try to facilitate change in someone else. This has become particularly evident in working with forensic populations who tend to be less motivated for treatment and more resistant or noncompliant while in treatment than other psychotherapy populations (Gerstley et al., 1989; Ogloff, Wong, & Greenwood, 1990; Rice, Harris, & Cormier, 1992). Some offenders in the criminal justice system experience the change process as so distressing that they are willing to sacrifice their freedom in order to maintain some (sometimes distorted) sense of security and well-be-ing as opposed to engaging in the change process.

One major difference between a general psychotherapy population and a forensic population is that forensic offenders are usually be-ing directed to change by a legal mechanism that makes changing a part of a legal mandate and forces them to participate under some degree of coercion. Therefore, forensic settings are typically less than optimal for inducing or maintaining motivation for be-havior, attitude, or lifestyle change, and in fact, these settings likely increase resistance.

What is Resistance?

Resistance is generally defined as the offender's subtle or overt opposition to changing his or her behavior. However, as Knowles and Linn (2004) pointed out, the term has an extensive history that includes definitions such as one's noncompliance with a di-rective (Newman, 2002); a desire to counteract someone else's attempt to limit one's choices (Brehm, 1966); an unwillingness to achieve insight about the real nature of one's thoughts or feelings (Messer, 2002); or the representation of the feeling of ambivalence about change (Arkowitz, 2002). "Therapists use the term resis-tance more generally to refer to offender behaviors that they view as antitherapeutic" (Turkat & Meyer, 1982) or to describe an of-fender who is unmotivated for change. Change agents often fail to consider that self-exploration and the disclosures that accompany the process can be very difficult, painful, and, for sexual offend-ers, dangerous. The most basic understanding of resistance is that it is a "reaction against change" (Knowles & Linn, 2004, p. 6). Greenson's (1967) definition of resistance has become the most known and utilized; "all those conscious and unconscious emotions, attitudes, ideas, thoughts, or actions which operate against the progress of therapy" (p. 155).

Resistance may manifest as a range of behaviors from simple avoidant behavior, such as showing up late to appointments, falling asleep during sessions, and conveniently forgetting to bring required assignments, to more overt hostility and rage directed toward the change agent or the therapy process itself. Resistance, however, is not always negatively expressed. In order to avoid the uncomfortable feelings that accompany change, resistance often takes the form of idealization, and a "feel-good" or "club" atmosphere, which can be recognized by an over-idealization of the therapist by the offender, or an over-idealization of the offender by the therapist. Regardless of its manifestation, and despite the negative overtones with which many change agents describe a resistant offender, it must be understood that resistance is a normal experience that occurs with virtually every person attempting to change a behavior or gain an insight.

The term "resistance" originated from Freud (1900), who stated "whatever interrupts the progress of analytic work is resistance" (p. 517). Freud believed that all resistance originated in the mind of the therapeutic offender. From the psychoanalytic perspective, the function of resistance is to keep from conscious awareness any, and possibly all, painful emotions. Freud stated that hysterical patients showing signs of memory loss as a result of a presumed traumatic event often claimed "not knowing" significant details of the event. Freud asserted, however, that these patients actually suffered from "not wanting to know" (1895, p. 269-270). Freud later added that resistance was not only an avoidance of remembering specific facts but was a way to guard against an awareness of unacceptable impulses (1900, p. 72). From this perspective, resistance serves to defend against anxiety. Freud used the term "anxiety" to describe a wide range of unpleasant emotions, such as shame, sadness, guilt, vulnerability, and inadequacy. In short, resistance was a form of self-deception whose sole source was to avert anxiety.

During the ensuing years, an important shift from psychoanalytic theory to empirically based behavioral treatment became a staple of most effective treatment programs. In the process of this shift, many of the original Freudian-based theories have fallen into obscurity with the exception of resistance. Strict behaviorists replaced Freud's client-blaming stance with an assertion that resistance is not self-induced but rather reflects flaws in the therapist's method. A behaviorist perspective contends that all behavior is a reaction to environmental stimuli. In the case of resistance, the behaviorist perspective posits that a resistant offender is merely engaging in avoidant behavior because he obtains stronger rewards from the environment for resisting change than adopting it. In other words, a reduction in resistance, and eventually behavioral change, will come as a result of rewards and punishments that are provided to the offender from the therapist and/or the environment, not from within the offender's psyche.

Evolving toward a more cognitive-behavioral approach, resistance is now believed to result from both present rewards and past beliefs that have been learned through repeated exposure and reinforcement. Shelton and Ackerman (1974), while adhering to traditional behavioral approaches, acknowledged that sound cognitive-behavioral practices need to consider the biases brought to the treatment setting by both the therapist and the client. Current cognitive-behavioral treatments also emphasize that simple contingency models of behavioral change are not fully effective when they fail to include motivation, coping style, and social supports (Horowitz et al., 2001). All aspects of change and resistance require a comprehensive evaluation of the individual's characterological structure, his/her immediate environment, and the context in which the individual lives his/her life.

Another important facet of resistance is the intensity with which we resist or acquiesce to change. Dollard and Miller (2004) pointed out that there is a push and pull between resistance and change and that the avoidance gradient is a greater force than the approach gradient. In order to facilitate change, a change agent must "increase approach forces or decrease avoidant forces" (p. 119). Therefore, resistance can be overcome by persuading someone about the benefits of changing or inhibiting the forces that increase avoidance.

Folded into an integration of these theories is the acknowledgment that people become resistant when faced with a need, or in some cases a mandate, to make changes in their behavior when they have not come to a definitive conclusion that changing is in their best interest. Resistance exists only when there is pressure generated, either internally or externally, to change. Without pressure to change there is no resistance. As put forth by Knowles and Linn (2004), resistance is correctly attributed sometimes to the person and sometimes to the situation. This perspective is consistent with a systems approach to resistance that acknowledges "resistance is an interaction of the components in the system" (Preston, 2000, p. 47). Regardless of its source, all of the "stuff" that builds resistance ultimately comes forth in the offender's relationship with therapy and the change agent. In order to overcome resistance, one must understand this relationship and provide a holding environment that adequately supports its expression, exploration, and finally, its extinction.

Sources of Resistance

Case Example

Frank is a 35-year-old Hispanic male with a long and varied history of criminal conduct dating back to age 14. He was referred to the sexual offender treatment program after serving 4 years of a 6-year sentence for attempted molestation of a 12-year-old female. Court documents state that he was identified by the young female as the man who approached her one day after school and offered her money to go on a walk with him. After she refused his request, the man pushed her under a stairwell of a nearby building and attempted to put his hands under her skirt. She screamed and the man ran. The girl ran back to school, and the police were notified. Frank was identified as the man matching the girl's description of the assailant and was arrested later that day. After being released from prison, he entered treatment, but only after his parole officer threatened parole violation if he did not cooperate.

Throughout the intake process he presented as angry and only superficially compliant. He repeatedly stated, "You know she probably confused me with someone else. Someone would have to be sick to do what they said I did." After being urged by the Caucasian psychologist to list the reasons for his noncompliance, he stated that he did not trust "white people" and felt that he could not benefit from participating in treatment because the staff was just interested in making money off his misfortune. He described his reluctance to discuss his case or any aspect of his sexual life for fear of being found out by other people on parole. He stated that he was severely beaten shortly after his arrest for being labeled a "Chester." He also stated that he had heard that if he won an appeal of his case he would not have to register as a sexual offender.

- Can Frank change?
- What specific challenges arise when attempting to facilitate change with him?
- Would you refer or accept him into treatment?
- What is your attitude or feeling toward him?

Denial

Working with and overcoming denial is one of the most difficult challenges reported by clinicians (Metzger, as cited in DiClementi et al., 2001). One of the greatest challenges for change agents is working, and maintaining a therapeutic relationship, with an offender who denies that he committed some or any inappropriate behavior. Many sexual offenders who enter therapy are unwilling to even consider that their behavior is a problem. More so than other clinical populations, sexual offenders who do not immediately convey full disclosure, cooperation, and accountability, as defined by the change agent, are regularly labeled hopelessly "in denial" or resistant.

It should first be acknowledged that denial and resistance are not automatically interchangeable terms. As discussed above, the term "resistance" refers generally to offender behaviors that are considered antitherapeutic (Turkat & Meyer, 1982) or reflect a lack of motivation for change. An offender's unwillingness or inability to immediately disclose all aspects of the offense behavior does not necessarily indicate that an offender is inappropriate for treatment or unmanageable in the community. In fact, reflexively labeling such an offender as in denial and unworkable is antitherapeutic and may undermine any attempt to work with the offender to reduce recidivism. The goal of change is to gain awareness into problematic behavior in order to reduce the likelihood of harming others and engaging in self-defeating behavior. Schneider and Wright (2004) expressed that requiring offenders to take full responsibility before entering treatment is synonymous with asking offenders to change on their own without help or supervision. However, offenders who do not take full responsibility for their offensive behavior should be treated in more intensive programs (ATSA, 2000, p. 20). It is also recommended that offenders who deny their offense should be regularly assessed to determine their progress and amenability to treatment.

There is little doubt that Frank (as presented in the case example) is resistant. He essentially says as much by indicating reasons for participating (e.g., winning a legal appeal). This does not, however, preclude the presence of denial. How can we distinguish between denial and resistance? Identifying whether or not an offender's denial undermines the potential for change requires an understanding of the term "denial." This is particularly important as it appears that the term is used in many different ways. "Denial" as defined by The Association for the Treatment of Sexual Abusers (2004) is "the failure of sexual abusers to accept responsibility for their offenses" (p. 60). This definition is far from a more traditional viewpoint that describes denial as a complex "unconscious defense mechanism for coping with guilt, anxiety, and other disturbing emotions aroused by reality" (Cohen, 2001, p. 5).

Recent literature, in an attempt to clarify, suggests that deliberate acts of deceit are more indicative of denial while faulty beliefs, social information processing deficits, and distorted perceptions of reality are indicative of cognitive distortions (Schneider & Wright, 2004). Using the ATSA definition as a springboard, we use the term "denial" to mean an intentional refusal to acknowledge all or part of the facts (for elucidation we use the term "willful denial"). Simply put, the willful denier states that he did not engage in a particular behavior or did not commit an offense when, in fact, he did. His sole purpose in maintaining the lie is to avoid detection. The motivations to maintain false innocence are numerous. For example, an offender may be intent upon appealing his offense. Even after serving a sentence for a crime and completing parole/probation, many offenders appeal their conviction in order to avoid state sexual offender registration laws, and/or to avoid the severe judgment that sexual offenders experience from both society and fellow parolees/probationers. For some, lying about offense behavior is a life skill developed in prison in order to avoid detection by other inmates and has become a deeply entrenched survival tool. Frank's resistance and possible willful denial appear to be influenced by both his desire to overturn his case and an adaptation to a hostile environment that predates on sexual offenders.

Cognitive distortions, or what we refer to at times as "clinical denial," are likely based in a distorted perception of reality. Usually a cognitive distortion is an automatic response, one that is not simply a lie or motivated by an effort to be willfully deceptive. Instead, cognitive distortions serve to block from conscious awareness information that is deemed to be intolerable to the offender. If the information were brought fully to awareness, it could provoke anxiety, feelings of rage, or shame that, psychologically, the individual is simply unable to tolerate. Breaking through cognitive distortions can also threaten familial or cultural beliefs that play a major role in defining the offender's identity. Consequently, the offender's ability to remain conscious of information fails or s/he distorts the information in order to maintain some level of functioning.

Cognitive distortions (clinical denial) and denial (willful denial) can manifest in many forms: denial of the offense, denial of victim impact, denial of the extent of the behavior (minimizing), denial of responsibility, denial of planning, denial of sexual deviancy, denial of relapse potential, and denial of the need for treatment or sanctions (adapted from Schneider & Wright, 2004). Distinguishing between a denier and an offender who is struggling with cognitive distortions can be a difficult process requiring several interactions to clarify the offender's intent. In some cases, outright lying (denying) is indistinguishable from cognitive distortions, and in some cases there is a mixture of the two. The key distinction is that the offender suffering from cognitive distortions is unaware of his erroneous perceptions, while the willful denier is intentionally deceitful.

A denying (lying) offender usually resists the change process, and special approaches need to be employed either to overcome the deceit or to identify alternative methods to reduce his/her risk of recidivism. In Frank's case, he may be motivated to lie about his offense for fear of being judged or beaten again. Although this presents an obstacle to treatment, interventions to overcome his denial might include trust and relationship building before a comprehensive undertaking of his offense can take place. If he continues to resist, the tools available to him (e.g., the therapist) will likely be ineffective and his risk will remain unchanged. Offenders with many cognitive distortions (clinical denial) are not usually resistant but rather have not been presented with convincing evidence that will correct faulty thinking patterns. In many cases, individuals with cognitive distortions can engage in an exploration of their thinking patterns.

It may be too early in Frank's treatment to determine to what extent his statements are influenced by clinical denial or willful denial. His statement that "someone would have to be sick to do what they said I did" reflects a conscious and harsh condemnation of the act. Is this a smoke screen or motivation to distort his perception of the events?

In all fairness, the possibility that some offenders are factually asserting their innocence should be considered because factual denial is also not resistance. Factual denial occurs when someone refutes an accusation, and in reality, is telling the truth. It is difficult to determine to what extent individuals participating in sexual offender treatment programs actually fall into this category; nevertheless the possibility exists, and even though change agents are not put into a position of determining guilt or innocence, this is an issue of which change agents should be aware.[1] Treatment should always

---

[1] Gross, Jacoby, Matheson, Montgomery, & Patil (2004) reviewed overturned convictions for murder and rape in the United States between 1989 and 2003. During that time, the authors report that 37% of rape convictions were overturned. Most exonerations (105 out of 120) resulted from the introduction of DNA evidence.

be approached from the perspective that the offender has been convicted of, and has engaged in, inappropriate behavior. If during an
initial intake evaluation an offender adamantly denies committing
any type of offense, objective measures fail to identify any deviant
sexual interests, there is no identifiable mental disorder, and the
offender has passed a polygraph examination, the ethical responsibility of the clinician is to seriously question the appropriateness of
sexual offender specific treatment.

Personality Disorders

Many offenders entering treatment present with some form of adult
antisocial behavior problems and will meet the criteria for various
personality disorders. The presence of a personality disorder will
likely contribute to an offender's resistance to participate in treatment. Although this may seem obvious to some, many change
agents reactively set limits based on the offenders' past sexual offense history and misinterpretations of behavior, rather than fully
consider the potential of an underlying mental illness that influences the behavior. As a consequence some offenders are barred
from participating in treatment despite the availability of specific
interventions that might address characterological issues. These
characterological issues likely contribute to offense risk. In short, it
is important to evaluate the presence of a personality disorder and
develop appropriate treatment plans that engage related resistance.

A personality disorder is traditionally described as a pattern of
behavior that began in early life and has remained persistent and
pervasive over time and situations. These behavior patterns are
marked by a significant deviation from the person's cultural norm
and lead to distress to the person, to others, or to society.

In terms of sexual offenders, Hanson's and Morton-Bourgon's
(2004) research indicates that an antisocial orientation (antisocial
personality, antisocial traits, history of rule violation) was the major predictor of violent nonsexual recidivism (d = .51). Antisocial
orientation was also a significant predictor of sexual recidivism (d
= .23). Additionally, Hanson found that a general category of "any
personality disorder" was also significantly related to sexual re-

cidivism. The presence of personality disorders in sexual offender populations is extremely common. In many cases, offenders are found to have features of more than one personality disorder (see Table 1.1). Lilienfeld, Van Volkenburg, Larnz, and Akiskal (1986) found that between 63% and 70% of individuals diagnosed with Antisocial Personality Disorder (APD)[2] also met the criteria for another personality disorder. Oldham et al. (1992) found that in a sample of 100 patients diagnosed with Antisocial Personality Disorder, 100% also met the criteria for Borderline Personality Disorder. In addition to APD and Borderline Personality Disorder, common disorders found among prison populations include Narcissistic Personality Disorder, Histrionic Personality Disorder, and Avoidant Personality Disorder (Widiger & Corbit, 1997).

Antisocial Personality Disorder by definition describes an individual who resists authority and rules and is prone toward proscribed behavior. Many of these offenders have extensive histories of engaging in behaviors that reflect such a profound tendency toward resistance that they have given up every opportunity for successful living that has been presented to them and have instead chosen to destine themselves and their families for a life of poverty and incarceration. It is therefore not surprising that their initial contact with a therapeutic environment will also reproduce their seemingly automatic tendency for resistant and noncompliant behavior. A similar pattern would be expected for offenders who exhibit features of Borderline Personality Disorder. The DSM-IV-Tr (American Psychiatric Association, 2002) describes several symptomatic features that would contribute to expressions of resistance, such as fears of abandonment, extreme mood swings, relationship difficulties, unstable self-image, difficulty managing emotions, and impulsive behavior. These behavioral patterns directly contribute to noncompliance in treatment. Table 1.2 outlines diagnostic features of com-

---

[2] The reader should be informed that although many sexual offenders have Antisocial Personality Disorder (APD), this should not lead to the conclusion that most persons with Antisocial Personality Disorder become sexual offenders or even that sexual offenders with Antisocial Personality Disorder are likely to commit new sexual offenses. Antisocial Personality Disorder is correlated with sexual recidivism, with a correlation coefficient .14 (Hanson, 2000).

Table 1.1
Comorbidity of personality disorders

Researcher	Percentage of individuals with ASPD who were also diagnosed with another Axis II Disorder									
	Par	Schz.	Szot	Brd	His	Nar	Avd	Dep	Obc	Pass. Aggr
Corbit (1993)* +	31	25	12	56	19	12	12	12	6	44
Friedman & Widiger (1989)* +	36	14	36	71	29	36	36	43	0	36
Morey (1988)* +	28	6	6	44	33	56	17	11	0	50
Oldham et al. (1992a)* +	25	0	38	75	62	50	25	62	12	0
Oldham et al. (1992b)* +	62	0	12	100	50	50	25	12	25	38
Pfohl &Blum (1990)* +	25	25	25	75	75	25	50	25	25	25
Zanari et al. (1987)* +	2	1	29	80	56	28	6	21	0	29

Notes. This table was adapted from a review study by Widiger & Corbit (1997). * indicates a Widiger & Corbit (1997) reference. + indicates that the researchers utilized the DSM-III or DSM-III-R (all others used diagnostic criteria from the DSM-IV).

Par = Paranoid Personality Disorder
Schz = Schizoid Personality Disorder
Szot = Schizotypal Personality Disorder
Brd = Borderline Personality Disorder
His = Histrionic Personality Disorder

Nar = Narcissistic Personality Disorder
Avd = Avoidant Personality Disorder
Dep = Dependent Personality Disorder
Obc = Obsessive Compulsive Personality Disorder
Pass Aggr = Passive Aggressive Personality Disorder

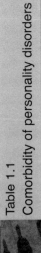

Table 1.2
Diagnostic features of various personality disorders

Antisocial Personality Disorder	• failure to conform to social norms • deceitfulness • impulsivity • irritability and aggressiveness • reckless disregard for the safety of self or others • consistent irresponsibility • lack of remorse
Narcissistic Personality Disorder	• grandiose • preoccupation with success, power, brilliance • beliefs regarding his "specialness" • entitlement • interpersonally exploitative • lack of empathy • arrogant
Borderline Personality Disorder	• frantic efforts to avoid abandonment • a pattern of unstable and intense interpersonal relationships characterized by alternating between idealization and devaluation • identity disturbance • impulsivity • affective instability • inappropriate and intense anger • transient, stress-related paranoia
Avoidant Personality Disorder	• avoids occupational activities that involve significant interpersonal contact • is unwilling to get involved with people unless certain of being liked • shows restraint within intimate relationship for fear of being shamed or ridiculed • is inhibited in new interpersonal relationships because of feelings of inadequacy • views self as socially inept, unappealing, and inferior • reluctant to take personal risks

Table 1.2 (cont.)
Diagnostic features of various personality disorders

Dependent Personality Disorder	• has difficulty making everyday decisions • needs others to assume responsibility for most areas of their lives • has difficulty expressing disagreement • has difficulty initiating projects • goes to great lengths to obtain nurturance and support from others
Schizoid Personality Disorder	• neither desires nor enjoys close relationships • has little, if any, sexual interest in sexual activities • lacks close friends or confidants • appears indifferent to praise or criticism • shows emotional coldness, detachment, flattened affectivity

(Source: DSM-IV-Tr, 2000)

mon personality disorders found among sexual offenders that may contribute to, or be falsely identified as, resistance.

Although more investigation is required, an assessment of Frank's childhood may indicate that he has engaged in antisocial behavior for a significant period of his life and may meet the criteria for Antisocial Personality Disorder. Although methods to deal with specific manifestations of resistance will be discussed in a later chapter, suffice it to say that an underlying mental disorder is present and specific steps will need to be taken to overcome this influence to his noncompliance in treatment.

Prison Enculturation

Many offenders develop resistance toward change as a consequence of the many years they have spent in prison. For example, in the case of Frank, it is possible that his many years of circulating in and out of the criminal justice system have jaded him in regard to the benefits of prison programs. He may have many underlying beliefs that prohibit trust and disclosure with anyone who works in conjunction with the parole or probation departments. Although it may be easy to argue that this aspect of his resistance is another symptom of an antisocial personality, the cultural environment in which he has been living has continually reinforced his refusal to participate in the treatment process. In addition, some suggest that the longer an offender is in prison the more likely he foresees criminality in his future.

Change agents must be sensitive to the enculturation that offenders may have endured for many years and be cognizant not to further cement these problematic beliefs by simply dismissing the power of the environment from which an offender, such as Frank, comes. In particular, many offenders have learned, in much the same way that most of us have, that trust is earned and not simply given. Attitudes supportive of treatment resistance, or mistrust of anyone associated with the criminal justice system, have likely been strengthened and reinforced for offenders who have spent extended periods of time in prison. Krosnick and Petty (1995) pointed out that the length of time that an attitude persists defines its strength, its ability to resist attack, and the force with which it guides related thoughts and behaviors. Knowles and Linn (2004) found from their research that attitudes were strengthened and people became more resistant to change when the attitude was based on beliefs that had large amounts of elaboration, were of personal relevance, and endured for longer periods of time.

Racial and Ethnic Considerations

It is also evident that Frank is entering treatment with biases about the therapist that will hamper effective treatment. The influences of culture, race, ethnicity, social class, gender, intellectual ability, religious preference, physical ability, sexual orientation, and others related to human diversity and oppression can greatly impact the psychotherapy process. Although this may be obvious to most change agents, not keeping cultural differences at the forefront of one's awareness can be detrimental to long-term change. As with all evaluations of resistance, the reader should be conscious that labeling a specific facet of an offender's bias as resistance could be problematic, particularly if the bias is accurate (e.g., some offenders are oppressed and judged harshly solely because of their race). However, change agents should be aware that some offenders might use the reality of racial discrimination as a way of resisting treatment (Kibel, 1972) and refuse work toward overcoming the conflict, thus sabotaging an environment that could be conducive to change. Fenster (1996) pointed out that issues related to racism may hide unresolved issues. Frank's bias regarding the therapist's ethnicity should be considered material for therapeutic exploration as well as an opportunity for the therapist to assess his/her own racial bias. Change agents and offenders must constantly work toward increasing awareness of their own preconceptions and biases in order to reduce resistance and move toward the attainment of goals (Addison, 1977).

Salvendy (1999) pointed out that many minority members are too inhibited to self-disclose in therapeutic settings because of concerns related to stereotyping and the potential negative implications that it may have for their ethnic group. He continued that offenders might see themselves as representatives of their ethnic group as well as individuals. For example, Frank may be concerned that he must assert qualities that he perceives as positively representing a Latino male or that he must present himself as a tough "gang banger" in order to maintain the image of the group with which he most strongly identifies. Salvendy also stated that self-disclosure for minority members will likely be difficult until they feel that others will relate to their personal histories.

Socioeconomic Status

An often-overlooked influence of resistance is socioeconomic status because its expression is often subtle and elusive. Many individuals entering mandated therapy perceive psychotherapy as an elitist and useless exercise reserved for wealthy individuals of privilege. Educating offenders of the utility of engaging in therapeutic exercises is often quite challenging but crucial to the process of overcoming resistance and encouraging life change. It is difficult for offenders to give of themselves if they cannot identify potential personal gains.

Change Agent Resistance

In the process of getting offenders to change, change agents must be aware of the ways in which they themselves contribute to the obstacles that inhibit change in offenders. That is, resistance for offenders to change exists within the change agent. The term "counter-resistance" is used to describe this phenomenon in psychotherapy (Langs, 1981). Exploring counter-resistance in change agents is not an easy task. For instance, we could begin this section by discussing the various personality disorders that are commonly found in psychotherapists, probation/parole officers, or anyone who might happen upon reading this book. However, such an approach may actually increase resistance and many would not read further. Instead, we encourage each of our readers to participate in a full psychosexual, psychological evaluation and engage in a therapy process themselves! In addition to fleshing out problems related to the presence of an Axis II disorder, certain empathy would develop for offenders who are asked to reveal their deepest and most disturbing fantasies. Although the above statements are made somewhat in jest, any therapist or other change agent willing to guide offenders into discussing the areas of their existence that are often shrouded by unconscious process and impulse should be willing to undertake such an examination of themselves.

Change agents working with sexual offenders experience the impact of working with this challenging population in many ways. Part of the goal in reducing resistance in sexual offenders is reducing the obstacles that the change agent brings to this very important process. Although one who enters the field of sexual offender treatment is not likely to be naïve about the potential toxicity of working with this population, many initially fail to comprehend how delving into the recesses of deviant sexual behavior will impact their perception of sexuality, the media, gender politics, and children. In addition to the challenges of working with this often difficult population of offenders, change agents face pressures from the environmental context formed by society and the criminal justice system. The change agents who work with sexual offenders are often pulled in many directions, both personally and professionally, because of the moral and reactive stance that many lay people, as well as other professionals, take in terms of sexual offending. Those of us who have been hired by either a prosecutor or a defense attorney to offer an opinion regarding reoffense risk or treatment progress can attest to the attempted influence imposed upon a clinician to draw specific conclusions that stray from the truthfulness of a case. Perhaps even Freud experienced such a pull away from appropriate treatment and diagnosis when, after proposing that a case of hysteria was caused by childhood sexual abuse, he was severely criticized by his fellow physicians. In an apparent response to his colleagues' rejections of his hypothesis, he restated the case claiming that the victim fantasized the abuse because she herself desired the sexual contact (Lerman, 1988). In short, change agents should be cognizant of implicit and explicit biased forces within the criminal justice system.

Criminal Justice System Resistance

In some instances, interventions within the criminal justice system are geared toward managing behavior while in the system rather than preparing offenders for when they are released (Severson, 1992). Working as change agents in the criminal justice system is different from any other system of change because, in addition to serving the needs of specific offenders, they must be particularly attuned to the needs of public safety. As a result, issues related to confidentiality and long-term goals are not solely offender-focused. It is also evident that, partly due to the political structure within which we work and the public reactivity toward sexual offenders, each change agent is potentially influenced by other change agents in different ways. Therapists, probation/parole officers, and judges, as well as the individuals who write the legal documents detailing the history of a sexual offender, are subject to bias. Belief systems and political agendas at each level of the criminal justice system play a role in shaping the opinions of countless others in terms of an offender's ability to participate in treatment (or the ability of sexual offenders in general to benefit from treatment). This includes his/her risk level, his/her ability to be maintained in the community, what the sentence for his/her offense should be, and even his/her status as a human being.

Sometimes these judgments are determined long before the change agent has had the opportunity to meet the offender. For example, Northey (1999) pointed out that with the intent to protect victims, many change agents have come to utilize the coercion of the court system to facilitate compliance in treatment. The power of a therapist to refer offenders back to their probation officers when they refuse to participate, or the ability of a probation or parole officer to place into custody those offenders unwilling to attend treatment, is invaluable. This intervention, however, should not be utilized too quickly. Northey continued that the ability to use court sanctions might cause therapists to disregard some of the most basic tenets of relationship development in treatment and adopt more adversarial roles. Therapists are often forced to focus on issues such as ensuring attendance and superficial compliance rather than actual change. The role of the therapist as change agent therefore becomes confused with the role similar to that of a beat cop. Similarly, as pointed out by Robinson (2001), legislative reforms intended to prevent future sexual offending have become increasingly punitive. He opined that it is not possible to "punish dangerousness:"

> To "punish" is "to cause (a person) to undergo pain, loss, or suffering for a crime or wrongdoing;" therefore, punishment can only exist in relation to a past wrong. "Dangerous" means "likely to cause injury, pain, etc.;" that is, dangerousness describes a threat of future harm. One can "restrain," "detain," or "incapacitate" a dangerous person, but one cannot logically "punish" dangerousness. (Robinson, 2001, p. 132)

Parole and probation officers are particularly caught in a bind between their roles as case managers and law enforcement officers. This conflict is so pervasive that while preparing for this book, we were unable to find two officers who defined their roles in the same way. Some of the parole/probation officers we interviewed were quite invested in the positive effects of treatment, identifying reduced reoffense risk and life enhancement as goals, while others admitted that they felt that treatment "could not hurt" but that their primary interest was increased containment and/or using treatment as a tool that provided structure for offenders who were less likely to return to prison if they were "busy." It has also become evident that some jurisdictions place a premium on keeping offenders out of prison regardless of compliance in treatment or risk. One officer cited the pressure on them to keep offenders "on the street" because it is too expensive to return them to custody. On the other hand, lower-risk, high-profile offenders whose cases have been highlighted in the media are at increased risk of being returned to custody for even the mildest of infractions.

In addition to the struggles imposed by the larger structure of the criminal justice system, many probation and parole officers bring their own biases and personalities to work, making them ambivalent to their role and the role of other change agents. There is little doubt that this ambivalence trickles into offenders' attitudes and motivations regarding compliance and change. Without clear policies and goals, both change agents and offenders will be limited in their ability to critically evaluate their needs and work together to promote prosocial, offense-free living.

Chapter Two

There are some duties we owe even to those who have wronged us.
There is, after all, a limit to retribution and punishment.
–Cicero

Punishment and Resistance

In the United States, we take pride in our system of justice, which balances the protection of the individual rights of the accused with the rights and safety of victims, families, and communities at large. When someone breaks the law and engages in illegal behavior, our system can respond in a number of ways. Sometimes we offer the offender opportunities for rehabilitation. Other times, we want to see that person punished.

Crimes involving violence, especially sexual violence, provoke strong responses from lawmakers, law enforcement agencies, the media, and the public. We seem to hear stories about violence, terror, and sexual abuse in the media time and again. We often go to bed horrified by yet another late news viewing of a child or woman as the latest victim of a "sexual predator." The stories are awful, and we fear that the short- and long-term effects are immeasurable. Often the gut response of "lock the sicko up forever" just feels right. Society has come to expect and want punishment for those who violate the rights of others sexually.

For the majority of convicted sex offenders, punishment happens in one form or another. Jail, prison, and/or commitment to state hospitals are common responses. While we have seen several trends in sexual offender management over the years, ultimately, most of these offenders end up back in our communities, living in our neighborhoods, as part of society again. Our hope and the main goal of our efforts is that they stop their abusive behavior completely and never offend again. To achieve this goal, significant federal and state legislation has been passed in an effort to help professionals in law enforcement, probation, and parole department increase their knowledge of the location of identified sexual offenders in their communities. In many cases, these efforts also allow citizens the right to obtain personal information about a sexual offender's whereabouts, with the hope that more information will lead to greater feelings of safety. Sexual offender registration Web sites, community notification through public news broadcasts and flyers sent out to neighborhoods where sexual offenders reside, and global positioning satellite surveillance systems are some of the more popular methods that have been employed across the United States. While every effort should be made to keep communities safe, even if it means increased legislation and monitoring tactics, we do believe discussion and analysis of these efforts are imperative so that objective data drives ongoing support for these projects and similar future efforts. As with any new community safety effort, tax payer dollars are at stake, and government officials should make sure their efforts are producing outcomes pursuant to their goals.

For example, although little evidence has mounted to date on the effectiveness of these systems, these interventions can have a significantly negative impact the offender and, at times, his/her ability to effectively reintegrate into society. As we'll discuss further in chapter 3, creating environments that actually increase an offender's risk level is not the goal. Additionally, we believe that government has a responsibility to gather data on how legislation and resulting policies and interventions impact the families of sexual offenders, victims, and their families, and communities where these practices are at work.

The goal of this chapter is to examine how current policies and practices might be impacting our ability to effectively work with sexual offenders and to assist in ultimately changing their future behaviors. To do so, we will:

- Take an historical look at how the criminal justice and mental health care systems have evolved in their responses to sexual offenders, with a critical look at the modern-day response.

- Review the effectiveness of the current models in leading to desirable changes in behavior.

- Explore criminological theories in an attempt to better understand sexual offender resistance from a more socio-cultural perspective.

Historic and Current Models for Working With Sexual Offenders

Walking the Punishment Continuum

Societies have always struggled with the dilemma of how to deal with people who break norms, rules, and laws, and how to justify the use of imposing consequences on transgressors. A number of models of punishment have been created over time, including retribution, incapacitation, deterrence, reintegration, and rehabilitation. Table 2.1 details these various models.

Modern-day society has moved from one end of the continuum to the other—like a pendulum—swinging back and forth between retribution and rehabilitation (Allen & Simonsen, 1995). With calls to make the offender pay and keep paying for what he did, we currently appear to be in the retribution model.

Danner (2001) explored theoretical models for punishment by distinguishing between two competing philosophical models that justify the imposition of criminal punishment upon individual offenders and guide the determination of how much punishment to impose in particular circumstances. The first model, "utilitarianism," evaluates punishment primarily in reference to an independent societal good and finds punishment justified only when the benefits to society outweigh the costs to the offender and to society. The second, "retributionism," by contrast, views punishment as a deserved response to wrongdoing and describes an appropriate sentence as one that is proportional to the seriousness of the crime. Other theorists have advocated hybrid theories of punishment that combine elements of utilitarianism and retribution.

Table 2.1
Models of punishment

RETRIBUTION: (just desserts) has the effect of stop the person and others (deterrence); retributive punishment attempts to right a past wrong; it responds either to the character of the act or the character of the person who committed it.

DETERRENCE: looks to the future results of today's punishment; it is designed to discourage would-be criminals; it may disable convicted criminals.

INCAPACITATION: stop the person (this goes with Gottfredson and Hirschi's [1990] work on the invariant idea of the age curve of offenders and crime).

REINTEGRATION: helps offenders transition back to the community by providing programming while incarcerated.

REHABILITATION: the offender needs to be "fixed" in order to belong to society; often but not necessarily set under a medical model, offenders were thought to be defective and it was—and is—the role of corrections to "fix" the defective offender before returning him/her to society; aims at future results by attempting to redeem someone who has committed a transgression.

For both utilitarians and retributionists, the harm caused by the defendant's action influences the determination of an appropriate, or optimal, sentence for that defendant's crime. In a retributive model, the link between harm and sentence is straightforward. A retributionist sentencing theory seeks to impose a sentence in proportion to a crime's seriousness, with seriousness generally measured by the degree of harm caused by the crime and the culpability of the perpetrator.

In a utilitarian model, the harm caused by a defendant's action influences the calculation of the costs and benefits both of punishing the defendant and of imposing a sentence of a particular length. The greater the harm caused by the crime, the greater the societal cost generated by its commission and threatened by its possible repetition. Nevertheless, the calculation of harm does not play as direct a role in the utilitarian model as in the retributive model because of utilitarianism's emphasis on punishment's effect on crime prevention, rather than retributionism's preoccupation with devising a punishment proportional to the crime committed.

Historical Responses to Sexual Offenders

An analysis of the United States' responses to sex crimes illustrates the full range of continuum responses. Three periods of public policy responses to sexual offenders have been described (Lieb & Matson, 1998). The first period, from the mid-1930's through the mid-1950's, was marked by a rehabilitation approach. By 1939, with the first organized mergers of psychiatry and criminal justice, sexual psychopathy laws were enacted in three states. The belief behind these laws was that sexual offenders had certain mental conditions that could not be influenced positively by criminal punishments. In other words, prison sentences would not change their behavior but treatment would. The therapeutic community applauded this approach, and at the time, it was received well by the public. As a result of these laws, many sexual offenders received long stays in mental health hospitals instead of prison beds. Once "cured," these men were then released back into the community.

The second period began to take shape in the mid-1970's and lasted through the early 1980's. Those who supported the idea of treatment instead of punishment from the first period, psychiatry and the public, for different reasons, began to question the value of the sexual psychopath laws. Victim advocate groups began to have a stronger voice in the development of policy for sexual offenders. As a result, laws were enacted to increase reporting of spousal rape, incest, and other types of child abuse. Specialized treatment was viewed as crucial for the sexual offender. While this also marked the beginning of treatment based on more objective data, little was known about what worked or didn't work with offenders in treatment.

The final wave, which could be viewed as starting in the late 1980's and continues through today, revolves around the creation and expansion of sexual predator laws. Since 1990, all states have passed sexual predator laws and have developed policies for how to handle dangerous sexual offenders. A significant amount of interest has been paid to this group of sexual offenders. Costly treatment programs have been set up within state hospitals. Yet, while empirically based treatment programs have been developed to house and treat these offenders, many choose not to participate in the programs, leaving hospital programs crowded with men refusing to comply with the therapeutic process. The current wave of intervention arguably has the greatest degree of punishment, as well. In support of this conclusion, Lariviere and Robinson (1996) cited how 76% of their Canadian federal correctional officers endorsed punishment as an important objective, whereas only 54% endorsed statements about the efficacy of rehabilitation efforts.

Although Lieb and Matson's (1998) three loosely constructed periods of sexual offender policy are important to consider, they do not fully address all of the interactions that most sexual offenders have with the criminal justice system, specifically with the post-release conditions of parole and probation, and their connections with other change agents such as mental health professionals and school and vocational program professionals. While some first-time and repeat offenders receive long sentences and might be considered for civil commitment, the majority of sexual offenders receive probation or parole after a short prison sentence.

A review of the history of sexual offender policy would be incomplete without discussing the social controls that exist once a sexual offender is released from prison. Consider for a moment that while most criminals receive their sentence, do their time, and complete a period of parole and/or probation, sexual offenders face several post-release/conviction sanctions in addition to the standard conditions of parole/probation. The number of expectations and punishments they receive, in addition to their probation sentence, can be very intense.

To illustrate these other systemic interactions, let's go back to our case example of Frank. In addition to having lived through the prison experience as a sexual offender, Frank is required by current legislation in many states to register with his local law enforcement office, undergo DNA testing, tell possible employers and family members about his sexual offense, and undergo a complete psychosexual evaluation which may include a sexual history polygraph and penile plethysmograph—all at the cost of several thousand dollars. In addition, because of the nature of his offense, signs are posted in his neighborhood alerting neighbors of his presence. If you didn't live close enough to see Frank's picture in your neighborhood, then you could find his street address, list of convictions (no dates included), and an outdated picture of him on the Internet. Finally, he's expected to get a job within a month, but he can't use the Internet, go to the local bookstore, or deviate from a weekly schedule he produced for his probation officer. When a potential employer calls and Frank can't get a hold of his probation officer, his choices are either to violate his probation or turn down the opportunity to get a job. Finally, he must pay for regular treatment sessions, which could range from $10 to $75 a week in offender programs around the country.

The authors recognize that Frank's "plight" likely pales in comparison to the lives left devastated by the sexual abuse he inflicted. As the reader, you might want to check in with how you are responding to the above paragraph. Maybe you have a very compassionate heart for the offender and his plight. Maybe you are somewhat out of touch with the realities of the average sexual offender released from an extensive term in prison. Regardless of your reaction, we are in no way asking the reader to feel sorry for or be mad at sexual offenders (or us)! Much like our efforts to assist victims to move forward again with their lives, we believe every reasonable effort should be taken to do the same for the offender who started the cycle of violence. Community efforts should be analyzed to help determine whether offender policies and intervention practices are moving offenders away from violence and toward being productive members in the community while at the same time keeping past or potential victims safe.

The Effectiveness of Current Models

So, how effective is our current model of punishment? As noted above, our current model is one that primarily relies on retribution. It could be argued that at no other time in recent history have sexual offenders received greater ongoing punishment, both institutional and societal, than today.

Some would argue that this type of punishment does not positively impact the underlying thought processes that produced the unacceptable behavior originally. The "badness" has merely gone underground. Punishment creates a push-back response, which is often seen within the therapy and supervision process.

> *"If you teach an animal a lesson by meanness or cruelty, don't be surprised if the animal remembers the meanness and cruelty and forgets the lesson!"* —an old cowboy saying

The research on punishment with children is inconclusive as to whether mild forms of corporal punishment hurt children. But it is clear that children who receive corporal punishment likely do not receive adequate amounts of positive reinforcement and other more effective parenting strategies (Gershoff, 2002; Parke, 2002). This is quite similar to many sexual offenders, who receive stiff sentences for dangerous behaviors, yet receive little positive reinforcement for gains they make in the community and treatment. Change agents are often surprised when an offender does well in treatment and/or makes significant changes to his life.

Groups like the National Center for Policy Analysis suggest that since the U.S. has taken a "get tough on crime" approach that the rates for many crimes have dropped significantly and that we should continue in this vein (Reynolds, 1999). Other more moderate and liberal groups would argue that our punishment efforts have only reinforced "bad behavior" and created outcasts to society. They contend that this has then led offenders to become alienated from normal interactions, as they face paralyzing scrutiny from the public when attempting to move back into mainstream society.

How Current Models Contribute to Resistance

Effectiveness research may not tell us the whole story about the impact of policies and laws regarding sexual offenders. Laws and policies created to structure sexual offender management may have unintended outcomes that were not considered. Based on Connell, Kubisch, Schorr and Weiss' (1995) theory mapping model, Pawson's (2000) work illustrated how sexual offender policies may not necessarily lead to their intended outcomes and that the unintended outcomes must be considered when developing policies.

Pawson's (2000) model would suggest the following line of thinking when discussing the purpose of Megan's Law from Connell et al.'s (1995) theories of change approach. For sexual offenders, the most significant intended consequence or goal that society hopes to obtain from current interventions (e.g., increased supervision, community notification) includes a reduction in recidivism rates. How is this expected to occur? According to Pawson, if the offender is constantly reminded of his awful behavior, this leads to an increase in shame and stigmatization and ultimately results in increased remorse. In turn, these thoughts and feelings will ultimately lead to a reduction in his offense risk. Secondarily, offenders are placed in mandated treatment programs because society hopes that if they become well adjusted they can begin to contribute to society again.

Unfortunately, however, any type of theory or policy has unintended consequences. We have found that these consequences are rarely discussed in sexual offender treatment and supervision circles. Pawson (2000) noted that for sexual offender policy, the offender often reacts to sanctions by offending elsewhere, moving and failing to re-register, being resistant to therapy, or relapsing under heightened anxiety. Sometimes offenders abandon treatment programs for fear of extended publicity. Perhaps the best example of unintended consequence is in California, where almost half of all sexual offenders who are supposed to register did not for several years. Those who registered were under much stricter surveillance than those who did not.

While the authors do not completely agree with Pawson's (2000) line of thinking, especially as it relates to the issue of shame production as an intended consequence, the model does provide a basis for all change agents to consider. Do we map out our theories and models before implementing them and consider the intended and unintended consequences of our policies and interventions? As Pawson questions, are we designing initiatives from an approach (theories of change approach) that includes a detailed plan and multiple steps to evaluate the progress of the plan's stated goals and specific intended outcomes? Do our models fully consider the realization that different systems of change and individual communities are complex and dynamic? While some jurisdictions may have efforts underway to meet Pawson's criticisms, little current research can answer his questions.

In a qualitative study of the effect of community notification on sexual offenders' treatment attitudes, 75% of subjects reported notification was a strong incentive not to reoffend (when surveyed while in treatment), while 60% said notification created a strong interest in relocating after release. On a positive note, the sexual offenders surveyed said notification positively impacted their own, and their families', motivation to obtain treatment (Elbogen, Patry, & Scalora, 2003). Elbogen and colleagues reported that "the framework of therapeutic jurisprudence also suggests that there may be ways in which community notification laws would promote mental health goals for sexual offenders" (p. 209.). That is, in a state that has a three-tier system of risk determinations and resulting notifications, mandatory risk assessments could be used as a therapeutic tool so that motivation to be involved in treatment is increased (as this factor could reduce risk determinations, thereby lowering one's risk level on the community notification tier and decreasing individual offender notification concerns).

At the same time, Megan's Law has some possible antitherapeutic effects. These include reducing the offenders' privacy, thus making them possibly less productive in life, which can increase stress and the chance of reoffense. Reducing the offenders' confidentiality and engendering self-labeling as ill, abnormal, or disordered, as well as without self-control, thus leading to less treatment or change motivation are other possible effects. Elbogen and colleagues (2003) agreed: "Benefit of Megan's Law is unknown because it is debatable whether victims of sexual offenders are typically strangers, known to the perpetrator, or both" (p. 210).

Elbogen et al. (2003) also found that the majority of sexual offenders had fears of embarrassment because of expected community notification upon release. Thus, they concluded, it could be inferred that a sexual offender might be embarrassed to return to the neighborhood in which s/he lived before. If this is the case, then the sexual offender's possibly negative attitude toward Megan's Law needs to be explored by a mental health counselor. Such adjustment issues may be salient to marital stability as well as familial adjustment—factors also relevant to relapse prevention. On a practical level, such considerations would seem critical to discharge planning, family meetings, and interactions with probation officers, as well (Elbogen et al.).

Finally, Elbogen and colleagues (2003) asserted that if a sexual offender in treatment voices his concerns or negative attitudes about notification (i.e., that it is unfair or he will be embarrassed), he runs the risk of being kept in the program longer or being seen as treatment resistant.

While many professionals wouldn't question the purpose of sexual offender specific interventions aimed at keeping our communities safer, often conflicts inherent in our polices significantly impact the sexual offender residing in the community. We've heard it said by many men in treatment, "If I'd only have committed murder, I wouldn't have to deal with all of this bullshit." While there is a degree of absurdity as well as cognitive distortion in this statement, we must be open to interpreting it from the offender's perspective. Perhaps he might be saying, "You're punishing me, over and over, for something that I feel badly about.... Please stop, and help me (get a job, find a healthy relationship, etc.)."

As noted above, one unintended consequence of current punishment models is resistance. As summarized by Goldstein (2001), resistance has been defined in the literature in numerous ways, such as an intra-psychic experience residing within the offender, as an interaction between the client and professional, or as a myth created largely by the professional's cognitive constructions of the change process. We are not naïve enough to suggest that no clients present with a host of clinical challenges that make working with them difficult. Neither do we wish to ignore the effects of our attitudes or beliefs about change as well as how such beliefs are transmitted through actions to our clients.

If we see our task as one of controlling the sexual offender's behavior through punishment, such a belief may distort the very working models from which we operate. That is, we can hold polarized views of the sexual offender that will preclude looking at multiple dimensions of sexual offending. Dichotomous thinking can inform our work. Rather than perceiving ourselves as the controller or the controlled or, conversely, that sexual offending is controlled or uncontrolled, our contention is that such thinking is too simplistic and ignores the multidimensional aspects of sexual offending that must be considered.

Kottler (1992) conceptualized resistance on a continuum, from seeing it as the enemy to the polar opposite of seeing it as a friend. He describes five categorizations:

a) The client does not understand what the therapist wants.

b) The client lacks the skills or knowledge to comply.

c) The client lacks the motivation due to previous failure experiences in treatment, a self-defeating belief system, or little or no perceived incentives to cooperate.

d) The client's defense systems are no longer working effectively and he sabotages treatment as he feels more fearful, embarrassed, or guilty, using compensatory strategies to cope.

e) Secondary gain and systemic (contextual) issues may be operating that help the client avoid change.

According to Kottler (1992, p. 13), "...when clients are difficult it is because they are trying desperately to maintain homeostasis in their lives."

Punishment and Control Theories

Certain criminological theories can help us understand why current policies and procedures lead to such unintended consequences, including the concept of resistance. By taking the time to examine some of the major criminal justice theoretical models of general criminal behavior, development, and reinforcement in more detail, we can learn ways of fashioning improved responses to the problem of sexual offending. The dominant theory of understanding deviance is control theory, followed by strain theory. Also important to our discussion are labeling and reaction theories. After explaining each theory, we'll then discuss how each theory relates to sexual offenders and the development of resistance.

Control Theory

Tittle's (1995) control theory offers a unique conceptualization of control. Briefly, Tittle claimed that all humans are concerned with the degree to which they can increase and exercise control in their lives. He contended that deviance or misbehavior is a reaction to a perceived or actual control imbalance. Control imbalances can manifest themselves in terms of a control deficit—where a person is subject to more control than s/he can exercise—or in terms of a control surplus—in which case a person is able to exercise more control than s/he is asked too withstand. For many sexual offenders, the reality of their lives is that they are under a significant amount of control from law enforcement and other supervision agencies, which leads to multiple restrictions (and reduced control). In reaction to increased sanctions and stipulations, we often see offenders exercise their control in unhealthy ways. Secrecy, manipulation, passive-aggressive behaviors—relevant in many ways to men who commit sexual offenses—often are exacerbated when significant controls are put into place. As change agents, we need to be aware of this process, predict it early in the supervision/treatment process, and offer the offender healthier alternatives.

Change agents work within systems that have created different types of offender control mechanisms. Part of our job is to help offenders learn how to navigate these systems in the most supportive and non-punitive manner possible (without sacrificing public safety). It's a delicate balance—much like being a parent to a teenager on the cusp of getting in with the wrong crowd. If you try to control them too much, they shut down—too little, they lack the skills to navigate life's challenges and sometimes make poor decisions. As difficult as it is, most parents can accept that their teenager will make a few mistakes on their path to adulthood. Change agents working with offenders do not have that luxury.

IMPLICATIONS FOR SEXUAL OFFENDERS: Some believe that the goals of the criminal justice system should be to provide punishment (prison/probation restrictions), offer support (positive reinforcement), and help remove roadblocks to success. Unfortunately, the system often adds roadblocks that enact inconsistent punishments. Sexual offenders have come to expect to be punished. Therefore, some may believe, "Why should I care?" or "Why should I want to get my life on track?" This ultimately leads them back to a place in their life similar to the time when they were offending. According to control theory, their lack of control may lead them into more deviance.

Strain Theory

Merton's (1968) strain theory notes that certain goals are strongly emphasized by society. At the same time, society also emphasizes certain acceptable means to reach those goals (such as education, hard work, etc.). Because everyone does not have equal access to legitimate means to attain those goals, Merton suggested that some people are more likely to end up alienated from society. This alienation, or strain, leads individuals to respond in different ways. Merton never meant to suggest that people who were denied access to society's goals would automatically become deviant. However, he did believe that their adaptive response depended on the individuals' attitudes toward cultural goals and the institutional means to attain them.

Merton's (1968) strain model also suggested that there are five modes—conformity, innovation, ritualism, retreatism, and rebellion—of adapting to strain caused by the restricted access to socially approved goals and means:

> According to Merton (1968), **conformity** is the most common mode of adaptation. Individuals accept both the goals as well as the prescribed means for achieving those goals. Conformists will accept, though not always achieve, the goals of society and the means approved for achieving them.

> Individuals who adapt through **innovation** accept societal goals but have few legitimate means to achieve those goals; thus

they innovate (or design) their own means to get ahead. The means to getting ahead may be through robbery, embezzlement, or other such criminal acts.

In **ritualism**, the third adaptation, individuals abandon the goals they once believed were within their reach and dedicate themselves to their current lifestyle. They play by the rules and have a daily, safe routine.

Retreatism is the adaptation of those who give up not only the goals but also the means. Individuals often retreat into the world of alcoholism and drug addiction. They escape into a non-productive, non-striving lifestyle.

The final adaptation, **rebellion**, occurs when the cultural goals and the legitimate means are rejected. Individuals create their own goals, and their own means, by protest or revolutionary activity (Merton, 1968).

IMPLICATIONS FOR SEXUAL OFFENDERS: Once convicted of a sexual offense, we believe that the offender's ability to achieve the "goals," defined under strain theory, are limited—especially early into a prison sentence and/or release into the community. One example occurs when an offender seeks employment in the community. Clinicians who have treated a non-sexual offender with a generic felony in their background understand that they must help their client adjust his/her expectations or be willing to undergo increased scrutiny by potential employers. For the sexual offender this scrutiny is even more extreme. While a person can explain a drug history or other misguided, young adult behavior and expect to receive some understanding from the public or potential employer, the sexual offender generally does not receive this same type of understanding. This lack of understanding and increased difficulty at obtaining employment can lead to extreme frustration, even for the person with great determination to obtain employment and become involved in other productive activities.

We recognize that the path of adaptation depends on many factors, everything from personality characteristics to personal history and other related criminogenic factors. While some sexual offenders in treatment do possess prosocial attitudes and good resources, many have always had limited degrees of these factors. We have seen many retreat into drugs, alcohol, and depression. We understand that many of the offenders we treat have always rebelled against authority and that the battle with them to internalize the beliefs we are suggesting is quite challenging.

Finally, at a minimum, we must accept the fact that the offenders we treat and supervise do have some serious limitations to achieving socially accepted goals. In line with the strain model, this could inevitably lead offenders to use various adaptive responses. Our goal as change agents should be to help them find healthy adaptive responses as we recognize that many offenders' chronic maladaptive response patterns are to rebel or retreat. These offenders need special attention in our treatment and supervision strategies. We must be careful to be fair and empathic, and hold out some hope that we will help them learn healthier ways of adapting and setting goals that are realistic, yet rewarding.

Labeling Theory

Another important theory to consider when working with sexual offenders is labeling theory. This model explores how and why certain acts were defined as criminal or deviant and why other such acts were not. Labeling theorists view criminals not as evil persons who engaged in wrong acts, but as individuals who have a criminal status placed upon them by both the criminal justice system and the community at large. From this point of view, the criminal acts themselves are not significant, but rather the social reactions to them. According to this model, deviance and its control involves a process of social definition that includes a response from others to an individual's behavior. This in turn leads to how an individual views himself. To help illustrate this point, let's briefly examine a crucial point made by sociologist Becker (1963):

> Deviance is not the quality of the act the person commits, but rather a consequence of the application by others of rules and sanctions to an offender. The deviant is one to whom that label has successfully been applied; deviant behavior is behavior that people so label (p. 95).

Taken a step further, labeling theory focuses on the reaction of other people and the subsequent effects of those reactions, which create deviance. When it becomes known that a person has engaged in deviant acts, s/he is then segregated from society and thus labeled, "whore," "thief," "abuser," "junkie," and the like. Becker (1963) noted that this process of segregation creates "outsiders," who are outcast from society, and then begin to associate with other individuals who have also been cast out. When more and more people begin to think of these individuals as deviants, they respond to them as such; thus the deviant reacts to such a response by continuing to engage in the behavior society now expects from him.

IMPLICATIONS FOR SEXUAL OFFENDERS: For the purposes of the present discussion, we won't disagree with the reasons that certain behaviors are regarded as deviant. Relevant to this discussion is how the labeling model impacts criminals in general, and more specifically, sexual offenders. The current trend of system responses that have been developed for most sexual offenders, regardless of their risk level, is lifelong—never to be removed. Drug offenders who have histories of physically abusing their children and spouses often serve little time in prison and have little of the post-release stigma attached to their future, and yet we could easily make a case that the impact of their crime was just as far-reaching as that of the father who commits incest.

Consider for a moment the following labels:

thief, prostitute, drug addict, sex offender, murderer...

Consider someone who committed murder or armed robbery, or embezzled millions from stockholders obtaining parole status:

What happens on the day of their release from prison?

Where can they go live?

With whom can they associate?

How much treatment do they have to pay for?

How long must they live by the label given to them?

Many sexual offenders do feel like outcasts. They can't see their families. They can't go to church. They must live in less-than-healthy living conditions. Many times there are rational reasons for the restrictions put into place for these offenders; however, these restrictions do, in many cases, limit the number of normal activities in which they can engage. One of the basic principles of behavior therapy is that in order to eliminate a behavioral excess, you must find a replacement behavior to fill the void. For most sexual offenders, the list of "do nots" is long. This leads to significant voids for them socially, financially, etc. For some offenders the void is filled with deviancy, since in many ways it is readily available to the sexual offender who does not have full access to the "healthier" (family, work, school) aspects of society. While it is a form of distorted thinking, many offenders take the cognitive stance of "I'm not going to try to fit in because I'll just be rejected." Many offenders, despite efforts to be viewed differently and make changes in their lives, have lost jobs and relationships because of their labels.

A man in treatment once asked me, "How come this is called sexual offender treatment? We talk about all types of things in here, everything from my relationships to how I cope with my feelings. Yet people think we're only talking about my offenses. Why don't we just call it treatment? I know why I'm here, and I'm working on understanding that." One interpretation of this man's appeal is that he is tired of the label, and he is working toward being known as something other than a sexual offender.

Reaction Theory

The final theory we would like to discuss is reaction theory. Lemert (1951) purported to show that deviance was a product of the interaction between individuals and the reactions of society to them. He preferred to think of his perspective as that of societal reaction, not labeling. One contribution of Lemert's work to societal reaction and labeling theory was his distinction between primary and secondary deviance. According to Lemert, primary deviance occurs when an actor engages in norm-violating behavior without viewing him or herself as engaging in a deviant role. The deviations "...are rationalized or otherwise dealt with as functions of a socially acceptable role" (p. 75). Secondary deviation, according to Lemert, occurs when a person begins to employ his deviant behavior or a role based upon it as a means of defense, attack, or adjustment to the overt and covert problems created by the consequent societal reaction to him. The general criminal takes on a victim posture because "people are out to get him."

IMPLICATIONS FOR THE SEXUAL OFFENDER: Similar to labeling theory, reaction theory focuses on the societal reaction to the sexual offender. Reaction theorists would propose that members of society come to expect sexual offenders to act out again, thus engaging the offender in the "drama of evil." Despite their best efforts, society doesn't allow the offenders to play a different role and thus reads deviance into every behavior they demonstrate. Smiling at a child, riding a bus, attending a church service—all are viewed within the context of their deviancy, which disallows the offender and others in society to experience him differently.

Case Example

Fred was arrested at the age of 18 for molesting a 16-year-old neighbor. While his initial crime by today's standards would be considered statutory rape, in most states he would be convicted of child molestation. Fred had to register and attend sexual offender treatment after a 5-year prison sentence. He had a difficult time accepting the label of sexual offender because his behavior with the victim at the age of 18 was consensual and age appropriate (confirmed by polygraph).

Once a promising auto mechanic as an adolescent, Fred had a difficult time finding work. He became addicted to alcohol, and was too scared to get into age-appropriate, sexual relationships. The treatment he was receiving at the time made him refer to himself as a sexual deviant. His parole agent referred to him as a pedophile. Fred reacted strongly to the deviant label and became extremely defensive.

Consideration of Theories Proposed

These theoretical models, rarely discussed in sexual offender management and treatment circles, can be helpful in shedding light on the experience of sexual offenders in society. These well-accepted theories within criminal justice research should be considered as we develop legislation that changes the degree of social control exercised against offenders. We were quite surprised that researchers are not discussing and evaluating sexual offender policy more often through the lens of these and other more multi-dimensional social-psychological models. One hypothesis to consider is whether these type of investigations and questioning would be accepted within the current political climate, as any attempt to provide alternative explanations for why sexual offenders struggle when they return to the community would be labeled as "pro sexual offender," which could lead to strong emotional reactions from the public.

In conclusion, we are proposing that change agents—therapists, probation/parole agents, policy officials, and others involved in the decision-making process—take an objective look at the models we have created and the implications they have for sexual offenders. Change agents as well as sexual offenders are faced with an uphill battle. Sexual offenders live their lives with the question of "What (punishment) is next?" While other treatment and supervision populations can see some end to their involvement with the criminal justice system, many sexual offenders will most likely continue to receive some type of punishment for the remainder of their lives. Control, strain, labeling, and reaction theories all shed some light on the processes that occur with sexual offenders (including resistance) and how they impact their place in society. Helping offenders work through and cope with this reality is often the first goal of treatment.

Chapter Three

To be alone is to be different, to be different is to be alone.
–SUZANNE GORDON, ALONE IN AMERICA

Individual Risk Factors:
How Societal and Change Agent Policies and Practices Potentially Influence Client Resistance and Risk Potential

At the heart of current intervention practices, both supervisory and clinical, is our desire to eliminate an offender's risk to reoffend. More realistically, we have gravitated toward models that seek to significantly reduce (not eliminate) this risk. Although some current treatment models do attempt to directly address individual offenders' risk factors, we find that our models have not adequately taken into account the societal and individual factors that lead to offenders' resistance to change.

To engage resistance effectively, change agents must understand the factors that lead to behaviors that we often label as resistant. Change agents must recognize those problematic behaviors that are created by the offender, and those that are common reactions to the conditions they face in their lives. This isn't to say that we should excuse an offender for problematic behavior, but how we approach the offender and his problem behavior might be quite different. For example, in the case of an offender's being late for group, we hope that change agents would have a different reaction to the offender who spent the night in the emergency room with his dying mother, than to the man who overslept for the 10th time.

Similarly, most professionals who work with sexual offenders know that being labeled a sexual offender has multiple consequences for the offender's life. As discussed in chapter 2, punishment for a sexual crime often continues for the remainder of an offender's life. Accordingly, chapter 2 discussed a number of different models from which to consider the sexual offender's plight in society, and shared different perspectives on why we observe certain resistant behaviors and attitudes from persons on probation/parole and in treatment.

While we have some anecdotal information about offenders' perceptions of treatment and supervision, the actual impact of the supervision and treatment process on an offender's ability to "get better" has rarely, if ever, been studied quantitatively. Put simply, are our intervention and supervision practices, as rooted in their social context, reducing risk on relevant risk dimensions? In an effort to move toward answering this critical question, this chapter will first consider the construct of social rejection or social exclusion, and then the relationship between social rejection and the ability of an offender to self-regulate. We will also evaluate how these constructs are connected to different dimensions of risk that change agents hope to impact in their treatment and intervention strategies.

How Social Rejection Affects the Offender

Social Rejection and Social Exclusion

An area of research studying the effects of social rejection has received considerable attention in the field of social psychology. Although it has relevance to work with sexual offenders, the idea of social rejection and its impact on the offender has rarely been discussed in sexual offender literature. Notwithstanding, Baumeister, Dewall, Ciarocco, and Twenge (2005), at Florida State University, have devoted years of research to a closely related phenomenon called social exclusion and report:

> Multiple studies have shown that being accepted versus rejected by social groups has a wide range of effects on individuals. Health, happiness, and well-being are strongly tied to whether one is accepted or rejected, such that people deprived of close social ties suffer more negative physical and psychological consequences than those with strong social networks (Cacioppo, Hawkley, & Berntson, 2003; Lynch, 1979; Myers, 1992). Ostracized individuals exhibit a broad range of distress and pathology (Williams, 2001).

In sum, whether the rejection is real or perceived, feeling rejected typically leads to unhealthy thoughts and behaviors. You may remember a time in your own life when you were not part of the most widely accepted group, or a time when your participation in something you were very interested in was not accepted and how that situation influenced your thoughts and feelings. In a related way, many persons who commit sexual offenses use thinking errors before, during, and after their offense behavior that revolve around this theme of rejection. Offenders sometimes think, "Since everyone already hates me, why should I care about others and be nice to them?" This type of maladaptive thinking is a common antecedent for many types of criminal behavior. We're confident that treatment providers reading this book will relate to hearing that type of thinking from the sexual offenders with whom they work.

Many treatment sessions are spent evaluating these types of thoughts, challenging their validity, and replacing them with healthier lines of thinking. However, offenders commonly feel rejected and scared about interacting with the world, especially when they initially come out of prison. The treatment team often has to work hard to get the offender back out into the real world with their families and friends, and to help them establish social networks that will enhance the possibility for job opportunities, healthy social interactions, and improved confidence so that they can live without committing crime.

In the past decade, sexual offenders' opportunities to enter back into the world unnoticed and without negative publicity has diminished significantly. Unlike other criminals who are released back into society, sexual offenders are introduced back into the community with their pictures, addresses, and histories on a Web site that can be accessed by just about anyone. Depending on the state in which you live, some sexual offenders have their pictures passed around the neighborhood where they will be residing, or police officers go door to door alerting neighbors of their arrival. In some cases this might be appropriate from a community safety standpoint; however, with the majority of sexual offenders there is no scientific proof that these interventions reduce recidivism. Proponents of these measure often ask the question, "Why should we care if society rejects these men—don't they deserve it?"

This is often where best practice responses to sexual offender management get confused. We once had a man in treatment who had exposed himself on one occasion while urinating after a night of binge drinking. The man had a history of domestic violence and drug abuse, but no other history of sexual misbehavior. The client was charged with a sexual crime and ordered to register as a sexual offender, attend sexual offender treatment, and live under the strict sexual offender parole guidelines. This client had languished in another program for almost a year prior to entering our program. Previous treatment providers attempted to force sexual offender treatment on him that had little relevance to his situation. He found the guidelines for treatment and supervision humiliating. His friends and family, who had been supportive of his getting help for his drug problems, were now scared of him and wanted nothing to do with him. In a session with his family, his mother starting crying and said, "I feel like I've lost my son.... He's one of those monsters my friends hear about on the news."

Not only did his family want nothing to do with him, but he was scared of applying for reliable jobs because of having to disclose his offense history. The amount of rejection this client felt from society was tremendous. His depression increased, his relationships became more distant, and he started to believe he was a predator.

In some ways, this case is pretty consistent with what is known about individuals (noncriminals) who experience a high degree of social rejection. Other studies attempting to compare those who experience social acceptance versus rejection have found some striking conclusions. Among these findings are the following:

- Rejected people are more likely than others to behave aggressively (Buckley, Winkel, & Leary, 2004; Twenge, Baumeister, Tice, & Stucke, 2001).

- Rejected people are less likely to act in pro-social ways, such as cooperating with someone or providing help (Twenge, Ciarocco, Cuervo, & Baumeister, 2003).

- Rejected people are less likely to approach and perform cognitive tasks with logical reasoning (Baumeister, Twenge, & Nuss, 2002). They engage in less meaningful thought.

- Rejected people show distorted time perception and an emphasis on the present rather than the future, are more passive than others, and lack self-awareness (Twenge, Catanese, & Baumeister, 2003).

- Rejected people demonstrate more self-destructive behaviors, as evidenced by increases in risk taking behaviors and unhealthy choices (Twenge, Catanese, & Baumeister, 2002).

Keep in mind that the subjects in these studies are typically from "normal," adult, noncriminal populations. Still, under the duress of social rejection, even prosocial individuals demonstrate significant reactions to being excluded from the mainstream or accepted "in" group. Additionally, consider that the social rejection experienced by these individuals was time limited, and that they knew they were involved in a research experiment. Despite all of these variables, they demonstrated many of the same behaviors that bring "normal" people to therapy every day. In summary, people, even nonoffenders, when faced with social rejection tend to

- Be more violent;

- Engage in less prosocial behavior;

- Be less logical in their thinking;

- Lack goal orientation, thinking only about now; and

- Be more likely to engage in foolish, risk-taking behaviors.

This list describes many of the offenders in the early stages of sexual offender treatment. Social rejection research should challenge us to think differently about our day-to-day decision making with sexual offenders. Improving intimacy deficits and general self-regulation skills are well-established as critical components of most treatment programs. Yet, we believe that treatment programs rarely acknowledge the rejection these men experience. The reaction is often, "If we validate their feelings in this area, then we're only supporting the persecutory thinking that leads them to victim posture."

Self-Regulation and Rejection

Baumeister has also gone on to investigate the process of self-regulation. Defined as the capacity to control or alter one's responses, self-regulation is a requirement for producing adaptive and socially desirable behavior (Baumeister et al., 2002). If rejection could be shown to impair or undermine self-regulation, then a broad range of socially undesirable behaviors might ensue, consistent with what has already been found regarding the behavior of rejected individuals. Baumeister's research has investigated three hypotheses attempting to measure the relationship between rejection and self-regulation. A summary of his research in this area demonstrating support for the three hypotheses and a discussion regarding the implications for offenders follows:

- The first hypothesis is that rejection impairs intellectual performance and cognitive processing when conscious executive control is required (Baumeister et al., 2002). Self-regulation is closely related to executive control (and, indeed, is probably one major form of it). Hence, the pattern of cognitive impairments indirectly involves self-regulatory deficits and can become a significant detriment for individuals.

- The second supported hypothesis in this line of research is that rejected participants exhibit more antisocial behavior and a reduced willingness to perform self-sacrificing actions such as helping others. Such findings depict rejected individuals as selfish. Yet other data show them also to be more self-defeating than other people. For example, rejected people take more foolish risks, make more unhealthy choices, and procrastinate more than others (Twenge et al., 2002). Selfishness and self-defeating behavior are seemingly at opposite ends of the spectrum of self-interested behavior. However, they both tend to involve self-regulation failures. So the data is mixed—are they more selfish or just emotionally unavailable to help others? Effective self-regulation is often needed to make people overcome selfish impulses and do what is best for others. Self-regulation is also needed for the pursuit of insightful self-interest, such as enabling the person to resist impulsive temptations. The most common form of self-defeating behavior involves seeking short-term benefits that are accompanied by long-term costs, such as overeating or smoking (Baumeister & Scher, 1988; Mischel, 1996). Self-regulation may have evolved to enable people to resist such impulses and cultivate long-term gains.

- The third hypothesis is that rejection appears to create a deconstructed mental state that may lead to diminished self-regulation. Twenge et al. (2003) found that rejected people had a distorted sense of the passage of time. Time perception is linked to effective self-regulation, and as self-regulation deteriorates, time is perceived as moving more slowly (Vohs & Schmeichel, 2003), just as it does among rejected persons. Likewise, rejection causes people to avoid self-awareness (Twenge et al.), and self-awareness is vital for effective self-regulation (Carver & Scheier, 1982). Self-regulation also benefits from meaningful thought, such as comparison with standards (Carver & Scheier), whereas rejected people exhibit decrements in meaningful thought (Baumeister et al., 2002). Thus, again, the pattern of effects of rejection is broadly consistent with the notion that self-regulation is impaired, though direct evidence is lacking.

The implications for this research regarding sexual offenders are profound. Social rejection, a likely experience for criminals in general, and even more likely for sexual offenders, has many negative effects that could directly or indirectly affect our ability to manage and relate to them. This social rejection and self-regulation research is significant in so many ways to our work with sexual offenders. In sum, unresolved social rejection doesn't usually lead to good things. As change agents, we can either ignore this reality or help the offender resolve it, hopefully in constructive ways. We would argue that helping offenders resolve these issues in a constructive manner may actually be one of the most important things we do to reduce recidivism.

Social Rejection and Risk Factors

As demonstrated in the discussion thus far, understanding social rejection and its impact on people in general should make us step back and ask the following questions:

- What does the social rejection literature mean for our clients in treatment?

- How does social rejection affect their risk?

- What can I do as a change agent to help offenders cope with social rejection?

- How do I talk with offenders about social rejection, while not giving them an excuse to misbehave?

- How can I use my knowledge about social rejection research to help me engage better with my clients?

As we work toward answering these important questions, consider the relevance of these questions as they relate to everyday practice and decision making. Treatment and supervision strategies targeting relevant risk factors are now a widely accepted model in the world of sexual offender treatment (Beech, Fisher, & Thornton, 2003). Helping offenders work on those factors most relevant to their offense behavior and other deficits in their lives also helps to engage clients. For example, requiring all men convicted of a sexual offense to go through drug rehabilitation may not make sense, especially for those offenders who never had a drug or alcohol problem. It may make them question the credibility of the treatment program. This is much like a person with a sore throat who goes to the doctor but is given medicine to treat an ear infection! In essence, to reduce resistance and increase buy-in from the sexual offender, interventions need to make sense to offenders. Change agents should take time to consider how they will explain the rationale of their interventions. While offenders may not initially accept our reasons, they will at least understand why we are taking a certain position.

The importance of engaging resistance—creating a desire within the offender to change—relates also to the dynamic, changeable risk factors of modern-day sexual offender management. Ideally, we introduce interventions into the offender's life that make sense, at least rationally, to the offender and to the supervisory team. However, we all know that balancing community safety with the necessary clinical interventions is a challenging task. Understandably and ultimately, treatment and supervision officials will make decisions on the side of community safety.

For example, a change agent team, consisting minimally of a therapist and probation officer, must attempt to make a decision about whether to allow a 28-year-old sexual offender attend the county fair with his girlfriend. This offender molested his 14-year-old niece on one occasion 10 years ago. Typically, a multitude of factors should be considered. The positive benefits of allowing the offender to go include engagement in an activity that is pro-social in nature; opportunity for the offender to develop an age-appropriate romantic relationship; and improved mood (cotton candy can have that effect). The negative aspects include access to children; potential access to alcohol; and a setting that is difficult to monitor. Without more information, it would be very difficult to make an informed decision about the question at hand. More importantly, without empirical evidence and case-specific information, we could in fact make decisions that would increase resistance and, potentially, increase risk.

If we hope to reduce resistance and create real changes in the offender, we must be aware of the process we engage in to make these decisions. In theory, if clients improve their functioning around these variables, can see the value in these changes, and are reinforced for these gains, then over time, the clients might become more compliant and less resistant with supervision and treatment expectations.

While this section predominantly focused on issues of social rejection and the sexual offenders, it is important to note that many victims experience similar reactions when they report the abuse they have suffered. Victims are sometimes ostracized from their families and community when they report crimes of sexual assault. Policy makers and victim treatment providers and advocates should be aware of the social rejection phenomena and consider it as they create legislation and models of support for these victims.

Overview of Dynamic Risk Factors for Sexual Offenders

Over the past decade, research has helped to determine which factors are most critical to focus on with offenders in treatment. The research has shown more clearly that when treating sexual offenders we must develop models of treatment that pertain to those variables that place an offender at highest risk to offend again. It is critical that change agents understand the various dynamic, changeable risk factors and how they are influenced by systemic (supervision and legislative policy) and therapeutic mechanisms. In practice, these variables could be grounds for additional resistance, and possibly increased risk, or positive therapeutic gain. In their critical 1998 meta-analysis, Hanson and Bussiére found the following categories of dynamic variables most pertinent to sexual offender reoffending:

- INTIMACY DEFICITS: Sexual offenders report low levels of satisfaction with their intimate relationships. Those who have not been in committed relationships are at higher risk.

- SOCIAL INFLUENCES: Offenders who have more criminal associations are more likely to recidivate in either sexual or non-sexual ways. We know that criminals are more likely to have other criminal friends than noncriminals. This places them at a higher risk to engage in criminal behavior.

- ATTITUDES TOLERANT OF SEXUAL ASSAULT: Sexual offenders who have strong attitudes or beliefs that are supportive of sexually assaultive behavior toward women and/or children are at higher risk to reoffend.

- SEXUAL SELF-REGULATION: Many sexual offenders have strong feelings of sexual entitlement and use this as an irrational reason for their need to act out sexually. Many sexual offenders have also learned to use their deviant behaviors as a way to reduce their level of stress. Behaviors that are problematic for men include excessive use of pornography (e.g., magazines, video, Internet); high frequency of masturbation; and using "paid for" sexual services (e.g., strip clubs, escort services, prostitutes).

- GENERAL SELF-REGULATION: Behaviors that can be described as impulsive or with little self-control are in excess among offenders in general. Offenders tend to smoke and drink excessively, use drugs, drive fast, quit school, and engage in multiple short-term sexual relationships beginning at an early age (Hanson & Morton-Bourgon, 2004).

- ACUTE RISK FACTORS: Factors that can quickly alter an offender's capacity to make safe decisions for his life include substance abuse, negative mood, anger resolution abilities, and proximity of potential victims.

Interestingly enough, others factors such as empathy, denial, and low motivation often create the battleground for increased resistance and are the least supported in terms of predicting reoffense. Hanson and Morton-Bourgon (2004) go so far as to suggest that denial could be interpreted as the offender's at least admitting that sexual offender behavior is wrong, while those who openly admit it may see nothing wrong with their behavior. Denial such as this is conscious rather than clinical. A more recent meta-analysis (Hanson & Morton-Bourgon) found some similarities to earlier research (Hanson & Bussiére, 1998) including factors such as sexual preoccupations, conflicts in intimate relationships, hostility, emotional identification with children, and attitudes tolerant of sexual assault.

As a result of current research findings, change agents now have valuable information that they can use when assessing an offender's offense dynamics and other life areas known to be relevant to recidivism risk. The verdict is still out on whether altering these specific risk changes alters an offender's recidivism risk. Some research demonstrates a small, insignificant change in an offender's treatment progress (Hanson & Morton-Bourgon, 2004), while other research demonstrates that positive changes on these significant dynamic risk factors is indicative of a reduction in risk to recidivate sexually and nonsexually (Beech, Erikson, Friendship, & Ditchfield, 2001; Marques, Day, Wiederanders, & Nelson, 2002).

While we should be careful not to draw final conclusions from the above findings, we do need to consider the data as we create and implement policies for working with sexual offenders. It is crucial that we, as effective administrators and professionals working in the field of sexual violence, provide the public with accurate information regarding the true risk of sexual recidivism among sexual offenders being lower than commonly believed. We need honest discussions amongst ourselves as we develop policies for the offenders we supervise. The variation in recidivism rates suggests that not all sexual offenders should be treated the same, and that most are not high risk to reoffend. Within the correctional literature, it is well established that the most effective use of correctional resources targets truly high-risk offenders and applies lower levels of resources to lower-risk offenders (Andrews & Bonta, 2003). Research has even suggested that offenders may actually be made worse by the imposition of higher levels of treatment and supervision than is warranted given their risk level (Andrews & Bonta).

More relevant to the current discussion is an understanding of how and why it is critical to make therapeutic and supervision decisions based on relevant risk factors for individual offenders. We believe that effective change agents can reduce offender resistance if relevant risk factors are addressed in a collaborative manner, and by helping the offender address the deficit around the risk factor. While this philosophy could apply to all risk factor categories, we will discuss this assumption by addressing three of the dynamic risk factor categories: intimacy deficits, social influences, and emotional regulation.

Intimacy Deficits

The research on this variable is pretty clear. Offenders who have a difficult time initiating, forming, and maintaining relationships are at a higher risk to reoffend. This premise is supported by several researchers (Marshall, 1993; Hudson & Ward, 1997). We also know that these offenders have a very difficult time knowing how to enter into and co-exist in a trusting, loving relationship. In addition to having poor skills in these relationships, a significant number of sexual offenders report little to no enjoyment in their sexual relationships (Seidman, Marshall, Hudson, & Robertson, 1994). Finally, sexual offenders who have never been married are at increased risk for recidivism (Hanson & Bussiére, 1998).

When considering intimacy deficits for sexual offenders, change agents should evaluate the different aspects of intimacy. The following categories should be assessed before coming to conclusions about the offender's overall deficits:

- How does the offender relate with intimate partners?

- How much does the offender identify (over identify) emotionally with children?

- What level of anger or hostility (overt/covert) does the offender display toward age-appropriate partners?

- How isolated and lonely is the offender? How much rejection has the client experienced or created in life?

- Is the offender capable of demonstrating care and concern for others?

Intimacy deficits, by definition, can also lead people to social rejection. They manifest in our clients through broken relationships with family members and previous friends, and the fear of new relationships. Often, men on parole or probation must tell any potential employer, lover, and person with whom they wish to spend significant time that they are a registered sexual offender. No wonder many offenders choose to stay away from jobs and close relationships during their time on supervision. This is a huge problem. How do we help offenders through these challenging situations?

Case Example

James, age 35, was on probation for 3 years after engaging in frotteurism with a client in the hair salon where he worked. James had never married, had been unsuccessful in most age-appropriate romantic relationships, and had a fear of trusting women. James was a "nice" guy, didn't cause problems for his probation officer, and had the attitude that he would just do his time on the street and get on with his life. He was intelligent and knew the right things to say, how to keep the focus off himself in group, and how to impress his probation officer. He never did anything, went anywhere, or asked for any privileges.

So what would be best for this client? On paper, James was the model client. He always showed up for appointments, never missed treatment, had clean drug tests, and never asked to do anything except go to a church service alone on Sunday nights—a service that did not include children. He actually had a girlfriend who was a strong, positive influence in his life. However, the management and treatment policies in place at that time supported his comfort-zone lifestyle of isolation and depression. The probation conditions included the following guidelines:

- You cannot have a romantic relationship without first having your potential partner go through a chaperone contract.

- You must stay in your residence from the hours of 7:00 p.m. to 7:00 am, unless otherwise approved by your probation officer.

- You must have no contact with family members unless they are first approved by your probation officer.

- You cannot enter malls or other places where families with children might congregate.

The list could go on and on—and many of these make sense for individual offenders. However, did they really make sense for James? While the treatment team could stress the importance of James' engaging in more socially appropriate environments with adults, the probation stipulations in many ways supported his desire for isolation from society and meaningful relationships. In the end, his conditions were modified to more fully support his need to engage in appropriate social interactions. But for the first 2 years of his probation, he did very little to work on his intimacy deficits outside of treatment. However, once the treatment team began individualizing treatment based on relevant risk factors, James was challenged by his treatment provider to address the concerns related to his maladaptive attempts to get his sexual needs met. James and his girlfriend participated in couples therapy during the latter stages of his treatment. Through these sessions, their relationship not only improved, but James came to recognize more about his problems with intimacy in general. James even commented toward the end of treatment that while he was initially scared to do couples treatment with his girlfriend, he knew it made sense. He discussed with his treatment providers and probation officers how he really felt cared for when the treatment team started helping him address the things he feared most.

It's also easy to see how addressing intimacy deficits directly impacts the degree of social rejection a person experiences. Without positive, corrective experiences in appropriate relationships, men like James are probably more likely to spend their lives alone and without the benefits that adults experience from close relationships. We believe that there is no better time than when offenders are in treatment to address these needs. The support, education, and guidance of a change agent team may provide one of the few times in an offender's life when s/he can make meaningful changes in this area.

Social Influences

Among the general criminal population, the number of criminal companions is one of the strongest predictors of recidivism (Gendreau, Little, & Goggin, 1996). Within this risk category, change agents should consider a number of factors:

- Who are the offender's friends? What are the criminal histories of these individuals?

- Did the offender have a gang affiliation?

- With whom does the offender wish to spend time now? What reasons does the offender give for wanting these connections?

- What positive social influences has the offender lost since his/her offense?

- What are the social influences at the offender's place of work? In his/her living situation?

For some sexual offenders, understanding and heavily scrutinizing their social network is critical. This risk factor may be extremely relevant with those who have committed sexual offenses in tandem with other offenders (i.e., gang rapes and pedophiles involved in pro-pedophilic networks, such as NAMBLA). Another example is the sexual offender who, in the past and currently, has appropriate and healthy social networks. The problem wasn't and isn't within the social network, but in the possibility of living two separate lives—one with a socially acceptable network and another in isolated deviance.

In the latter cases, we believe it is critical to engage the positive aspects of the offender's social network and not put up constraints to these relationships. The case example below demonstrates an example of this situation.

> Mike, 37, had recently been released from prison after serving 10 years for molesting his 12-year-old stepdaughter. Mike had been an active member of his church during the time of his offenses, and the church was devastated when they heard about his crimes. The minister of his church visited him regularly throughout his prison sentence and helped him find an apartment when he was released.
>
> At first glance, the change agent team was very skeptical of his church involvement. Although the victim and her mother no longer attended this particular church, this was around the time when significant publicity was taking place in the media about the sex crimes committed by priests. Change agents in the case initially denied Mike's request to attend church on the basis that many of the members had stayed in contact with him throughout his prison sentence. Change agents assumed that because the members wanted ongoing contact with Mike, they must not think his crimes were significant. After closer examination and meetings with several of the church members and clergy, the change agent team came to some very different conclusions. They discovered that a group of men in Mike's church wanted to mentor and hold him accountable for his actions.
>
> In Mike's case, the people from his church were concerned about having Mike back in their congregation. They welcomed education from the change agent team. Mike signed releases of information so that key members of the church could be

communicated with about events that Mike wanted to attend. Without these church members, Mike would have had literally no positive social influences in his life. Without the help offered from church members in finding him an appropriate living situation, Mike would have likely had to live in a halfway house with other convicted felons.

A common mistake made among change agents is blaming and being skeptical of any person who wants to be close to the offender. There are cases where family members, friends, and social group members do collude consciously or unconsciously with the offender during his offending period. However, in many other cases these people really didn't know there was a problem or didn't have the skills to intervene. When given the right information and guidance on how to form a different kind of relationship with the offender, these individuals can be extremely valuable in engaging a client in treatment and adding an additional layer of supervision to the change agent team.

In summary, change agent teams should look critically at an offender's social influences. A thorough review of their past and present friends and family members is a good place to start. Finding ways to engage and strengthen positive social influences while discouraging negative influences should be a goal of any change agent team. If these two goals are met, change agents will gain valuable information about the offender's progress around a key dynamic risk variable, and could reduce the amount of resistance experienced from the offender and their social network. Most importantly, the change agent team could help the offender escape long-term social rejection and the consequences associated with this phenomena.

General Self-Regulation

In addition to problems with intimacy and engaging in helpful social relationships, many sexual offenders also have problems regulating their daily behaviors. This dysregulation often manifests itself in the form of impulsive behavior, which is common among criminals in general. Gottfredson and Hirschi (1990) proposed that impulsivity or low self-control is one of the common links among all illegal behaviors. "Offenders are more likely to abuse drugs, drive recklessly, fail in school, smoke, have financial problems, and have histories of multiple short-lived sexual relationships." The Hare Psychopathy Checklist–Revised (Hare, 1991) and Level of Service Inventory–Revised (Andrews & Bonta, 1995), two scales used to predict criminal recidivism, feature several items related to impulsive decision making and general lifestyle instability. Key research (Hanson & Bussiére, 1998) has also demonstrated that general criminality predicts sexual offense recidivism among sexual offender samples.

Overall, sexual offenders may actually have fewer problems with lifestyle instability than other offender groups. However, with certain types of sexual offenders, impulsivity can directly or indirectly contribute to sexual offending. For example, impulsivity can contribute directly when a pedophile sees a child, has a deviant fantasy, and finds a way to be alone with that child. Indirectly, impulsivity can contribute to a situation where an offender makes a decision to go buy some legal pornography that might trigger deviant sexual thoughts, or when an offender buys drugs that could lower sexual inhibitions.

As change agents, these are the behaviors we often see in our offices or hear about in group therapy. Many offenders attempting to reintegrate back into society lack the skills necessary to manage daily responsibilities. If an offender can't pay his bills, get to work on time, or resist temptations to engage in other destructive behaviors, it's quite likely that he will add another layer or two of the social rejection he is already experiencing by the mere fact that he is a sexual offender.

As change agents, we should consider a number of things when helping an offender address this dynamic risk factor. First, change agents should be aware that for some people impulsivity is due to a bio-chemical mechanism within the brain. We know, for example, that individuals with attention-deficit with hyperactivity disorder (ADHD) experience high degrees of distractibility. When appropriately medicated, patients have demonstrated a significant reduction in these symptoms (Nigg, 2001). For offenders under our care, we must consider whether a referral for medication might be appropriate. We have seen cases where offenders, never before medicated, began medication treatment for ADHD and showed a significant reduction in their levels of impulsivity. With the help of additional self-management strategies, some of these clients begin to realize that they can gain control over their behaviors. This provides positive personal and social rewards for offenders who have struggled with impulsivity for their entire lives.

Second, we should dedicate treatment time to this critical area. Some sexual offender treatment providers still have the mindset that if they are not talking about an offender's actual offense, they aren't doing sexual offender treatment. In addressing impulsivity, it's helpful to think about the purpose of the actual behavior. Many offenders engage in the impulsive behavior in response to an uncomfortable or uncontrollable emotional state. The reputation developed by individuals with these characteristics leads them to be social outcasts, and in a sort of social "black hole." Helping them out of the hole is the job of change agents and can help reduce further chances of recidivism.

Finally, we should consider how to manage highly impulsive men and give them the additional supports they need in order to be successful in the community. Referring offenders to credit counseling, AA, and anger management groups could be supports that would offer additional accountability, as well as increased positive social interaction. Because some highly impulsive offenders are at a much higher risk to recidivate sexually and non-sexually, we must consider the array of options for supervision that are available to us. Regular maintenance polygraphs, more significant surveillance strategies, drug testing, and credit checking may actually help the sexual offender stay crime free and in the community. Of course, without self-management gains made in treatment, these strategies may only help prevent further crimes while the offender is under formal supervision.

For sexual offenders who have difficulties just maintaining life, we have an opportunity to show them another way to live. How we approach this task will have some bearing on the outcome. Change agents working with highly impulsive offenders should acknowledge this fact early on, and then work with the offenders to help them find other ways to meet the needs they are trying to obtain through destructive behaviors.

Moving Toward Social Inclusion and Reduced Risk

As change agents we are faced with a daunting task as we attempt to protect society and help sexual offenders make positive changes in their lives. Sometimes these goals seem to contradict one another; e.g., making a protective decision for society further alienates and increases an offender's risk on another dynamic risk factor. We hope change agents will consider the social rejection research as they develop supervision and treatment plans. Helping offenders reintegrate into society through positive contributions could significantly reduce the direct and indirect negative affects of social exclusion.

Stated in a different way, Singer (1997) notes that "we should provide offenders with other-centered pursuits. In doing this, we provide socially excluded offenders with a feeling of connection to or an embeddedness in the world around them." Not only must an offender accept prosocial norms and behavioral expectations in order to go straight, but society must figure out a model by which it eventually comes to accept the offender as well (Maruna, 2001, p. 119). The challenge exists, however, because employers, change agents, and members of the community at large have little confidence in their own ability to discriminate between genuine and dishonest claims of an offender's reform. As a result, the safest option when faced with the struggle of interpreting any offender's claim to being a "new man" is to label the offender a charlatan and his behavior changes as superficial. The risk of seeing the offender as a new man could open oneself to being hurt, manipulated, abused, and criticized or being made to seem a naïve player of the social game (Maruna). For change agents, this is a big risk.

As ex-offenders learn to navigate the world without criminal behaviors, they may need to experience some level of personal success in the conventional world before they realize that they do not need the criminal lifestyle to feel relevant and important. Falling back into the criminal lifestyle is no longer a matter of simply going back to the "devil they know," because the ex-offender now sees options and alternatives that are equally or more rewarding and, most importantly, personally attainable (Maruna, 2001).

While much progress has been made, the sexual offender treatment and supervision community needs more examples of how to effectively translate risk prediction research into plausible treatment and supervision models. System administrators face the challenge of developing models that allow change agents the time they need to develop individualized plans of treatment and supervision that will: maximize the offender's chances of reclaiming a place in society; reduce the offender's risk to reoffend; and provide society with accurate assurance that they are doing everything possible to protect past and potential victims. In making these efforts transparent to offenders, we believe that these changes can lead to reduced resistance from offenders and greater opportunities for these individuals to make the necessary changes to their lives.

Chapter Four

What man actually needs is not a tensionless state but rather the striving and struggling for some goal worthy of him.
–VICTOR FRANKL

Changing:
The Transtheoretical Model and Offender Change

Change is difficult because there is no single way that people change, nor is there a predetermined step-by-step process to transform behavior. This is particularly true for sexual offenders because, as most agree, sexual offending is caused by multiple factors that vary depending upon the individual. The challenges for change agents mount when offenders are resistant to change and to the change process itself. This can culminate in a feeling of hopelessness and the belief that offenders cannot change. In some cases, offenders are labeled "in denial." Tierney and Mc-Cabe (2002) point out that while "denial [may be] considered to reflect low motivation [to change] and vice versa, there is no empirical evaluation of this relationship." In fact, some offenders may exhibit signs of denial (e.g., minimizations, blame, and a whole slew of other cognitive distortions) and still wish that they were different and able to change. Many times offenders' seemingly resistant and incorrigible behavior may simply reflect their own desire to change and the frustration of not knowing how.

When offenders do not know how to change, some change agents seem to believe that it is easier to simply change their behavior for them (e.g., limit their actions, keep them incarcerated or under strict supervision). Although controlling their behavior may suppress inappropriate behavior for a while, it does not help offenders learn to control their own behavior or help them live nonharmful lives when they are finally out of the system or in a situation fraught with triggers and risks. The ultimate goals would be to instill in offenders the ability to get their needs met in healthy ways as well as to thwart urges toward inappropriate behavior by instilling a personal motivation to do so.

Since no one-size-fits-all plan instills lasting change in offenders, change should be viewed as an art form. Enduring and prosocial change must begin within the individual and express itself as a manifestation of the individual's own sense of meaning and purpose. Therefore creativity is required in developing clear and applicable plans that blend both overarching goals (no harmful behavior) with the offender's inner goals (e.g., subjective meaning and happiness). This perspective parallels Maruna's (2001) statement that "to successfully maintain... abstinence from crime, ex-offenders need to make sense of their lives." Maruna's conclusions were based on comparative evaluation of offenders who changed their behavior patterns against those who did not. He found that offenders who changed established "redemption scripts" containing core beliefs that illustrated a person's "true self," an optimistic perception of personal control over one's destiny, and the desire to be productive and give something back to society (p. 88). Those who did not change maintained a victim stance in which behavior was viewed as out of their control and a product of external sources which Maruna referred to as "condemnation scripts."

Although offenders need assistance and guidance in the change process, change itself must be self-directed. As Ward (2002) expressed: "Offenders need to make their own choices." The guidance that change agents provide might come in the form of helping offenders identify long-term goals. In addition, change agents can make available to the offender all of the known strategies of success. Most importantly, change agents can offer the knowledge of how change occurs and the support necessary to navigate the process. Understanding the change process can also assist change agents in goal planning and assessing progress.

The Transtheoretical Model

One popular and comprehensible model of change is the Transtheoretical Model (TTM), also known as the "stages of change." The model was developed by James Prochaska (1982) in an effort to understand the process of change that transcended adherence to a single theoretical orientation. Since its inception, the TTM has been applied to a variety of change processes including psychotherapy, health care, and substance recovery. Its ability to be applied to so many different settings likely rests in its applicability to the individual's abilities, awareness, and current readiness to change. Prochaska, DiClemente, and Norcross (1992) asserted that traditional treatment programs treat all individuals like they are ready for change and open to therapeutic intervention at the outset. In addition, although "unconditional positive regard, authenticity, living in the here and now, confrontation of beliefs, social interest, conditioning and contingencies" are valuable tools, these interventions do not sufficiently explain therapeutic change (Prochaska & DiClemente, 1992). According to TTM, change is facilitated, in part, by identifying core stages, processes, and levels of transformation. Scott and Wolfe (2003) asserted that an individual's placement in the change process reflects a number of variables, including motivation, denial, and willingness to seek help. Therefore individualized interventions are required to facilitate change. This is consistent with Levy's (1997) perspective that "treatment outcome is much improved when treatment is tailored to the individual. In particular, it seems that tailoring treatments to an individual's readiness or stage of change greatly improves treatment outcome" (p. 278).

The Stages and Processes of Change

According to Prochaska and DiClemente (1982) change occurs in a series of steps or stages. The stages are precontemplation (not thinking about changing), contemplation (considering changing), preparation (getting ready), action (making efforts to change) and maintenance (sustaining change). Each stage represents the state of the individual and his/her decision making process, cognitive experiences, behavior, and emotions as opposed to external or social influences of change. In addition, the stages are not necessarily linear; that is, individuals may demonstrate signs of advancement onto the next stage only to return to a previous stage.

For this reason TTM usually takes the form of a "spiral" (see Figure 4.1). That is, some individuals will move linearly through the stages of change from contemplation to preparation to action and then to maintenance, but most individuals will spend time in one stage and then regress to an earlier stage before finally advancing. Movement between stages results from a struggle between the pros and cons of changing. This struggle is often referred to as Decisional Balance (Janis & Mann, 1977). Individuals should be supported through this process so that demoralization and increased resistance can be averted (Prochaska & DiClemente, 1992). Ideal progression through the stages will accompany increased awareness of triggers and potential lapses to earlier stages.

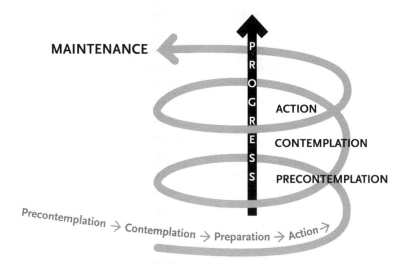

Figure 4.1: The Spiral Model of the Stages of Change

Adapted from Prochaska and DiClemente (1992).

Processes of Change

The stages of change represent levels when individuals are ready to engage in specific steps toward long-term change. The processes of change represent strategies or interventions that can assist in healthy transitions from one stage to the next (Prochaska, 1991).

Prochaska, DiClemente, and Norcross (1992) highlight nine specific processes that are used to facilitate lasting changes. It is important to note that some of the processes are cognitively based while others rely on behavioral tactics. Table 4.1 illustrates the processes as associated with specific behavioral goals at each stage of change. Table 4.2 delineates when the processes are likely to take place.

Table 4.1 The process of change	
PROCESS	DEFINITION
Consciousness Raising (Cognitive)	Increasing the individual's knowledge about self and the problem. This includes an awareness of the impact of the behavior on self and others. This process can be applied via psychoeducational groups, bibliotherapy, and respectful confrontation.
Helping Relationships (Behavioral)	Identifying and utilizing appropriate and prosocial people, e.g. support groups, family, friends, therapists, etc.
Dramatic Relief (Cognitive, Behavioral)	Experiencing and expressing feelings about one's problem and solutions.
Self-Liberation (Cognitive)	Choosing and committing to action and experiencing a belief that one has the ability to change. This can be accomplished through collaborating with treatment planning, goal setting, and contracting.
Self-Evaluation (Cognitive)	Assessing emotional experiences and beliefs regarding the core problem. Encouraging corrective emotional experiences.

Table 4.1 (cont.)

PROCESS	DEFINITION
Social Liberation (Cognitive, Behavioral)	Raising awareness regarding alternative, healthy behaviors that are available in society. This is particularly crucial for those who are deprived of healthy social opportunities. Advocating for rights of repressed, empowering, policy interventions, involvement in restorative justice, and restitution.
Counter-Conditioning (Behavioral)	Substituting alternatives for problem behaviors with healthy self-coping skills such as stress management, relaxation, desensitization, positive self-statements, healthy sexual relationships/outlets.
Stimulus Control (Behavioral)	Avoiding or countering stimuli that elicit problem behaviors via restructuring one's environment (e.g., minimizing antisocial associations, or pre-offense stimuli), avoiding high-risk situations.
Reinforcement Management (Behavioral)	Rewarding oneself or being rewarded by others for making changes: contingency contracts, overt and covert reinforcement.

*Adapted from Prochaska, DiClemente, and Norcross (1992)

Table 4.2
The common processes applied at each stage of change

	PRECONTEMPLATION	CONTEMPLATION	PREPARATION	ACTION	MAINTENANCE
P R O C E S S	Consciousness Raising	Self-Reevaluation	Self-Liberation	Reinforcement Management	
	Dramatic Relief			Helping Relationships	
	Environmental Reevaluation			Stimulus Control	
				Counter-Conditioning	

*Adapted from Prochaska, DiClemente, and Norcross (1992)

The Applicability of the Transtheoretical Model to Sexual Offenders

The utility of the model with sexual offenders was discussed at length by Tierney and McCabe (2002), in addition to various other authors (Kear-Colwell & Pollock, 1997; Long, 2002; Dewhurst & Nielsen, 1999). Tierney and McCabe undertook the task of assessing offenders' readiness for treatment by adapting the Stages of Change Questionnaire (SOCQ) (McConnaughy, Prochaska, & Velicer, 1983) to sexual offenders. These researchers found that the questionnaire adequately assessed an offender's readiness for treatment as well as his/her stage of change. Importantly, the scale did not appear affected by offenders' social desirability or attempts to present in a favorable light. The researchers additionally assessed decisional balance simply by evaluating the offenders' perceptions of the advantages and disadvantages of changing. As noted by Tierney and McCabe, more research is needed; however, their study concluded that the SOCQ was particularly helpful in determining treatment readiness and determinations about treatment planning. For example, denying offenders (in the precontemplation stage) would likely benefit from consciousness-raising interventions as opposed to a relapse prevention program.

The above suggests that in addition to providing a construct for understanding change, TTM can be used as an assessment tool as well as a foundation for sexual offender specific interventions. Knowing when to apply specific interventions is crucial in the early stage of treatment when dropout is so high. The Transtheoretical Model has been compared to traditional methods of predicting early termination from treatment. Most efforts to predict treatment dropout used client characteristics. Prochaska (1991) suggests that the stages, processes, and the decisional balance offered by TTM can act as an assessment of one's progress. It appears that premature terminators tend to perceive more disadvantages than benefits of change.

Smith, Subich, and Kalodner (1995), not surprisingly, found that a sample of general psychotherapy patients entering treatment at the preparation stage were more likely to complete treatment versus those that entered at the precontemplation stage. In addition, these researchers found that individuals utilizing particular processes (self-reevaluation, self-liberation, helping relationships, consciousness raising, dramatic relief, and social liberation) had the lowest rates of premature dropout. Interestingly, the use of stimulus control processes was not correlated with termination. This may be because simply changing one's environment or avoiding problematic stimuli is not enough to either abandon or stay in the change process. If these results can be applied to sexual offender populations, it appears that change agents who frequently assess the offender's stage in the change process, as well as the processes/interventions utilized, can identify potential dropouts and apply more intensive strategies. For example, if offenders are assessed as highly endorsing precontemplative thoughts, the change agent can emphasize consciousness raising and self-reevaluation techniques, which can help the individual progress to the contemplation stage (Prochaska, 1991). If the decisional balance is shifting in the direction of not changing, the change agent may have to apply even more persuasive techniques.

In addition, this model can be used to assess progress. Tierney and McCabe (2002) found that the use of the processes of consciousness raising with offenders dramatically reduced the number of deniers in a program from 31% to 2% and with those offenders who minimized their offense from 32% to 11%. Again, more research on this topic is needed, but these findings are encouraging. Research, although not based on sexual offenders, shows that successful self-changers demonstrated an ideal pattern of utilizing the change processes over time. In particular, successful self-changers tend to use cognitive processes in the contemplation stage and then transition to behavioral processes in the action and maintenance stages (Prochaska & DiClemente, 1992).

The following case example will be used to illustrate each of the stages as applied to sexual offender treatment.

Case Example

Trudy, a 26-year-old Caucasian female, was referred to a program after serving a prison sentence stemming from charges that she forced two adolescent boys to have sexual intercourse with her at knife point. During the initial intake, Trudy asserted that the incident was a consensual sexual encounter, and that she resorted to showing a weapon out of fear for her own safety when the minor victims became aggressive with her. She said she never intended to harm them but showed the knife to let them know that she was not going to let them hurt her. Despite arguing with them, she stated that she knew the boys wanted to have sex with her because "every boy would want to have sex with a grown woman" and said, "If I hadn't initiated the sex, they would have." When the intake worker attempted to gather more information about the offense, Trudy became exasperated, stating, "When is this going to be over. It's nice outside and I want to go for a walk."

The first 5 months of treatment were marked by Trudy's sporadic attendance and general apathy toward the process. She repeatedly stated, "I don't know why I have to come here—it's boring." Her participation increased after she watched a television special on the effects of child sexual abuse. She came to treatment with a lot of questions about the impact of such abuse. Her therapist took the opportunity to provide general education regarding both the short- and long-term impact of sexual abuse. Consequently, she became willing to explore her own sexual victimization as a child. After acknowledging her own fear while being sexually victimized, she vaguely acknowledged that the boys may have in fact felt threatened by the presence of the knife. However, she still asserted that the sex was consensual and that she needed to carry a knife with her for protection: "Where I grew up you have to carry a knife." During a group session she became angry with another member for challenging her on the need to carry a knife and dropped out of the program, stating that she did not need to change.

After a few days, Trudy returned to the program and requested to participate in the anger management component of the program. She stated that she felt overwhelmed by being confronted by another group member, and it reminded her that she frequently gets into conflict with others and ruins every relationship she gets into, even when people are trying to help her. She added, "The only people I end up hanging out with are those who I get into trouble with. Maybe I need to get away from them." She apologized for her behavior to the group and expressed anxiety and uncertainty about her ability to change. Trudy assessed her patterns of behavior and her skills and tried to learn better ways of dealing with her fear and anger than resorting to, or threatening people with, violence. She began to express hope and asked for additional guidance. She became more interested in the entire program and rejoined the female sexual offender group. Trudy had perfect attendance for the next 6 months and completed all homework assignments.

It was difficult, but with the support of other offenders and her probation officer, Trudy began severing ties with former negative peers and reestablishing contact with her supportive family. Although previously not compliant with requests for a psychiatric evaluation, she now regularly took a prescribed mood stabilizer. She also rejoined the women's sexual offender group and took responsibility for her behavior.

By connecting her own feelings of being abused with the experience of her victims, Trudy eventually acknowledged full culpability for her offense and its impact. She worked through each stage of the program and even asked to participate in a "beginners" sexual offender group to act as a mentor. She added that she wanted to make a commitment to help others and also wanted to remind herself of the process that she went through to keep her motivated toward a healthy lifestyle. When Trudy was released from her probation, she requested supportive sessions to assist her in managing her behavior in the future. She added that she found that participating in therapy eventually became crucial to her mental health and also a rewarding experience that she wanted to continue.

Stage One: Precontemplation

The precontemplation stage of change has been referred to as the "huh?" stage. It represents a period in the change process when the individual is unaware of the need to change. Perhaps the individual believes that her current behavior is acceptable, right, or simply the only option. Some offenders may believe that they are unable to change and are discouraged as a result of failed past attempts at modifying their behavior (Tierney & McCabe, 2002). In some cases these individuals are labeled "in denial," and although this may be accurate in some cases, another perspective is simply that they have not been presented with information that is compelling enough make them consider changing. Prochaska (1991) asserted that these individuals may see more benefits to their behavior than negative consequences. As a result, these individuals make no self-initiated efforts to change or participate in the change process. In terms of those mandated to treatment, they may show up for treatment simply because they are forced to and present as passive, guarded, and avoidant. Many are caught in the precontemplation stage for a long time and may cycle back through the prison system before they are able to contemplate the costs of their rigid adherence to dysfunctional living.

In Trudy's case, she demonstrated signs of the precontemplation stage during the intake process and during her first few months of treatment. Specifically, in terms of cognitive indicators of this stage, she justified her behavior by attempting to normalize it. She further minimized her use of a weapon as an acceptable way of managing her fear. It was also evident by her annoyance with the interviewer that she had little or no emotional investment in exploring, let alone changing, her abusive conduct. Behaviorally, Trudy's poor attendance speaks for itself. Participating in treatment and changing was not a priority for her.

Without the offender's self-motivation to change, many change agents feel forced to expend all resources on behavioral management via external forces as opposed to facilitating inner growth, understanding, and healthy functioning. Behavioral management is crucial when working with sexual offenders, particularly with those offenders who do not identify their behavior as problematic. Efforts also need to be made to educate, if not convince, the offenders that their behavior is both harmful and self-defeating. Efforts in the precontemplation stage should be geared toward getting the offenders to at least consider that they have a problem and need to change.

A pivotal point in Trudy's transition from precontemplation to contemplation occurred after watching a television program that triggered an introspective process.[1] The therapist took advantage of Trudy's emotional and intellectual response to viewing a television program on sexual abuse. This provided fertile ground to engage in **consciousness raising** and educate Trudy about the impact of her behavior on her victims. She also identified a source of emotional pain and possibly a contributor to some of her misbehavior. Finally, being confronted by a fellow group member caused her to reassess her behavior. Trudy's emotional reaction to the group also provided **dramatic relief,** facilitating an introspective process, followed by an expression desire to change. Trudy's graduation on the contemplation stage was ripe when she began to reflect on the influence of the environment in which she lives and with whom she associates.

Stage Two: Contemplation

Once the individual enters into a dialogue (even a healthy debate) regarding the merits of her behavior and considers the possibility of change, she has entered the contemplation stage of change. At this stage of change the individual often vacillates between the ideas of changing and defending her old behavior. Despite the desire, some offenders feel they are unable change and that their old behavior is their only choice. However, the ability to contemplate change allows the change process to be owned or personalized as opposed to being imposed. If the individual is not convinced that change is in his/her best interest, it is not likely to facilitate true or long-standing change.

As this stage progresses, the desire to change becomes solidified as the individual begins to recognize the harms that s/he has brought to him or herself as well as to others. Some divulge that they have made attempts to change in the past but have failed (Prochaska et al., 1992).

Trudy's acknowledgment that she needed help and her expressed concern that she might not be capable reflects **self-reevaluation**. It

---

[1] It is important to acknowledge that most change occurs outside the therapeutic venue. Although her relationship with the change agent may have facilitated a willingness to explore the issue of child sexual abuse, it is equally plausible that it did not.

is important to point out that she did not do this before regressing back to her old "I-do-not-need-to-change" position and back to precontemplation. By her own efforts, she was able to reenter the contemplation stage and began to prepare for true change by rejoining the group and asking for help.

Stage Three: Preparation

The preparation stage is demarcated by clear, cognitive planning. The individual is no longer ambivalent about making changes and makes serious efforts to develop strategies to correct behavior. At this point, an offender is seriously thinking about change and also beginning to take some action. In effect, she is ready for change because she has resolved the indecisiveness of the contemplation stage. The individual can visualize goals and success. Individuals may express a desire for direction and insight from others. During the preparation stage, individuals may experiment with change processes such as "trying out" a group or making mild disclosures. In some cases, individuals will report past attempts at changing and explore the lessons learned from these past attempts (DiClemente et al., 2001).

Trudy's transition into the preparation stage was facilitated by **self-liberation**, which was evidenced by her improved attendance, her requesting to join the anger management group, and her disclosure to the group that she had erred. She also disclosed a pattern of relationship and behavior problems and expressed the need for support and direction. Once in the group, she appeared hopeful and invested in the change process. This transition was crucial because it led Trudy to acknowledge the need for change and reach out to others. This combination created an environment of collaboration where change agents were utilized as opposed to reacted to. Although true transformation is measured by actual life changes, her work in the group was readying her to take meaningful action.

Stage Four: Action

Graduation to the action stage is measured by observable lifestyle changes. This includes an obvious investment in the change program as well as concrete changes in one's everyday life. Thinking and planning will likely and hopefully never go away, but none of it counts until the individual takes actions to integrate what has been learned. Although it is important to continue to think and plan, life is not an intellectual endeavor. Learning and commitment to change must be applied and acted on. The action stage challenges individuals to abstain from past behavior and adopt new ways of being. In the case of sexual offenders, this would mean cessation of high-risk, preoffense, and offense behaviors. Such changes would likely relate directly to the dynamic variables that contributed to offense conduct (e.g., intimacy deficits, self-regulation, substance use, sexual regulation, cognitive errors, etc.). Levy (1997) points out that the action stage requires a commitment of time to the change process. In addition to honing skills for successful change, steps need to be made to prevent a regression into past behaviors as the likelihood of relapse is high (DiClemente et al., 2001).

In our case example, Trudy engaged in the process of **helping relationships** by taking steps to reestablish a relationship with her supportive family. She also engaged **stimulus control** by identifying and terminating unhealthy associations. In addition, she began taking medication to assist her in regulating her emotions and behavior.

Stage Five: Maintenance

The maintenance stage is attained when the individual has been successful at replacing undesirable behavior with healthy positive behavior. However, at this stage the individual also acknowledges the history of problematic behavior and recognizes that steps need to be made to foster ongoing beneficial behaviors. As is true with a smooth-running car, maintenance is required to assure both current well-being and longevity. Relapse into problematic behavior needs to be prevented by remaining cognizant of the strategies that prevent harmful and self-defeating behavior. Achieving success without challenges is rare. In fact, relapse is a common and normal occurrence in most behavior change attempts (Prochaska et al., 1992) and may occur numerous times before the change is stable (Brownell, Marlatt, Lichtenstein, & Wilson, 1986). Ideally, relapse can be completely prevented or limited to preoffense behaviors. As a result of the potential risks, the maintenance stage requires that the individual heed caution. Specifically, any false belief that one is "done" with treatment or has permanently eliminated problematic behavior can result in a hasty termination. Premature termination from a structured change process may actually reflect a regression back to the precontemplation stage.

At any stage, even during the maintenance stage, a lapse may occur. In such an event, the lapse should be viewed as an opportunity to learn and enhance change and maintenance skills. Change agents should be cognizant that lapses may be an inherent part of the change process. The role of the change agent is not to shield the individual from the consequences of the behavior but to use the individual's experience and the consequences as lessons in the change and learning process.

Trudy evidenced moving into the maintenance stage by requesting "booster" sessions as well as wanting to act as a mentor to others. In addition, her desire to help others serves as a type of **reinforcement management**, or reward, to herself for all of her hard work.

Stage Six: Termination

Throughout the years, the fundamental constructs of TTM have remained the same; however, discussion regarding a termination stage has been added to some applications of the model, e.g., in terms of changing smoking behavior (Rossi et al., 1989) and exercise behaviors (Prochaska & Velicer, 1997). These applications define the termination stage as an extended period of time in which no desire to engage in the problematic behavior exists and no effort is needed to abstain from it. However, DiClemente (2005) points out that one should not confuse the dimensions of the TTM with the reality of the phenomenon being examined. Therefore, in terms of sexual offenders, the harm of relapse (reoffense) is too great and too unpredictable to allow offenders to graduate from the maintenance stage. Offenders should be encouraged to participate in lifetime maintenance of their potentially highly unpredictable and harmful behaviors.

Exercise

Trudy remained in the clinic for an additional year. Two years after her termination from the program, she returned at the direction of her probation officer. She stated that her probation officer was concerned about her dating an 18-year-old who was still in high school. What obstacles might Trudy face at each stage of change? What process or interventions would you employ?

Precomtemplation?

Obstacle –

Interventions –

Contemplation Stage?

Obstacle –

Interventions –

Preparation Stage?

Obstacle –

Interventions –

Action Stage?

Obstacle –

Interventions –

Maintenance Stage?

Obstacle –

Interventions –

The Transtheoretical Model offers much promise in terms of providing a framework for the change process with sexual offenders. In addition, it allows for an assessment of progress and suggests specific strategies for facilitating long-term change. Most importantly, the model empowers the offender to participate in the change process in ways that require specific decisions to be made by the offender. In other words, the offender guides the process based on his/her own desires, goals, decisions, and intent. If this is not the case, we are setting up offenders to simply "play along" and not engage in meaningful change. At the same time, the model requires a collaborative relationship with the change agent. Change agents should neither dominate the process nor be passive bystanders. Instead change agents actively participate in the process by offering guidance and information that is specific to a distinct individual (not just another offender). Based on Prochaska and Norcross's (2001) principles in attaining optimal change outcomes, change agents should constantly assess an offender's stage and readiness of change and apply the appropriate interventions that are relevant to identified goals and one's stage of change. In addition, it is crucial that change agents do not treat all offenders as if they are in the action stage. Instead, change agents should acknowledge the art of the work and engage offenders accordingly.

Chapter Five

Things do not change, we change.
–HENRY DAVID THOREAU

Changes in the Change Agent

Engaging offenders in a process of change is crucial to reducing future offending. It has been suggested that offenders who do not cooperate with supervision and do not attend sexual offender treatment are at greater risk of reoffending (Hanson & Harris, 2000). Even though the effects of sexual offender treatment have been widely debated (Rice & Harris, 2003), many studies in recent years show that sexual offender treatment can be effective (Huot, 2002; Looman, Abracen, & Nicholaichuk, 2000; Nicholaichuk, Gordon, Gu, & Wong, 2000; McGrath, Cumming, Livingston, & Hoke, 2003; Zgoba, Sager, & Witt, 2003). However, if offenders do not participate with supervision and treatment requirements, their risk of reoffending will remain unchanged and they will not progress through the stages of change.

Risk reduction and successful completion of supervision relies on overcoming an offender's resistance toward adhering to the conditions of parole or probation, participating in treatment, and working in partnership with change agents. In terms of treatment, Long (2002), while studying the impact of motivation on sexual offenders' progress in treatment, found that offenders' motivation to participate significantly influenced their progress in treatment. Long also found that the more motivated an offender was, the more consistent his/her self-appraisal was with that of the treatment providers. This suggests that the alliance between the clients and the change agents aided in successfully engaging offenders in treatment. However, as discussed in previous chapters, one contributor to offender resistance is the resistance, or counter-resistance, that exists within the change agent. Counter-resistance, as defined in chapter 1, is any obstacle to change that exists within the therapist (Langs, 1981). In order to maximize change among offenders, change agents must constantly work toward gaining insight into their own counter-resistance and take steps toward managing it.

Why Is Changing the Change Agent Important?

There is little doubt that much of society holds sexual offenders in disregard. Some of this disregard is a consequence of the abhorrent actions that sexual offenders have engaged in. Some of this disregard is out of realistic fear, and some is out of a misunderstanding regarding offenders' potential for future offense. Garfinkel (1956) expressed that societies often ritually denounce people based on collective "reasons" in order to identify and categorize them for the purpose of placing them "outside," making them "strange." He adds, "this paradigm of moral indignation is public denunciation. We publicly deliver the curse: 'I call upon all men to bear witness that he is not what he appears but is otherwise and in essence a lower species'" (p. 421).

Many of the attitudes and beliefs held by society and change agents adversely affect sexual offenders' self-evaluation and their belief in their ability to change. Some evidence suggests that negative societal beliefs may become self-fulfilling prophecies because people may act in ways that reinforce the negative judgments foisted upon them (Lott & Saxon, 2002). Steele and Aronson (1995) coined this effect as stereotype threat. That is, people who are the target of stereotyping realize that widely held negative stereotypes apply to them in a given situation regardless of their actions. They recognize that their behavior will be subject to the idiosyncratic interpretations and misperceptions of others, regardless of what they do. As a result, they act in accordance with what they believe is thought or expected of them either out of fear, hopelessness, or an unconscious desire to comply. Similarly, theorist Edwin Lemert (1951) explained how this "secondary deviance" becomes the driving force behind sexual recidivism. For example, once an offender accepts the label he is given, he allows it to significantly influence his actions. Common labels applied to sexual offenders include monster, predator, lost cause, untreatable, in denial, and difficult. It is not surprising that those of us working with sexual offenders hear reoffenders identify the thought "Screw it, who cares?" as a significant factor in their decision-making process.

How these stereotypes get personified and can be influenced by the change agent has been explored. For example, Kottler, Sexton, and Whiston (1994) have examined how the interactions between the change agent and client, as well as the authentic engagement and projected images or attributions held about the client, can promote or impede therapeutic outcomes. Kottler and Uhlemann (1994) challenged change agents to examine what is meant by the concept of a "difficult client" and how perceptions might influence one's work. Finally, Kottler (1994) discussed how change agents might respond to diagnostic labels, such as "borderline personality disorder" and how this can cause change agents to view a client as "an enemy." On a similar note, Marshall et al. (2003) have opined a major characteristic of poor outcome cases is change agent hostility in response to offender negativity. That is, those change agents who express anger toward their offenders experience disrupted relationships and decreased therapeutic progress.

Fedoroff and Moran (1997) point out that sexual offenders already have difficulty establishing lasting relationships and finding gainful employment after conviction because they are ex-convicts. In addition, some offenders fear that they will be subject to vigilantism once the community is notified of their presence. As a consequence, many relocate and opt not to register with local law enforcement when they arrive at new locations. Once in a new location some make special efforts to avoid detection by limiting social ties, and thus healthy social supports, increasing the chance of reoffense. Understanding the impact that change agents have on sexual offenders can assist in maintaining rapport and a collaborative relationship with them. Otherwise, offenders remain alienated and disconnected.

How Attitudes Guide Interventions

In order to successfully affect change in sexual offenders, those of us who work with them must be willing to evaluate, understand, and sometimes change our approach. This evaluation begins with an investigation into our own beliefs and thinking patterns.

Thoroughly consider the following questions:

What automatic beliefs and views do you hold about sexual offenders?

Do the views that you hold about sexual offenders help or hinder their progress?

How do you define progress in terms of sexual offender change?

Do you believe that the risk sexual offenders pose can be reduced? If so, how?

Should sexual offenders be allowed to return to the community after serving their prison sentence?

Do sexual offenders in the community need to be punished and controlled in order to prevent further offending?

Are most sexual offenders merely misunderstood men who have made a mistake?

Where do your opinions come from? Are these opinions valid?

Could you reasonably support your beliefs and opinions to other professionals?

Our beliefs and thinking patterns, and ultimately our behaviors, are shaped by a variety of influences. Before deciding on a course of action, or settling on an opinion, most of us filter our impulses and judgments through a decision-making process that includes (but is not limited to) our social and professional roles, our past experiences and insight, and the perceived consequences of holding certain attitudes. One model that is useful in examining our decisions and behaviors is Ajzen's theory of planned behavior (1991). According to Ajzen's theory, human action is guided by three kinds of considerations: beliefs regarding the expectations of others (normative beliefs), beliefs regarding the possible consequences of a behavior (behavioral beliefs), and beliefs regarding perceived control over the outcome (control beliefs).

NORMATIVE BELIEFS result from perceived social pressures. In other words, people intend to behave in ways that they believe others think it is important for them to behave (Ajzen, 1988). People are likely to develop ideas about sexual offenders based on how they believe their peers think about sexual offenders, as opposed to forming their own opinions.

For example, if a new therapist joins a treatment team that believes only harsh, punitive confrontation can facilitate change in sexual offenders, the new therapist may develop similar views because s/he believes those views are important to his/her peers.

> What views do your peers and colleagues hold about sexual offenders?
>
> When you compare your views and beliefs about sexual offenders with your peers and colleagues, what are the similarities and differences?
>
> Do you feel pressure, either overtly or covertly, to adopt the views and beliefs of your peers?

BEHAVIORAL BELIEFS are formed by linking a particular behavior with an anticipated outcome. These beliefs then produce a favorable or unfavorable attitude toward a particular behavior. According to Ajzen (1988), a person who believes that performing a given behavior will lead to mostly positive outcomes will also hold favorable attitudes toward performing the behavior. On the other hand, a person who believes that performing the behavior will lead to mostly negative outcomes will hold unfavorable attitudes toward the behavior. Behavioral beliefs can be developed and/or strengthened by a person's past experiences or by vicarious learning. For example, the new therapist's first offender is highly resistant and angry. She reports to her colleagues that she attempted to empathize with him but made no progress and he remained hostile and uncooperative. Her colleagues inform her that all sexual offenders are resistant and resentful and that is why most offenders cannot be successfully treated. They suggest that aside from a few incest-type offenders, psychotherapy for sexual offenders is really intended to help the probation department keep track of the offenders' activities.

The goal of a sexual offender therapist, according to her colleagues, is to get offenders to talk about their weekly activities, set limits by admonishing them when their behavior is inappropriate, and then report their behavior to the probation officer. She is told that if the offender thinks he's being watched, he is less likely to offend. The therapist is then reminded of a 1989 study by Furby, Weinrott, and Blackshaw and the reported results from a SOTEP program in California (Marques, Wiederanders, & Day, 2005), which point out that sexual offender treatment does not work. Consequently, she develops an attitude of discouragement and futility, influencing her to abandon an empathic stance and exchange it for a punitive one.

> Which specific interventions do you use with sexual offenders in order to facilitate change?
>
> Which of these interventions are most effective? How do you know they are effective?
>
> Which of these interventions are least effective? How do you know they are less effective?
>
> Which interventions produce negative feelings in you? Why?
>
> Which interventions produce positive feelings in you? Why?
>
> What is the purpose of each of the interventions you listed?
>
> Do these logically, or empirically, facilitate prosocial change in sexual offenders?

CONTROL BELIEFS relate to one's perceived ability to overcome obstacles and successfully engage in a behavior. People who believe they do not have the resources, support, or know-how to successfully complete a task are not likely to develop the intention or the attitude necessary to follow through with a job. Conversely, those who feel confident that their efforts will pay off are more likely to engage and complete a course of action. For example, the new therapist finds that her punitive interventions are increasing her offender's resistance. She eventually comes to believe that it is impossible to do any kind of change work with sexual offenders, let alone get them to be more disclosing. She believes that she did her best and even sought consultation from her colleagues. She begins to feel helpless about the work and begins to approach her sexual offender group as a rap session. She eventually quits her job.

Another, more optimistic example might be that the therapist refuses to give in to her treatment team's bias, seeks outside consultation, reviews current research, and uses empirically sound interventions. As a result, she develops a sense of mastery over her work and despite some expected and normal resistance from her offenders, she continues doing therapy with them and persistently seeks effective interventions.

> Do you feel confident that the training that you are currently receiving or received in the past adequately prepares you to be successful in affecting change in sexual offenders?
>
> Do you feel that you have access to the necessary resources to employ effective interventions and/or management strategies with sexual offenders?

As illustrated in the above examples, the environment within which one works and lives can potentially influence how people interpret and evaluate others and situations (Asch, 1940). In addition, having extensive experience working with a particular population does not make one immune from developing misguided preconceptions and stereotypes about that population. In fact, there is little doubt that the beliefs that professionals hold facilitate long-standing and often contagious stereotypes about forensic populations. In particular, the stereotypes held by forensic professionals have been found to affect the quality of services employed and the amount of inter-professional consultation relied upon in instances of sexual crimes. Specifically, how individuals within a profession, or a group of professionals as a whole, view the meaning underlying sexual assault and abuse affects their choice of treatment regime, investigative approaches, and efforts to engage in inter-agency collaboration. Ward, Connolly, and McCormack (1996) concluded that "professional attitudes toward sexual offenders impact social service delivery and in particular, the nature and quality of services provided" (p. 39). Finkelhor, Gomez-Schwartz, and Horowitz (1984) found that while child protective workers prefer a wide range of resources (i.e., medical, mental health, school), mental health professionals less frequently engage other disciplines. Unfortunately, forensic mental health professionals evidenced the least effort in connecting to other professional groups. In some cases, mental health professionals, particularly those who work in isolation, may not be aware that other professionals (i.e., social workers, probation officers, etc.) are actively involved in the offender's life.

Although poorly researched, it is also evident that parole and probation officers have varying confidence in the efficacy, or even the need, for sexual offender treatment. Some also view sexual offender treatment as nothing more than a punitive measure and an extension of the offender's sentence. Consequently, some criminal justice professionals do not engage, or at least under-utilize, mental health professionals in understanding sexual offenders.

> What stereotypes, or snap judgments, do you hold about sexual offenders in general?
>
> What stereotypes do you think individuals from other disciplines (i.e., lawyers, law enforcement, judges, probation officers, parole agents, therapists) hold about sexual offenders?
>
> What efforts have you made to discuss these stereotypes and their validity with colleagues or other professionals?
>
> Are you confident that you are aware of other professionals and their role in the management of sexual offenders?

The Puzzle

To many, the system within which sexual offenders navigate is a complex puzzle. Consider the steps that a sexual offender goes through: initial investigation, arrest, assessment (maybe), trial, sentencing, prison, release from prison, parole, registration, assessment, treatment, and release (often with indefinite registration). By the end of this sequence, offenders have interacted with so many different professionals and agencies that it is often difficult for the professionals charged to monitor them to keep track. In order to explore and address the problems that undermine proper sexual offender management and change, a full and comprehensive evaluation of the system within which sexual offenders are required to participate is necessary. It begins with an understanding of the conditions under which sexual offenders are expected to change and the roles of the players involved. Although some may argue that the scope of this book overreaches its audience by including many different aspects of the criminal justice system, we assert that it may be possible to change sexual offenders' behaviors and attitudes at any point during their journey through the system. In fact, the likelihood of change is greater if the system works together, creating unified and specific goals to guide offenders from entrance to discharge. In too many cases, offenders are released into the community, sometimes after many years of incarceration, to face for the first time mandated interventions designed to reduce reoffense risk. To some offenders these interventions are unexpected and include intensive outpatient sexual offender treatment or civil commitment procedures. Sending offenders into a system intended to contain them for many years that is fraught with unexpected twists and turns undermines a basic tenet of behavioral change. Specifically, interventions are most effective when they are clearly understood and applied immediately after a consequence. Effective change and management of sexual offenders requires collaboration between each part of the system and the offender, and should provide a clear understanding of the roles of all the parties involved.

Pieces of the Puzzle: Change Agent Role and System Collaboration[1]

Every person who works with offenders either directly or indirectly plays a role in shaping their future even though some individuals and agencies have differing goals. It is important to keep in

---

[1] The reader should be aware that we are not purporting to be experts in each of the disciplines described. Our goal is to encourage self-evaluation and collaboration in the context of creating a safe society, while at the same time enriching the lives of those who have been affected by past, present, or future sexual offending.

perspective that each component of the criminal justice system enforces its own philosophy and agenda. Even within a particular discipline, individuals may define their roles differently. It is crucial that each party communicate with the others in order to understand the roles and agendas that each piece of the puzzle is intended to fulfill. Following are brief descriptions of some of the players involved in the life of a sexual offender.

Attorneys

Attorneys are intent upon debating points of law as they pertain to a particular case from a specific point of view. A defense attorney is charged with assuring that her offender is treated fairly and, if necessary, attempting to reduce the negative impact of punishment. On the other hand, the prosecutor is charged with representing and protecting the community and victims, and prosecuting the accused to the fullest extent of the law. These agendas create an adversarial relationship that is essential to the fairness of jurisprudence. The manner and intent of the attorney's actions can play a significant role in the offender's life.

Defense attorneys can take steps shortly after an arrest has been made to assure that their clients get treatment if it is needed. In the case of juvenile offenders, Imhoff and Associates (1998) suggests, "A defense attorney can take immediate action to assure that rehabilitation of the juvenile is a priority for all parties involved. This action can be taken when initial allegations are made, prior to the filing of criminal charges. This is a crucial stage of any case, and in particular, a juvenile case. Defense attorneys often overlook the impact that can be made in a juvenile case prior to the filing of criminal charges. Because the prosecutor makes the final decision on whether to file charges, a defense attorney has the opportunity to convince him, through informal negotiations, to seek alternative measures, such as counseling. These informal negotiations may consist of phone calls, written documentation, and out-of-court, in-person meetings." Defense attorneys can also be instrumental in informing offenders about the expectations of supervision and the requirements that they will need to adhere to if convicted of a sexual offense.

Prosecutors, while maintaining focus on the accomplishment of justice and community safety, can be influential in making recommendations for the conditions of an offender's probation. These conditions may include adhering to federal and state registration requirements and/or recommending that the offender participate in sexual offender specific treatment. Prosecutors can also be instrumental in having offenders placed in facilities where sexual offender treatment is available.

Forensic Mental Health Evaluators

As with law enforcement, the task of the forensic evaluator is to bring forth facts and scientifically based opinions. These opinions are meant to represent, as much as possible, the objective reality of a case as opposed to the agendas of a specific party. In most cases, forensic psychologists are called, usually during pretrial or presentencing proceedings, to assess the probability or risk that an alleged offender will cause certain types of harm, under particular conditions, within varying periods of time (Schall v. Martin, 1984; Hess & Weiner, 1999). Sexual offender specific evaluations may also include recommendations for treatment as well as recommendations concerning the safety of victims and the community.

Forensic Treatment Provider

The forensic clinician is intent upon pursuing the truth and facilitating behavioral change, accountability, and insight. Although forensic mental health clinicians work closely with law enforcement (particularly when the offender needs containment and management in the community), their focus is on addressing issues that contributed to the offender's behavior and working toward reducing the risk of the offender's repeating the offense.

Being aware that there is no "cure" for sexual offending behavior, forensic psychotherapists understand that their primary goal is the public's safety. In order to sustain this goal, forensic clinicians assess risk on an ongoing basis and are prepared to intervene when offense behavior is probable. Another crucial goal is bringing to light the intellectual, social, and emotional meaning of the offender's behavior. This includes identifying and addressing the dynamic issues related to the offender's harmful behavior. (The dynamic variables were discussed in chapter 2 and include intimacy issues, cognitive distortions, impulsivity, social influences, and ability to manage one's behavior). The forensic clinician must focus on the truth, the totality of the behavior, and factors that contribute to reoffense risk as opposed to the criminal charge for which an offender was convicted. (Many offenders who have been charged with a sexual offense plea bargain to a lesser charge that does not fully reflect, or even describe, their actual behavior.)

Parole and Probation

Parole and probation officers are often designated with the task of monitoring the offender's behavior and in some cases managing the offender's life after release from prison through placement, vocational instruction, mental health treatment, and registration. Parole and probation officers are also often charged with the task of monitoring issues related to victim protection and interfacing with the community regarding offender presence. This includes representing and enforcing the law as it pertains to the conditions of the offender's release. Some agents have expressed that part of their role is acting as social work case manager and counselor.

Victim Advocates

The victim advocate provides services to victims regarding restoration and safety. The victim advocate plays a role in educating other parts of the system regarding victim issues and offense characteristics. These advocates also keep us focused on the true purpose of the work.

> Do you understand the roles that other professionals have in the life of a sexual offender?
>
> Do you value the role that other professionals have in the life of a sexual offender?
>
> What efforts have you made to make contact with other professionals?
>
> Are there specific professionals with whom you avoid making contact? Why?

Are you reluctant to share your perspective on your role with other professionals? Why?

Resistance Versus Collaboration

Each individual involved in a sexual offender's case can potentially influence an offender's motivation or resistance in terms of taking responsibility for his actions and ultimately changing his behavior. Collaborative efforts among change agents can assist the development and implementation of effective intervention and prevention strategies. However, the concept of collaboration to groups of individuals who are often philosophically opposed can be met with resistance. For instance, at a meeting of diverse professionals who work with sexual offenders (i.e., social workers, police, therapists, parole/probation officers, attorneys), a prosecutor disapprovingly asked, "Why do we have the public defender here?" The public defender responded, "I know more about these guys than anyone—they tell me everything." Excessive and knee-jerk divisiveness drives a wedge in the system and potentially weakens effective interventions, as well as the integrity of the system as a whole.

As discussed above, the criminal justice system is by nature adversarial. Viewing other parts of the system as permanent enemies leads to system breakdowns and missed opportunities to employ effective interventions. Some defense attorneys, particularly those who are savvy to the benefits of early treatment, have successfully directed their offenders into immediate treatment. On the other hand, it has also been observed that some offenders are taught early by their defense attorney to "Never admit anything," or are told "What happened doesn't matter; it's what looks like happened that counts." These offenders can develop complex defenses that endure for many years after their conviction, based on irrelevant legal details that are extremely difficult to overcome, often undermine the goals of treatment, and may increase reoffense risk. Another example is the well-intentioned, kindly therapist, who approaches sexual offender treatment from the "just let them talk" perspective. These therapists do not challenge or engage offenders in a dialogue that is relative to sexual offending. In some cases, they maintain strict seclusion from other therapists and professionals in an attempt to protect their offender's confidentiality, as well as their own unempirical, specialized style. Unfortunately, these professionals collude with minimizing and ignoring past offenses and may actually increase the potential for future offenses. These examples are not intended to single out therapists and attorneys as leading sources of resistance because each of us, as individuals and as change agents, can either hinder or help in the process of monitoring, managing, and changing sexual offender behavior. It is therefore crucial that agencies involved with sanctioning, managing, and treating sexual offenders, as well as those responsible for protecting and treating victims, work together to raise awareness regarding effective and ineffective practices.

According to The Center for Sexual Offender Management (2002),

> "collaborating partners should be in contact with one another about developing policies on sexual offender management, assessing the impact of those policies on victims, and seeking the input of one another on the most effective ways to hold sexual offenders accountable while providing support to and safety for victims. Increased information sharing, limited confidentiality, and an overall willingness to work more closely with other organizations should characterize all collaborative efforts. Resistance can be reduced by identifying common interests, frustrations, and shared goals, and clarifying roles of each agency and ways they can contribute to the prevention of future victimization."

Considering each of the change agents involved with the sexual offenders with whom you work, what attitudes limit or enhance your ability to collaborate with them?

Are your interventions designed to include other professionals who are working toward the goal of preventing future sexual offenses?

The ultimate goal of collaboration in sexual offender management is public safety. Increasing public safety can be achieved by encouraging offenders to cooperate with each component of the system because every change agent can assist them in changing patterns of behavior that in the past have been harmful. A system that is oppositional and antagonistic to offenders adds to their stress and resistance in regard to prosocial change and increases their likelihood of reoffending. Although offenders themselves are ultimately responsible for their behavior, a collaborative approach that increases their participation in the system contributes to public safety. One collaborative model that is becoming widely used in sexual offender treatment is the containment model. The containment model asserts that in order to increase public safety, sexual offenders must be managed by an interdisciplinary team of professionals who are committed to the case management and control plans that are individualized for each offender. This team utilizes consistent and informed public policies, and assures the quality control regarding the implementation of policies that enhance program functioning. The containment model will be discussed in more detail in chapter 8, but it is important to understand that if breakdowns in communication occur between relevant agencies or adequate services are not provided to offenders, they are at greater risk to reoffend and are less likely to live meaningful and fulfilling lives. This approach is not meant to simply oppress and track offenders, but rather to assist them in utilizing the resources available to them in establishing productive, safe lifestyles. A collaborative approach allows feedback from related but different specialty areas regarding goals, roles, and responsibilities in the context of the entire system within which offenders exist.

Our Piece: Change Agent Change

Within a system that is constantly shifting due to legislative, financial, and personnel influences, change agents work in a constantly changing environment. Individuals working with sexual offenders need to constantly evaluate and adapt their work to assure that they are adhering to current practice standards. Additionally, personal and institutional perspectives can either aid or obstruct the process of change. Systems, and individuals within a system, that are not contemplating potential pitfalls, and those refusing to stay in motion with the rest of the system, will likely fail to contribute to effective sexual offender management and public safety. Understanding the origins of particular attitudes and beliefs is a crucial first step to evaluating the efficacy of our actions as agents in sexual offender management.

As previously discussed, the expectations that others have for us (normative beliefs), our beliefs regarding the potential positive or negative consequences for our actions (behavioral beliefs), as well as the confidence we have that we will be successful (control beliefs), play a role in our approach to the task. In addition to our perceived, if not assigned, role in the life of a sexual offender, we likely possessed beliefs about what works and what doesn't work with sexual offenders before entering our field of work. In fact, most people in our society have some opinion regarding how sexual offenders should be treated and managed. These opinions include lifetime incarceration, lifetime registration, castration, public notification of their residence and employment, and forcing offenders to have pink license plates on their vehicles (a proposal by Rep. Michael DeBose, (D) 12th District Ohio, to the Ohio legislature, May, 2005). In order to be effective, our strategies should be developed out of knowledge and experience, not unsubstantiated opinions.

Origins of Attitudes Toward Sexual Offenders

Understanding the origins of beliefs and opinions regarding sexual offenders is an enormous undertaking even for those who work with sexual offenders daily. The following section is intended to describe some of these potential influences and facilitate an exploration into your own attitudes and beliefs.

Media and Society

There is little doubt that many of the opinions and beliefs that people hold regarding sexual offenders come from information provided by the media. Whether or not the popular media is a credible source of information has been, and will always be, a topic for heated debate. However, few would argue, as Reiner (2002) points out, that the creators of media reports are intent upon achieving an audience response. In an ever competitive news market, the media is forced to choose news items that will appeal to, and captivate, a broad audience. In many cases, the lines between the news and entertainment have become increasingly blurred (Manning, 1998; Ferrell, 1998). This is evidenced by "reality" television which depicts real criminals being arrested, or popular crime dramas that fictionalize actual events that closely parallel, but do not accurately reflect, the true crime. This is not to suggest that the media is creating fictionalized accounts of actual events, but the manner in which the news is presented is intended to arouse interest, if not emotionality, in as large an audience as possible. As a consequence, information is presented in a standardized manner that sacrifices detailed explanation. The media consumer is therefore often left having to interpret and assess the reporter's intended meaning based on incomplete or distorted facts.

The ambiguity with which the news is presented can have significant effects on public perception. While studying group standards and social influences, Smith (2004) found that a newspaper article's social influence increased when words in the article possessed more ambiguity and decreased when the article possessed less ambiguity. Further, Frenkel-Brunswik (1954) describes a cognitive syndrome she calls "intolerance of ambiguity" that relates to the tensions and pressures which bring out authoritarian characteristics. In other words, when one is confronted with ambiguous, incomplete, or confusing information about a particular group of people, attitudes are formed to facilitate a feeling (albeit false) of understanding and control. Frenkel-Brunswik's ground-breaking work ultimately resulted in numerous research studies regarding anti-Semitism, authoritarianism, attitudes toward minority groups, and xenophobia. Inaccurate and ambiguous information regarding sexual offenders and the strategies used to address sexual offending will undermine our goals and keep sexual offenders and the issue of sexual offending marginalized by society and policy makers.

One source of ambiguity regarding sexual offenders likely rests on the fact that the news and fictional television concentrate overwhelmingly on serious violent crimes against individuals, albeit with some variation according to the medium and market (Reiner, 2002). The media also regularly fails to identify success stories among sexual offenders, or identify the types of sexual offenses that tend to have lower recidivism rates, leaving many readers to assume that all sexual offenders are high risk or predatory. In addition to shaping public perception of sexual offenders, newspapers stimulate public anxiety that eventually influences changes in policy and criminal justice practices, which appear to confirm the reports of increasing sexual offense frequency by processing more offenders: a self-fulfilling spiral of deviancy amplification (Hall, Critchley, Jefferson, Clarke, & Roberts, 1978).

No one is immune from the potential influence of the media or public perception. For example, the influence of the media on jury verdicts and sentencing practices of judges has been regularly debated (Brushke & Loges, 2004; Campbell, 1994; New, 2003). King (2005) asserts that the pressure on judges, created by public criticisms and media treatment, may be negatively impacting the judiciary's detachment and impartiality. King continued, "Judges are human. They have to mix socially and, in the course of their personal relationships with people, are influenced by unfair and inflammatory criticisms published in the media." Another example of media influence on public perception is the phenomenon of pop psychology on television, exemplified by television self-help personality Phillip "Dr. Phil" McGraw. Michael Petrunik (2003), while discussing the influence of public attitudes on public policy pointed out that Dr. Phil, after showing a film of his meeting with an imprisoned pedophile, explained to his viewers that he had to wash his hands after he shook the pedophile's hand. Examples of public degradation of sexual offenders undermine an exchange of information between science, the public, and legislators. It should be made clear that popular media is not the enemy; there are an abundance of examples of well-intentioned and well-informed stories in the media (see "The Making of Molester" by Daniel Bergner, New York Times, January 23, 2005). It is therefore incumbent upon change agents who know the reality of risk, intervention, and prevention to communicate with those able and willing to disseminate impartial and accurate information to the public.

Most professionals working in the criminal justice system are aware of the pressures that shape attitudes and beliefs, and they attempt to take steps to put safeguards in place. Nevertheless, media and social influences are so pervasive that constant attention must be paid to these types of pressures and our reactions to them.

To what extent are your beliefs regarding sexual offenders influenced by television or news media?

To what extent are your beliefs regarding sexual offenders influenced by empirical data?

Do you find yourself more or less reactive to cases where more information is available, or where information is missing or ambiguous?

Social and Work Environment

Pessimistic attitudes and false stereotypes that are developed and strengthened by social and work environments can undermine effective management of sexual offenders and collaborative efforts. Research indicates that the general attitude held by correctional officials and workers toward prisoners is important "because it is likely to influence the way prisoners respond to the (correctional) regime and the effectiveness of attempts to help prisoners change their offending behavior" (Hogue, 1993, p. 27). Epps (1993), for example, stressed that it is important for those who work with sexual offenders to be aware of their biases toward offenders. They also need to acquire a variety of specific skills while remaining realistic about the nature of sexual offending. Additionally, Radley (2001) concluded that it becomes important to assess not only the attitudes of staff toward sexual offenders prior to their exposure to such individuals, but also to determine their ability to model appropriate attitudes to others. Ward et al. (1996) opined that attitudes held by professionals working with sexual offenders impact the quality of the services provided for the victims of abuse and those associated with them. The risk is that such attitudes can become part of the framework of expert knowledge. The potential for change agents to act in inappropriate and hostile ways toward offenders is ever present.

What stereotypes or snap judgments do your professional colleagues and/or agency hold about sexual offenders?

What are the beliefs and attitudes held by your coworkers regarding sexual offenders?

How do these beliefs and attitudes influence your interactions and interventions with offenders?

Is there diversity of thought among your colleagues?

Are the discussions that you have about sexual offenders explorative or authoritative?

The content of the work can also have a profound influence on one's ability to manage stress. Undoubtedly working with sexual offenders can be an extremely stressful endeavor and can lead to burnout. Epps (1993) noted both the professional and personal stress associated with working with perpetrators and victims of sexual assault. Edmunds (1997) pointed out that clinicians who work with sexual offenders often assume feelings of responsibility to victims, society, and the offenders. While studying a multidisciplinary sample regarding the impact of working with sexual offenders, Edmunds found that over a period of one year more than a third of her sample reported an increase in cynicism, sleep disturbances, general irritability, and using private time to think about work. Clarke (2005), while examining the impact of working with sexual offenders, reported a lengthy list of negative consequences that includes disrupted cognitive schemas, heightened fear and anxiety, rumination, intrusive visual imagery, decreased sense of safety, hypervigilance around strangers, increased cynicism, difficulties in interpersonal relationships, increased difficulty in making decisions, and reduced sex drive.

Similarly, English (2005) reported that the results of an anonymous survey of sexual offender therapists included feeling victimized by the offender's hostility; annoyance with coworkers; feeling their own power and control issues had been triggered; feeling life is unfair and the system does not work well; feeling betrayed by offenders; developing more conservative attitudes about sexual activity; feeling like they are doing more work than the offenders; and feeling confused about what constitutes normal sex.

The work environment can be an additional burden. The stress of working in an environment that is often judged by outsiders and others within the correctional system to be unproductive and useless can only serve to frustrate and exhaust even those with the best training and intentions. Lea et al. (1999) found nearly one quarter of their sample of professionals working with sexual offenders "articulated the view that they continually have to work around the stereotyping of sexual offenders by both professionals and lay persons and that this hampers their practice" (p. 111). As Lea et al. stated, "those who work with sexual offenders are vulnerable to attracting a courtesy stigma" (p. 113) because they are judged to have sympathy for sexual offenders.

> Do you spend excessive time thinking about offenders when you are not at work?
>
> What impact has working with sexual offenders had on your sexual, romantic, and interpersonal life?
>
> Is your supervisor or a respected colleague available to discuss your thoughts, beliefs, and perceptions regarding the sexual offenders with whom you work?
>
> Do you feel that your colleagues understand and support your role?

Personal Experiences

Many of the attitudes and beliefs that we hold about sexual offenders may be influenced by our past experiences. A national survey of 250 female and 250 male clinical and counseling psychologists showed that over two thirds (69.93%) of the women and one third (32.85%) of the men had experienced some form of physical or sexual abuse (Pope & Feldman-Summers, 1992). A follow-up study performed by Pope and Feldman-Summers revealed that among psychologists, childhood abuse (either sexual or nonsexual) was reported by 28.6% of the female participants and by 17.9% of the male participants, equaling 23.9% of the sample. Of the participants in this study who reported having experienced childhood abuse, 40.5% reported that there was a period of time when they could not remember some or all of the abuse. Another study of juvenile sexual offender counselors by Carone and LaFleur (2000) found that counselors preferred to work with perpetrators who had histories of being sexually abused over perpetrators with no abuse history. Further, counselors who were not sexually abused chose to work with the nonabused offender more frequently than the counselor with a history of sexual abuse.

According to Carone and LaFleur (2000), the similarities in the backgrounds of the sexually abused counselors and the physically abused offenders might have influenced the counselors' objectivity in working with the offenders because some sexually abused counselors have been reported to experience a lack of trust, fear, and guilt toward other people (Allen & Brekke, 1996; Emerson, 1988). Considering the prevalence of sexual abuse, it is likely that many change agents have themselves, or vicariously through the experiences of those close to them, been impacted by sexual victimization. How these experiences impact attitudes and beliefs in regard to working with sexual offenders is likely to be varied. Clarke (2005), while studying impact issues for sexual offender treatment providers, reported that in her sample of 181 prison service treatment providers from various disciplines, treatment providers who disclosed sexual abuse as a child did not score significantly different from those who did not disclose sexual abuse. Treatment providers who experienced sexual abuse as an adult demonstrated a stronger negative reaction to offenders and were more vulnerable to rumination than those who did not report being sexual abused as an adult.

We must be cognizant that personal experiences either related directly or indirectly to the victimization of sexual abuse have the potential of influencing change agents' attitudes and approach in working with sexual offenders.

> Prior to or during your work with sexual offenders, what personal experiences have you or someone close to you had with sexual abuse and victimization? If any, in what way did this experience influence your beliefs or attitudes about offenders?
>
> Since working with sexual offenders, what personal experiences have you or someone close to you had with sexual abuse and victimization? If any, in what way did this experience influence your beliefs or attitudes about offenders?

Aside from sexual victimization, what personal experiences shape your attitudes and beliefs about sexual offending?

How have these experiences influenced your attitudes and beliefs about sexual offenders and sexual offending?

Reducing Change Agent Facilitated Resistance: Practical Application

Thus far, this chapter has been about identifying and understanding how attitudes and beliefs promote counter-resistance among change agents, and we've recommended a few ways that counter-resistance can be overcome. The following section is intended to assist change agents in making specific changes in their approach to sexual offender change.

Many factors promote resistance in offenders. Many authors have argued that resistance should not be seen as primarily a psychological characteristic but, rather, as an adaptation to the environment in which a person has to survive (Maletzky, 1991; Haley, 1973; Watzlawick, Weakland, & Fisch, 1974). To understand all of the factors involved in offender change, each change agent must have more than adequate understanding of the environment within which offenders must change, a comprehensive understanding of oneself, and an understanding of the needs of sexual offenders. The environment may include the current political and media environment, the laws and regulations of a particular region (federal, state, or county), the philosophies of the local law enforcement and management agencies (probation and parole), and the attitudes and beliefs of treatment providers.

Understanding the environments in which offenders are required to change can be extremely challenging. As discussed previously, the offender interacts with many different professionals who often have differing agendas and personalities, but all of whom have great influence over the offender's life. Therefore effective change agents make efforts to collaborate with other professionals in order to work toward specific and common goals. The following is a partial list of professionals with whom change agents should be collaborating:

- Probation and parole agents
- Other treatment providers
- Social workers
- Housing agencies
- Attorneys
- Law enforcement
- Polygraph professionals

Entering the therapeutic process is difficult for anyone. Melamed and Szor (1999) indicated that across all areas of health care between 33% and 50% of patients do not comply with treatment. Wierzbicki and Pekarik (1993) in a meta-analysis of 125 studies found that an average 47% of psychotherapy patients prematurely drop out of treatment. Comparably, Abel et al. (1988) found a dropout rate of 34.9% in their sample of 192 pedophiles. Similarly Browne, Foreman, and Middleton (1998) in their study discovered a dropout rate of 37%. Treatment compliance appears to be difficult for everyone. Nevertheless, the contempt many change agents hold toward offenders who are initially resistant in treatment is palpable and leads to labeling offenders in negative ways. Many offenders may have little or no experience with the psychotherapy process and need specific coaching as to how to participate in and use the therapy process or other resources made available to them through parole or probation departments. Many therapists underestimate the difficulty offenders have in acknowledging themselves as sexual offenders (Tierney & McCabe, 2002).

Murphy and Baxter (1997) pointed out that clinicians who provide little guidance to offenders early in treatment fail to reduce offender resistance. Those who prematurely label offenders' unconscious motivations rather than gather information or reflect feelings also fail to reduce offender resistance. The most effective change agents are informed of, and acknowledge, current laws and regulations as they apply to sexual offenders. Change agents also consider how these laws impact sexual offender management and change. For example, in many states new legislation is requiring longer prison sentences, stricter parole/probation conditions, and more intensive treatment. As a consequence, pressures on change agents to emphasize control may cause some to neglect the needs identified by the offender, such as housing and employment. In California, many offenders express that the emphasis put on notification (e.g., Megan's Law) far outweighs the emphasis put on assisting them in getting housing or employment. Change agents can recognize and enforce legal mandates while at the same time identifying and compassionately addressing the obstacles that offenders face. In short, change agents must be cognizant of the system requirements and, at the same time, help create an environment in which offenders can change.

- Regularly review current information concerning changes in the law regarding sexual offender sentencing, reporting, placement in the community, and registration.

- Consult with other professionals and offenders about how the law impacts the offender's ability to transition into the community as well as risk of reoffense.

- Research obstacles in the change process from sexual offender specific literature as well as literature based on randomized samples.

In terms of treatment, change agents must adhere to the basic tenets of therapeutic practice. Even though mandated treatments can make developing a therapeutic relationship challenging, change agents understand the therapeutic relationship makes change possible. Drapeau, Korner, and Brunet (2004) found, per interviews with sexual offenders in treatment, that the most important factor in treatment and to change was the interpersonal factor and not the therapeutic techniques. For example, disagreements between offenders and therapists were seen as the result of the treatment process and not overt offender resistance to treatment. As a result, offenders expressed that they were able to "understand themselves better because the therapist understood them" (p. 3).

Change agents who listen and attend to the needs of offenders may find higher rates of compliance. Drapeau et al. (2004) found that offenders who felt able to participate in their own treatment

planning maintained a greater sense of mastery. Further, these offenders asserted that therapists must be strong leaders who are capable of being authoritarian, can ensure group order, and are respectful and open to discussion while being caring and willing to admit their own mistakes. Offenders also stated feeling safe, assured, and at less risk of "acting out" when the program was solid, well structured, and the staff followed the rules. Program rules should include clear policies regarding attendance, punctuality, behavior, appropriate communication (no verbally abusive behavior), and clinical goals focused on sexual offending.

Fernandez and Serran (2002) added that an effective sexual offender therapist embodies the necessary, but insufficient, characteristics initially highlighted by Carl Rogers (1951)—genuineness, empathy, and warmth. These authors also suggest that therapists who provide support, encouragement, directiveness, flexibility, and self-disclosure are most successful in facilitating change. Horvath (2000) noted the effectiveness of genuineness, empathy, and warmth, as well as a number of other features, and referenced cumulative evidence supporting the contention that treatment outcome is to varying degrees dependent upon the interpersonal skills of the professional. Other effective characteristics associated with positive outcome include support, as reflected in encouraging and positive statements; confidence in treatment efficacy; and encouragement of emotional expression by offenders. Similarly, W. Marshall and L. Marshall (2005) expressed that effective therapists are directive, rewarding, supportive, and warm. On the other hand, therapists who aggressively confront sexual offenders to break down their personal defenses with the aim of achieving an admission of guilt end up with a sexual offender who responds with disagreement, resistance, poor cooperation, dropping out of treatment, insincere agreement, and/or adopting a position of "not having a problem."

- Focus on specific issues that relate to an offender's sexual offense.

- Allow room to discuss dynamic variables in the offender's life that may influence his/her risk of reoffense.

- Maintain good boundaries regarding appointment time, attendance, behavior in the program, and appropriate communication.

- Develop characteristics of an effective change agent: genuineness, empathy, and warmth.

- Provide rewards to increase compliance and motivation.

- Consider that no evidence supports heavy-handed, harsh confrontation as effective in changing offender's behavior.

- Use consistent and compassionate but firm interventions.

Change agents who are willing to include the offender in management and treatment planning are likely to improve compliance and therefore success. Including the offender in a collaborative process of change will enhance the change agent's abilities to address offender needs, increase compliance, and reduce future sexual offenses. Such collaborative discussions should clarify and address issues related to confidentiality, the roles of each agent of change in the offender's life, nature and purpose of treatment, evaluation procedures, and regular updates regarding legal mandates.

In order to maintain an enduring perspective that promotes prosocial change in offenders, change agents must engage in an ongoing process of self-care. This includes constantly attending to the impact of the work on one's professional and personal life. Roger (1995) published a Personal "Risk" Profile intended to assess one's susceptibility to stress and emotional control. Roger's work examines one's propensity for rumination, emotional inhibition, sensitivity perspective taking, and detachment under stress. Clarke and Roger (2005) took this work further and developed a specific assessment of the impact of working with sexual offenders on various types of professionals. This Assessment of Dynamic Adaptation measures negative reactivity to offenders (NRO) and ruminative vulnerability (RV). The assessment is intended to allow an ongoing appraisal of one's well-being at any given time and provides an opportunity for ongoing self-assessment and management. The authors found that high levels of NRO and RV are significantly negatively correlated with detached coping. Detached coping is the ability to remain objectively aware of one's stress and its causes while maintaining control over one's emotions.

It is also important to regularly assess the reasons why you do the work. Clarke (2005) pointed out that various studies indicate that between 75% and 96% of treatment providers describe their work as a rewarding and positive experience (Clarke; Edmunds, 1997; Ellerby, 1998). Many providers also highlight that the opportunity to play a role in addressing a very difficult and important social issue is fuel for keeping perspective on the work and maintaining a healthy attitude about working with sexual offenders. Other healthy motivations to continue the work include a healthy curiosity, a connection to colleagues, and the satisfaction of providing protection to an innumerable number of potential victims.

In terms of establishing and maintaining a healthy work environment, numerous examples in the literature endorse ongoing support of colleagues as invaluable and a help in maintaining sound professional health and avoiding burnout (Ennis & Horne, 2003). English (2005), for example, found that sexual offender clinics that did not have strong, supportive team relationships experienced excessive interagency conflict, increased scrutiny of offenders' motives, and coworker hostility. Recommendations for change agent health include

- Regularly taking an inventory of the reasons why you chose this work.

- Regularly evaluating your personal relationships.

- Regularly assessing the impact of working with sexual offenders.

- Regularly assessing your work environment.

- Seeking support and regularly consulting with colleagues.

- Engaging in process and discussion with others who do similar work.

- Maintaining a balance between personal and professional time.

- Maintaining a sense of humor.

- Engaging in regular physical exercise.

- Having fun.

In conclusion, change agents can greatly influence resistance. Resistance always occurs within an environment. Change agents who understand the influences they bring to the process and take responsibility as an active part of the change mechanism will more likely facilitate offender change. Taking responsibility begins with the willingness and ability to engage in self-examination. The Change Agent Inventory (Appendix A) is intended to assist change agents in evaluating their motivations and practices in regard to sexual offender change. Additionally, the inventory will assist change agents in identifying if and how working with sexual offenders modifies beliefs, attitudes, and lifestyle choices. Finally, as previously discussed, a supportive and collaborative working environment (within and between agencies and disciplines) promotes effective practices, change agent sustainability, and the reduction of counter-resistance. The Change Agent Inventory is intended to assist in evaluating existing partnerships with offenders, other professionals, and agencies. Partnerships with other agencies will be further discussed in chapter 7.

Chapter Six

To fly we must have resistance.
–MAYA LIN

Specific Interventions for Overcoming Resistance

Resistance is normal, common, expected, and healthy. In addition to the often painful challenge of confronting dysfunctional beliefs and thought patterns, resistance to change is often reality based and appropriately self-protective. Cullari (1996) explained that it is not surprising that people are reluctant to cooperate with health care professionals, considering the useless and even dangerous methods that have been employed in the past. In fact, those who resisted such medical treatments as bloodletting, hydrotherapy, and psychosurgery were probably better off. From a sexual offender's perspective, current treatment and management practices can be just as invasive, considering the use of antiandrogens, physical castration, and sexual arousal/interest-testing methods. Many offenders express that simply being a sexual offender in the criminal justice system places social limitations on them that they believe undermine their attempts to obtain employment, develop prosocial relationships, and maintain a residential location. It makes sense that offenders are reluctant to involve parole and probation officers in every aspect of their lives. When entering mandated treatment, they are hesitant to focus solely on the behavior that brought them into treatment and instead want to concentrate on pragmatic life-style issues or their lack of trust in you and the system.

While some resistance is a function of an inability to tolerate negative emotions, to be conscious of thoughts, or to control urges, one should not discount that some of the offender's resistance is a natural skepticism that, when addressed properly, can be used as a powerful tool in facilitating introspection, understanding, commitment, and change. Exploring offenders' skepticism may be the first opportunity to forge a working relationship with them and sets a tone of open communication and collaboration. It is also through the power of skepticism that the limits of understanding are often revealed. In many cases, the offenders are unwilling to change their behavior or engage in the change process because they do not trust or understand the change agent's motivations and have not been presented with personalized and/or compelling reasons to do so. Instead, offenders may perceive attempts to quash their resistance as punishment and oppression facilitated by an uncaring criminal justice system. If offenders can be taught what is expected of them and can identify meaningful reasons to change, their motivation and commitment will increase.

Case Example

James was referred to treatment as part of his probation requirement. Five years previous, he was convicted of molesting a friend of his teenage niece and then threatening her with physical harm if she told anyone. He had a long history of threatening behavior and refused to participate in any prison program. Once released, he was mandated to attend sexual offender treatment. Efforts to enroll him in treatment failed until, after 4 months, he was told that if he did not attend sexual offender treatment, he would be returned to custody.

At his first appointment, he entered the therapist's office, walked past the chairs and stood silently looking out the window of the four-story building. The therapist walked over, stood next to him, and asked, "What's up?"

James replied, "I was just wondering what would happen to you if I threw you out of this window."

The therapist replied, "I don't know, but what would happen to you if you threw me out of the window?"

James replied, "What?"

The therapist clarified, "If you threw *me* out of the window, what would happen to *you*? Would you end up on the run, would you go to prison? Both?"

James looked flustered and sat down. The rest of the session was spent discussing the rules of the program and expected behavior. James was also encouraged to identify goals that he wanted to work on in therapy.

After four sessions that vacillated between marked silence and complaints about being forced to attend treatment, a discussion regarding his role in creating his life situation ensued. Discussion topics that related to his self-defeating lifestyle and years of missed opportunities to obtain stability in his relationships had a profound effect on James. His initial resistance to show up for treatment and the eventual threat to be re-incarcerated were also discussed.

James soon asked for coaching in regard to interviewing skills so that he could get a good job. The therapist agreed as long as issues related to his offense behavior took priority. After a bit more discussion he admitted his offense, explored its precipitants, and entered group therapy. He gained insight into his propensity to resort to hollow threats when he felt powerless and inadequate. He also discovered that he used intimidation and domination to compensate for poor social skills and his desire to be liked. James was provided with resources for vocational training and some therapy time was spent discussing interviewing skills.

Over time, he became a strong member of the group. At the completion of his probation he requested additional sessions to assist him with maintaining good relationship and intimacy skills.

By engaging an offender in an exploration of his resistance, he can learn the utility of the therapeutic process, comprehend and buy into defined goals, and commit to an offense-free lifestyle. Once this is accomplished, the goal of therapy is to implement the changes and contain harmful behavior. Though simply said, this is not an easy or guaranteed process. For some, resistance to change never goes away completely or at all. Some never get past the resistance to the change process itself, while others eventually buy into the process but are unable to achieve its goals and need ongoing maintenance. It is therefore crucial to address issues related to resistance early in the change process.

Creating a Space for Exploration

In order for change to occur, a "space" needs to be created for offenders to change. In psychotherapy, such a space is referred to as the "frame." The frame is defined as any aspect of the treatment program intended to create an environment in which change is possible. In its simplest form, the frame includes the structure of the program and expectations regarding behavior, communication, punctuality, payment, etc. The therapeutic frame could also include interventions intended to instill a process or method by which change is possible. Myers (2000) described the frame as ground rules for therapy or special values, social principles, and standards of action that are applied to a social setting. When a frame is in place, both the change agent and the offender know what is expected of them as well as what is and is not appropriate; they also know what is and is not productive and relevant to the change process. One example of this is the rule that it is appropriate to express anger, resentment, or hostility toward someone in a psychotherapy group, but it is not appropriate to threaten them. Such rules create a protocol for communication that promotes awareness and consistency, as well as emotional and physical safety.

Although the concept of the frame is traditionally used in psychotherapy, it can be applied to any setting intended to provide an environment where change and communication are possible. When a probation agent defines her role to an offender, describes the rules of probation, and informs the offender regarding potential consequences of violations, a frame is developed. Setting limits in regard to developing social relationships with an offender is another part of the frame. Being a good change agent never involves stepping outside your role as a change agent.

Another function of the frame is to create a meeting place where offenders and change agents can learn to understand each other.

This begins with acknowledging that most offenders speak a different language from change agents. Some change agents have worked with hundreds of offenders over many years. One cannot expect to engage in collaborative change with a novice who understands neither the process nor the language used by the agent. In fact, it should be expected that an offender would resist a process that he does not understand. Providing guidance to an offender early in the process engages him and reduces resistance. Labeling or harshly confronting an offender's motivations rather than gathering information or reflecting feelings only thickens the wall between change agent and offender. Educating the offender regarding roles, goals, the change process, and expected obstacles (including resistance itself) sets a tone of collaboration, compassion, and exploration, and thus increases cooperation. It is important to remember that resistance is normal, common, expected, and to some extent, healthy. However, in order for change to occur, the process must occur within the frame. A solid frame that creates a common understanding and a common reality will eventually help define communication that is both overt and implied (Berger & Luckmann, 1966; Harré, 1980; Heidegger, 1971; Winograd & Flores, 1987).

Change agents must develop the frame with intentionality. That is, change agents must themselves know how the frame is to be defined and have a plan for implementing it (see Table 6.1). This will likely include clearly written rules, expectations, and goals. In addition, the change agent must impart that the offender and the change agent are working together toward mutually understood and accepted objectives: prosocial living and no further harm.

Manifestations of Resistance

Resistance can manifest in many forms. Sometimes it is obvious and sometimes it is extremely subtle. At times, resistance is directed toward the process of change while at other times resistance is about the intrapsychic challenge or pain of gaining insight. This distinction is important because resistance, as long as it occurs within the frame, can be addressed. If it occurs outside of the frame (e.g., not showing up for sessions, acting out) it may be

Table 6.1
Defining the frame

Treatment Examples	Supervision Examples
Attendance and Punctuality Requirements • How many missed appointments will result in termination from the program?	**Conditions of an Offender's Supervision** • What steps need to be taken to assure adherence to allowed social contacts, working environment, Internet use, travel, etc.?
Expected Behavior • What are the limits of acceptable behavior? • What will get someone discharged from the program? • What are the group therapy rules? • Are there specific facility rules?	**Expected Behavior** • What are the limits of acceptable behavior? What behavior will result in a violation of their conditions? • What behaviors will lead to increased privileges?
Limits of Confidentiality • With whom does the therapist share information? • What information gets released to the probation/parole officer?	**Notification** • How much contact will the agent have with the offender's family, friends, employers, neighbors, and treatment providers?
Language • Are the terms used in treatment understandable to everyone involved?	**Consequences** • What are the consequences for specific types of violations?
Reporting Laws • What type of information will trigger a mandated report to the authorities?	**Cost** • Does the offender need to pay restitution?
Cost • Does the offender need to pay for treatment?	**Supervision Objectives** • What and how will behaviors and tasks be performed?

impossible for change to take place. Identifying the motivation for the resistance is crucial to developing a plan to address it. James' failure to attend therapy represented his resistance to the change process. Making threats also reflected his resistance to the change process. Rules and consequences needed to be clear before he could enter the frame. Fortunately, the therapist's willingness to explore James' resistance as well as James' ability to reflect and consider its consequences brought him into the frame and the change process could start. It is quite possible that if James' initial resistance had not been addressed properly, he would not have invested in the change process and made the progress that he did.

At times, behavior that obstructs the process of treatment is misinterpreted as reflecting profound flaws in the offender or the offender's inability to cooperate. For James, the four-session period during which he complained incessantly represented a gray area. It appeared as though his complaining about the system kept him out of the frame, but it eventually served as a trial period during which he learned that he could express himself and trust the therapist. He entered the frame by offering self-disclosures. Had he remained out of the frame, his ability to benefit from treatment would need to be questioned.

How an offender resists can tell us a lot. For example, coping style, fears, beliefs, communication skills, locus of control, perceived strengths, etc. are revealed by the offender's resistance tactics. The chosen path of resistance can be diagnostic and indicate patterns of behaviors that contributed to the offender's being referred to treatment in the first place. But again, in order for the change process to occur, the offender must be able to function within the frame. Most people going through a change process shift from positions within the frame to outside the frame and back before committing to the change process. Sometimes it is difficult to distinguish between a resistance that is within the frame versus resistance out of the frame. Table 6.2 gives a list of common manifestations of resistance that are "out of the frame;" however, any of these could be "in the frame." The only way to determine if it is in or out of the frame is to identify its effect—whether or not it contributes to or facilitates the change process.

Table 6.2
Common manifestations of early resistance (out of the frame)

Acting out
- Expressing one's feelings, thoughts, attitudes through behavior rather than verbally.
- Posturing (standing, walking, sitting in a way that is threatening), being argumentative, verbally threatening, showing up to appointments drunk or high, etc.

Focusing only on emotional experience
- Refusing to integrate insight or understanding; incessant complaining and expressing anger, remorse, depression, anxiety, etc.

Clowning around
- Frequently telling inappropriate jokes, being sarcastic or silly during therapy or meetings with change agents.

Silence
- Refusing to respond to questions and giving the "cold shoulder treatment" to change agents.

Being tangential or "chatty"
- Frequently changing the topic to irrelevant or superficial topics such as movies, media, friends, weather, sports, etc. in a manner that subverts the purpose of the interaction.
- Focusing solely on problems that are not part of the treatment plan.

Displaying false ignorance
- Pretending not to know obvious information specific to their case, supervision requirements, rules, social mores, etc.

Acquiescence (faking)
- Giving in to the change agent simply to get through the interaction or the process without truly considering the content.
- Faking cooperation and adopting a façade of "Whatever you say— you're the man."
- Being seductive or sexually provocative, flirting, and/or inquiring about the change agent's personal life.

Lack of engagement
- Being silent or setting up dynamics in which others (the therapist, group members, probation officers) must do most of the talking.

Table 6.2 (cont.)

Controlling the interaction
- Maintaining control of the content or tone of the interaction by being threatening, condescending, and dismissive, or by being nice, complimentary, and friendly.
- Excessively nice, polite, overly formal, and/or repeatedly (and often groundlessly) complimentary to the change agent in order to avoid disclosure.

Making it about the change agent
- Repeatedly representing the change agent as bad (victimizing the offender) or focusing on the change agent's weaknesses.
- Criticizing the change agent.

Arguing
- Being belligerent and consistently challenging the statements of change agents often without adequate reason.
- Defying or contradicting anything others say.
- Challenging the relevance of the criminal justice system or the need for treatment.

Not showing for appointments
- Forgetting, calling in sick, or scheduling other appointments at the same time as therapy or probation appointments.

Frequent tardiness
- Frequently missing the bus, not finding parking, or being subject to family or personal crises that prevent punctuality.

Intellectualizing
- Presenting legalistic, philosophical, or academic arguments in order to dispute or rationalize behavior.

Blaming others
- Repeatedly failing to take responsibility for any type of behavior, including offense behavior.

Forgetting to make payments for therapy or restitution

Lying

Is Denial Resistance?
Is It Inside or Outside the Frame?

The term "denial" is used in reference to sexual offenders more than it is with other clinical populations. Regrettably, the term denial is too commonly used pejoratively and erroneously. As discussed earlier, we often hear "denial" used to describe an offender who is simply difficult. The use of the word denial to describe an offender whom one does not like or who is difficult to manage is not accurate and is a misuse of the term.

One of the first tasks in working with a denying offender is to attempt to evaluate the offender's denial. Specifically, is the offender lying (willful denial) or exhibiting cognitive distortions (clinical denial)? The differentiation would allow change agents to more accurately evaluate progress and compliance, as well as reduce the likelihood of letting fakers complete the program. Unfortunately, it may be difficult to distinguish between the two as they may manifest similarly (see Table 6.3). Even though both types of denial could motivate someone to resist the treatment process and stay out of the frame, individuals experiencing clinical denial are more likely to be invited into the frame and engage in an exploration of their beliefs.

Table 6.3

Types of denial that can be motivated by willful denial or clinical denial

- Denial of the offense
- Denial of victim impact
- Denial of the extent of the behavior (minimizing)
- Denial of responsibility
- Denial of planning
- Denial of sexual deviancy
- Denial of relapse potential
- Denial of the need for treatment or sanctions

(adapted from Schneider and Wright, 2004)

The frame is the best place to evaluate the type of denial an offender is manifesting. Both clinical and willful denial can be motivated by frank psychological issues and emotional pain. At the outset of a change process, it is important to understand that it is the offender's ability to engage in the process that makes change possible, not an immediate disclosure of his offense. In some cases, the change agent's ability to be observant, empathic, and curious is enough both to identify the type of denial and to serve as an effective intervention. Evaluators who are rigorous in their observations of the offender's statements can steadily explore inconsistencies. In some cases, the willful denier is unable to keep up with the discrepancies and eventually will concede, while the clinical denier's distortions become more evident or break down. In both cases, the offender enters the frame.

The process of distinguishing between types of denial and upending it can also be accomplished by engaging the offender in a discussion regarding lying. When an offender is extremely guarded, an objective approach that does not require direct self-disclosure can be useful to introduce him to the topic without provoking feelings of threat and causing entrenchment. For example, general discussions regarding "why people lie," or "why offenders lie" can be particularly useful in revealing underlying motivations to maintain the deceit.

Another similar tactic is to introduce a dialogue regarding the pros and cons of maintaining "the lie." This can be done by assisting the offender in completing a "cost-benefit analysis." This allows him to identify and discuss the potential positive and negative consequences both of telling the truth and of lying. Table 6.4 provides an example of a cost-benefit analysis completed in a deniers' group. This exercise is usually done using hypothetical examples or "what ifs" (e.g., "If you were lying, how would it benefit you?"). Even if the offender is unwilling to provide personal examples at the outset of the exercise, his thinking patterns and motivations are often revealed. (It is interesting to note which area the offender concentrates on most, truth or lie.) An offender's participation in the exercise assists him in reflecting on his own decision to be honest or deceitful. (Again, not all of the change process will be immediately visible to the change agent. Introspection in the

Table 6.4

Pros and cons of maintaining the lie

	PROS	CONS
Telling the Truth	• Lasting relationships are built on credibility and trust • Honesty is integrity • Relief • Progress and change • The foundation of lasting friendships	
Maintaining the Lie	• Less likely to be shamed by others • More likely to maintain physical safety • Better chance of appealing case later • Less likely to be rejected • Maybe get out of program if you convince them you don't have a problem	• You'll never know that you won't be caught • Paranoia, worry, and stress (must be on constant guard) • One lie leads to another • Constant effort • Loss of credibility about everything when caught • Getting caught is a sign of weakness/stupidity • Puts those who defend you at risk of rejection, shame, and judgment • You don't feel good about yourself

privacy of the offender's mind might be needed before he is willing to share anything with the change agent.)

The use of objective measures can assist change agents in gathering information about an offender's denial. Such tools include the Multiphasic Sexual Inventory-II (MSI-II), The Abel Assessment of Sexual Interest (AASI), and the Paulhaus. Both the MSI-II and the AASI provide reasonably valid measures of cognitive distortions and dissimulation (lying), while the Paulhaus provides an assessment of an individual's propensity to provide socially desirable responses. The polygraph can also be extremely valuable in assessing an offender who denies his offense. Although hotly debated, notable evidence shows that the use of post-conviction polygraph is useful in eliciting disclosure and honesty. Two studies in particular (Hindman & Peters, 2001; Ahlmeyer, Heil, McKee & English, 2000), found a significant increase in the disclosure of additional victims with the introduction of polygraph. Further, Kokish, Levenson, and Blasingame (2005) found that program participants reported that the polygraph requirement helped them to be more honest in their lives and that it had a positive effect on their relationships. In addition, although somewhat anecdotal, we have observed a few sexual offender groups in which members experienced enhanced cohesion regarding pending polygraph examinations and thus supported each other in passing it via truthful disclosure.

In conclusion, distinguishing between willful and clinical denial is difficult. Strategies to work with those in clinical denial are not necessarily the focus of this book, and the reader is encouraged to seek out literature on cognitive distortions and defense mechanisms (see Schlank & Shaw, 1997; Brake & Shannon, 1997). However, many of the interventions to assess willful denial are also useful in shaking rigid cognitive distortions found in clinical denial.

Should We Treat Willful Deniers?

The issue of treating offenders who have been convicted, but deny their offense, is one of the most controversial and divisive topics in the management and treatment of sexual offenders. One side of the debate is driven by comments such as, "If they're not admitting it, what are you treating?" and "He'll never change anyway." The other side asserts, "There is no evidence that admitting is related to recidivism." Though not empirically based, few points of view have led us to the conclusion that it is reasonable to keep (some) offenders who deny their offense in treatment. First, as previously discussed, denial is a complex mechanism that is motivated by many forces. Distinguishing those offenders who are in willful denial from those who are expressing clinical denial may take extended periods of time. Secondly, keeping in focus the goal of public safety, if offenders who deny their offense are refused treatment, they are likely to remain in the community with less supervision and monitoring than those offenders who actively participate in treatment and possibly pose a lesser risk of reoffense

(Brake & Shannon, 1997). Thirdly, although most (including the authors) agree that offenders who are accountable are easier to treat, assess, and assist in promoting a group and program culture of accountability, there is little empirical evidence that account-able offenders who participate in treatment reoffend at a lower rate than those who admit to their offense (Seager, Jellicoe, & Dhaliwal, 2004). In fact, Maletzky & Steinhauser (1998) found that treated categorical deniers had a similar recidivism rate to treated admit-ters, and were much less likely to reoffend than untreated deniers.

Additionally, addressing issues related to sexual offending, such as cognitive distortions and dynamic risk variables (i.e., intimacy deficits, social influences, attitudes supportive of sexual offending, sexual self-regulation, general self-regulation, substance abuse etc.), does not necessarily require that one admit his offense. Finally, and probably most importantly, it has been our experience that some offenders who initially deny their offense later admit to it even after extended periods of treatment.

As discussed by Brake and Shannon (1997), allowing denying offenders to stay in a program indefinitely runs the risk of build-ing antisocial confidence in their ability to "get away with it." It is our recommendation that denying offenders who participate in treatment should be constantly assessed (with a formal evalu-ation every 3 months) in regard to the benefits of being in the program. Although complete disclosure may not come within that period of time, observable movement in the direction of reduced risk must be observed if treatment is to be continued. In addi-tion, the goal of accountability should also remain a priority. Our experience has been that a time period of 6 to 12 months is usually sufficient to observe and assess amenability to change. However, each case should be evaluated individually. The use of pretreat-ment programs have been shown to reduce denial in offenders by 58% (Brake & Shannon). In addition, interventions such as those described by Schlank and Shaw (1997) are encouraged. Finally, program completion requirements should include full disclosure and accountability.

Case Example

Dominic was accused of molesting a 13-year-old, runaway, homeless boy. He allegedly met the minor on the street and offered him a place to stay. During the night, Dominic repeatedly molested the boy. The following day the boy went to the police and Dominic was arrested. He denied his offense throughout his trial but was eventually convicted. After serving time in prison, he was referred to an outpatient sexual offender treatment program. After his initial assessment, he was found to exhibit a sexual interest in prepubescent males. Nevertheless, he persistently denied his offense. Dominic was placed in a deniers' group that was scheduled to last approximately 9 months—at which point Dominic's progress and his appropriateness for treatment would be reassessed.

At the outset of the group he was extremely resistant. Despite attending every session on time, he was condescending, non-disclosing, and trivial. The facilitator respectfully and diligently challenged his statements about his offense and his lack of ever having any sexual thoughts. During one session about 6 months into his treatment, a discussion about prison life and the marginalization of sexual offenders arose. He began to talk about the pressures to live a double life and hide his past for fear of being harmed or killed. He added that, although he was innocent, it made sense to him that the others in the group would not admit their offense. Dominic started the following group session by describing how years of lying had become habitual but also tiring. He then proceeded to describe his offense in detail, using the "offense chain" format that he had been taught a few months earlier. By the end of the session one other member also admitted his offense.

After the 9-month period, Dominic was placed in a sexual offender group with others who were accountable. Two years later, Dominic was off parole and voluntarily participating in the program. He has been a guest presenter to other denier groups in the program.

Identifying Resistance

Identifying resistance early in the process is crucial. Such an evaluation will likely include an evaluation of an offender's character and interaction styles. It is important to sort out behavior that may be perceived as resistance but is not. For example, an offender who asks many questions regarding the efficacy of a particular therapeutic practice or assessment technique may not necessarily be resisting change (although he may). Most of us would likely find it disconcerting if a physician or psychologist mandated that we participate in an assessment or treatment procedure that we had never heard of or did not understand. Disagreeing with a change agent is not necessarily resistance to change; it may reflect healthy self-preservation. An offender may also be labeled resistant when in fact he is unable to participate because he does not comprehend information due to cognitive or neurological deficits.

A proper assessment of the individual's cognitive and psychological functioning could provide valuable information regarding an offender's ability, and willingness, to participate in treatment and

Table 6.5
Issues that are falsely identified as resistance to change

- Axis I mental health conditions
- Neurological conditions (e.g., memory or intellectual deficits)
- Legitimate health conditions
- Disagreeing with the change agent
- Language barriers
- Appropriately bringing new personal problems to treatment
- Not knowing how the change process works
- Not having the financial resources to pay for treatment or transportation to treatment
- Attachment or characterological issues that the offender is willing to explore in psychotherapy

supervision. Some offenders are unable to cooperate fully because they have intellectual and neurological deficits that inhibit participation. These offenders often fall between the cracks in the system and are labeled resistant or difficult. Although some offenders may have legitimate problems that limit their ability to cooperate, caution should be made to identify those offenders who present with disabilities but are in fact malingering or feigning psychological or neurological conditions (see Table 6.5). A proper assessment would include a thorough review of collateral information, including document review from any institution where the offender was previously placed (we acknowledge that such information is often difficult to obtain but encourage efforts to obtain it), interviewing friends and family members, and consulting with previous treatment providers or supervision agents.

Assessment Tools to Identify Obstacles to Treatment and Supervision[1]

Facets of Sexual Offender Denial (FoSOD)
> This measure assesses various dimensions of denial. It assists in differentiating between offenders who are responsive or unresponsive to treatment (Schneider & Wright, 2001).

Multiphasic Sexual Inventory–II (MSI-II) (Nichols & Molinder, 1984)
> This measure is designed to identify the sexual characteristics of an adult alleged to have committed a sexual offense or sexual misconduct. The measure assesses various aspects of sexual knowledge, self-reported sexual interests, and cognitive distortions (or problematic thinking patterns).

Millon Clinical Multiphasic Inventory–III (MCMI-III) (Millon, 1987)
> This is a structured psychological measure that assesses personality styles and patterns, psychopathology, and psychosocial stressors.

---

[1] This is not an exhaustive list of assessment tools. The authors also assert that a conclusion should never be based solely on the results of a single test, but rather on an integration of various sources of information.

Minnesota Multiphasic Personality Inventory-2 (MMPI-2) (Butcher, Dahlstrom, Graham, Tellegen, & Kaemmer, 1989)
This well-known and well-respected personality assessment is often used to accompany neuropsychological tests to assess personality and emotional status that might lend understanding to reactions to neurofunctional impairment (particularly, the F, Fb, and Ds scales).

Wide Range Achievement Test (WRAT) (Wilkinson, 1993)
Provides level of performance in reading, spelling, and written arithmetic. The reading and spelling tests are often used in estimating pre-morbid intellectual functioning.

Kaufman Functional Academic Skills Test (Kaufman & Kaufman, 1994)
A brief, individually administered test designed to determine performance in reading and mathematics as applied to daily life situations.

Structured Interview of Reported Symptoms (SIRS) (Rogers, Bagby, & Dickens, 1998)
This is a structured interview designed to detect malingering and other forms of feigning of psychiatric symptoms.

Test of Memory Malingering (TOMM) (Tombaugh, 1996)
This instrument is designed to provide a reliable, economical first step of a full psychological battery to help assess whether an individual is falsifying symptoms of memory impairment.

Weschler Adult Intelligent Scale (WAIS-III) (Weschler, 1997)
This set of 13 separate "subtests" produces measures of memory, knowledge, problem solving, calculation, abstract thinking, spatial orientation, planning, and speed of mental processing. In addition to summary measures of intelligence, performance on each subtest yields implications for different neurofunctional domains. The set of tests takes about an hour or more to administer. The WAIS-III is often the foundation for a comprehensive neuropsychological assessment.

Halstead-Reitan (Reitan & Wolfson, 1992)
A set of tests that examines language, attention, motor speed, abstract thinking, memory, and spatial reasoning is often used

to produce an overall assessment of brain function. Neuropsychologists use some or all of the original set of tests.

Cognistat (Kiernan, Mueller, Langston, & van Dyke, 1987)
This screening test examines language, memory, arithmetic, attention, judgment, and reasoning. It is typically used in screening individuals who cannot tolerate longer or more complicated neuropsychological tests.

Paulhaus (Paulhaus, 1991)
This instrument measures the tendency to give socially desirable responses, useful for identifying individuals who distort their responses.

Abel Assessment of Sexual Interest (AASI)
The questionnaire portion of the AASI allows for an assessment of the subject's intent to appear socially desirable. The Abel also has a Denier-Dissimulator Scale that is intended to identify those individuals attempting to conceal having sexually abused a child.

Sources of Resistance

Offenders resist change for a number of reasons including, first and foremost, the emotional challenge of admitting something that places them on the margins of society to be ridiculed and despised. Additionally, issues related to shame, guilt, and fear motivate some to not comply and/or flee. In many cases, these fears are directed toward change agents who are seen as part of a system that oppresses them. In some cases, offenders fear retaliation or being used as a scapegoat by other offenders more than they fear disclosing their offense details to change agents. As one offender said after being asked why he would disclose his offense to his parole agent but not to the offenders in his treatment group, "Are you kidding me? That could get me killed. My private stuff is valuable information to someone who is trying to protect himself."

Some offenders are motivated to resist change because they are convinced that the antisocial way of life that they have chosen is more beneficial to them than "living a straight life." As discussed earlier, while some resistance can be extremely functional (such as resisting bloodletting procedures), at other times it is dysfunctional (refusing to register as a sexual offender after being directed to do so). At some point in time, the offender perceived the resistant behavior as beneficial even though it produced negative consequences. For some offenders, dysfunctional behavior patterns provide positive rewards, such as a sense of safety, power, confidence, or enhanced masculinity, and they will pursue such rewards despite the potential for harmful and self-defeating consequences. Effort therefore needs to be made to help offenders identify the underlying goals that motivate resistant behaviors and then to direct them to develop healthy prosocial ways to meet these desires.

Resistance can also be a product of dysfunctional character. As Hanson and Morton-Bourgon (2004) pointed out, the presence of a personality disorder is a major predictor of sexual recidivism. An offender's inability or unwillingness to bond with change agents and engage in a change process may be symptomatic of a personality disorders. The symptoms associated with these disorders should be primary targets of the treatment plan. It is also important to define resistance according to observed behavior and its effect (that it obstructs the process of change) rather than relying on a label (e.g., the offender has borderline personality disorder and therefore is resistant to change).

Another source of resistance is prison acculturation. Many offenders have spent significant amounts of time in prison without participating in activities that would assist in their transition into the community (e.g., sexual offender treatment, vocational training, etc). Offenders have, however, participated in a system that is adversarial and divisive. Many enter treatment unwilling to participate in a system that they feel does not respect or care about them. A profound lack of trust instills attitudes that promote resistance to anything suggested by the system.

Interventions to Overcome Resistance

Overcoming Resistance With a Plan
Some would argue that sexual offenders provoke intense countertransference. The previous chapter discussed various ways for

change agents to remain cognizant of motivations, beliefs, and feelings while working with sexual offenders. Being aware of counter-transference issues, as well as potential counter-resistance, will reduce change agent resistance. The most effective interventions directed toward overcoming resistance are intentional. Interventions that are knee-jerk, emotionally charged responses usually undermine the change process and increase resistance. Intentional planning includes developing a frame, establishing specific treatment goals, placing offenders in appropriate treatment modalities, and finally, approaching each interaction with meaning and purpose.

Teaching Communication Skills

The frame is reliant upon teaching sound communication skills. Kahn's (1995) work on conversational skills with college students is a particularly useful tool when taught to offenders. Kahn studied different ways that seminar styles might or might not be successful in exploring new ideas. Adapted from Kahn's work, four conversational styles can be observed in both individual and group interactions. They can be particularly useful in teaching offenders how to communicate in group settings.

The first is called **Free-For-All**. In a free-for-all, there is no structure to the conversation; anything goes. The goal of the speaker is to win something. It could be enhanced self-esteem, the facilitator's approval, acknowledgment as the disruptor, etc., and this might be accomplished by being smarter and more assertive than everyone else. Being smarter could also mean making others look dumb. Another style is the **Beauty Contest**. In the beauty contest the goal is seeking admiration by looking and sounding the best. While one person is parading their ideas, everyone else is preparing their next idea; therefore, no one is really listening—except to themselves. **The Club** style is motivated by the desire to develop a "feel good" atmosphere. Everything that is said is accepted and nothing is challenged. Then there is the **Barn-Raising Conversation**. Barn-raising is comprised of an openness of expression but also permission to engage in challenges and critical thinking. The conversation thrives when participants contribute equally. When someone has an idea to share, even if it is incomplete, it is the project of everyone involved to develop it or figure it out. If there is a disagreement, it is each participant's responsibility to explore it equally. In a barn-raising discussion the frame is supported by each participant.

Solid barn-raising communication relies on mutuality and trust. If the offender is unable to have confidence in the process, he will likely not invest in change. The most efficient way to maintain confidence is to know the limits of the frame and remain consistent, while at the same time allowing the offender to test the limits and explore. This does not mean that the change agent must tolerate verbal abuse or threatening behavior, but it does require room for expression of genuine feelings and skepticism. Inviting ambivalence, hostility, cynicism, concern, doubt, and differences into the dialogue can be the first demonstration of a collaborative exploration. It is also an opportunity to teach appropriate communication skills regardless of the difficulty or emotionality of the topic. An offender who pretends that the change agent is immediately trustworthy and easily goes along with anything the change agent says may be providing the first sign of false compliance and a hidden refusal to engage in the process.

Free-For-All Conversation
- The goal for each member is to win.
- Winning usually means looking smarter or tougher than everyone else in the group.
- Winning is accomplished by making other group members or the facilitators look dumb or weak by being sarcastic, condescending, indifferent, or aloof (having a "whatever" attitude).

Beauty Contest Conversation
- The goal for each member is to gain admiration.
- Admiration may mean pleasing the facilitator or getting others in the group to pay attention to you because you look or sound good.
- Admiration is sought at the expense of gaining or sharing any meaningful insight because how you present yourself is not about being truthful. Group members in a "beauty contest" are interested in looking good or getting attention by giving others what they think others want.

Club Conversation

- The goal is to recognize and validate everyone's worth and uniqueness.
- Recognition and validation may take the form of appreciating everyone's openness and honesty.
- Recognition and validation is accomplished by making others feel good about themselves and about sharing. However, in this model, recognition and validation are often accomplished at the expense of critical thinking. Identification of faulty thinking and errors in perception are ignored in order to create a "feel-good" atmosphere.

Barn-Raising Conversation

- The goal is for each member to build a sound structure of ideas and behaviors both individually and as a group.
- The structure is built with ideas. Each member brings their ideas, and there is equal responsibility among group members to develop, explain, and defend the ideas until they are sound. For example, if a group member brings a dilemma to the group, the dilemma belongs to the whole group. When one person is stuck and can't tie concepts together, it is the task of the entire group to help clarify or educate.
- A sound structure of ideas is accomplished by equally participating in every idea, concept, or problem that arises. Equality is not determined by how much you speak but by disclosure—all members must share all their thoughts.

Establishing Goals

Sexual offenders seem particularly adept at avoiding the issues to be addressed in order to reduce their risk of reoffense. The development of a strong and consistent frame with clear, definable goals will encourage offenders to stay on task and participate in the change process. Goals that are ambiguous or not steadily addressed may facilitate noncompliance. The literature suggests that goals should be specific rather than vague, demanding rather than easy, and accompanied by feedback (Locke, Shaw, & Saari, 1981; Miller 1985). One offender expressed that he felt the most resistant when treatment sessions did not adhere to their stated goals. Such occasions contributed to the belief that he should not take the goals seriously if the facilitator did not. He said that sessions that appeared aimless or easy made him feel that the facilitator was only there to make money and didn't really care abut him.

Cullari (1996) pointed out that the development of treatment goals should utilize four guidelines: 1) Goal Relevance, 2) Goal Importance, 3) Goal Attainability, and 4) Emotional Salience.

Goal Relevance refers to goals that are pertinent to a particular offender's risk factors. For example, most offenders will not state during the early stages of treatment that their goal is never to offend again (because they believe they will never offend again). Nevertheless, it is appropriate to assert "no offending" as the primary goal. Relevant additions may be never to harm anyone, to abstain from viewing deviant sexual material, and to develop honest, age-appropriate relationships.

Goal Importance works toward identifying goals that are personally significant to the offender. These goals could relate to dynamic factors that contributed to the offense but are also identified by the offender as goals that would contribute to his personal happiness and stability. A goal such as maintaining a job or establishing a healthy, enduring relationship would fall into this category.

Goal Attainability refers to goals that the offender believes can be achieved. Re-establishing a committed and loving relationship with his ex-wife in two weeks and sustaining it for one year is an unrealistic goal for an offender recently released from an extended prison term. An attainable goal would include the development of healthy communication between the offender and his ex-wife. Developing a short-term goal for a pedophile never to think of children in a sexual way again may set the offender up for failure and eventual indifference to treatment goals. An attainable goal would be abstaining from masturbating to deviant stimuli and contacting a support person when an urge arises.

Emotional Salience refers to setting goals in which the natural rewards are obvious to the offender. For example, does the offender know, or believe, that he will feel good about attaining the goal? If the offender is participating in social skill development to address relationship problems, is the offender confident that he will have more emotionally fulfilling relationships?

As with the attainment of any life-changing goal, those goals that are easy to attain often have less meaning to the individual. Cameron, Pierce, and So (2004) found that performance and intrinsic motivation increased when rewards were given for succeeding at a moderately difficult task while rewards given for achievement on a task of low difficulty reduced performance and motivation. On the other hand, goals that are far beyond the ability of the offender will not increase engagement or achievement (Cullari, 1996). For this reason, packaged curriculum materials or treatment protocols that are rigid often fail to match the offender's ability. Change agents should be cognizant of the offender's skill level and present goals and psychoeducational materials accordingly. Prepackaged curriculum materials, for example, should be presented by facilitators in a way that meets the needs of the offenders; materials should not be presented in a rote or formulaic manner.

Allowing offenders to participate in treatment planning will decrease resistance since change is more likely if the offender takes personal responsibility for goal attainment rather than having the goals imposed upon him. For example, efforts should be made to get offenders to buy into sexual offender specific goals and the offender should be encouraged to add a few personal goals, such as reducing anxiety at work or increasing concentration.

Additionally, aspects of the treatment plan should be established before the offender is released from the institution. Many offenders are not informed of the requirements of their parole or probation until after their release. Informing offenders of requirements as well as the goals of their supervision and/or treatment before implementing a plan will greatly assist in the change process.

Addressing Mental Health Issues

Successfully changing offenders often means identifying and addressing coexisting psychological disorders that contribute to offense behavior or simply pose a threat to treatment compliance. Offenders with serious mental health conditions should be referred for full psychological, psychiatric, and medication evaluations. Table 1.1 in chapter 1 highlights various characteristics of Axis II disorders that often contribute to resistance. Treatment plans should clearly outline how behaviors related to a character disorder will be addressed (see Table 6.6).

Individual Treatment Versus Group Treatment

As expressed in various forms through this book, the authors strongly suggest that all sexual offenders be given the opportunity to participate in sexual offender therapy. According to the California Coalition on Sexual Offending (2002), empirical research has not established the comparative efficacy of group versus individual therapy. It seems likely that varying modalities work best for addressing particular issues with particular offenders. At present, when to use which modality remains a question of clinical judgment.

An alliance between an offender and change agent is more likely to develop during the course of individual sessions than in group settings. Schwartz (1988) suggested that individual therapy provides more confidentiality and may be used to develop trust and basic social skills, and assist in overcoming reticence. However, one-to-one settings such as individual psychotherapy may be more prone to entrenched and adversarial interactions as opposed to a group setting where the offender has to present his ideas to many people. When done properly, one of the most effective methods in addressing resistance is peer inquiry. Addressing issues of compliance in a group of peers, as opposed with the change agent in a one-to-one setting, reduces the "you're just part of the system" mentality that keeps many offenders disengaged from the process. Utilizing "working group members" to be role models can also set a tone of disclosure and cooperation that can be beneficial in reducing resistance in some of the most stubborn offenders.

Working together with other offenders also provides valuable, experiential education regarding how groups work and guidelines to establish a frame. As discussed earlier in this chapter, educating

Table 6.6
Specific interventions for various Axis II disorders

Disorder	Interventions
Antisocial Personality Disorder	• Decrease impulsivity • Set clear limits regarding the rules for treatment • Point out and prohibit manipulative behavior • Teach anger management skills • Increase coping skills • Provide insight into consequences • Increase interpersonal sensitivity • Challenge distortions regarding criminal thinking • Instill self-skills to assess social influences and triggers
Narcissistic Personality Disorder	• Set clear limits regarding the rules for treatment • Praise genuine interaction • Explore underlying feelings of inadequacy that may be masked by grandiosity • Increase accurate self-image based on true strengths • Explore low self-esteem • Identify and correct cognitive distortions • Increase social skills • Provide empathy training
Borderline Personality Disorder	• Increase interpersonal relationship skills • Build trust • Increase problem-solving skills • Instill reality-checking mechanisms • Decrease suspiciousness • Address issues related to self-image • Decrease self-defeating and self-destructive behaviors • Increase coping skills • Reduce impulsivity • Link behaviors with underlying feelings • Increase appropriate expressions • Increase boundary-setting skills • Decrease manipulative behaviors • Confront splitting immediately if it arises • Address all-or-nothing thinking errors • Use consistent interventions • Don't get pulled into arguments

Table 6.6 (cont.)

Disorder	Interventions
Avoidant Personality Disorder	• Create a working alliance • Provide support regarding feelings of inadequacy • Decrease cognitive distortions • Increase coping skills • Provide assertiveness training • Increase self-esteem • Decrease interpersonal sensitivity • Improve social skills • Don't pressure them too quickly
Dependent Personality Disorder	• Increase independent decision-making skills • Decrease reliance on others • Increase coping skills • Decrease feelings of hopelessness • Address cognitive distortions • Improve self-efficacy and self-esteem • Identify fears of independent behavior • Don't pressure them too quickly

offenders regarding which kinds of groups work can reduce the mystery of group process and increase engagement. The barn-raising approach is the most useful for the purpose of developing a functional group because it promotes disclosure and community effort. Most groups shift between the different types, but being able to identify them when they occur will assist the group in getting back on track.

Purpose and Meaning

Approaching interactions with offenders with clear goals will facilitate participation and reduce resistance. It is also important to pay attention to which interventions or interaction styles increase participation and which interventions increase resistance. One way of conceptualizing this process is the approach and avoidance model. Dollard and Miller (2004) pointed out that there is a push and pull between resistance and change. The forces that motivate one to avoid something (or resist it) tend to be stronger than the forces that motivate one to approach something (or change it). In order to facilitate change "a change agent must increase approach forces or decrease avoidant forces" (Knowles & Linn, 2004, p. 119). This means resistance can be overcome by enlightening an offender about the benefits of changing and/or the disadvantages of resisting.

According to Knowles and Linn (2004) certain strategies can be used to meet these goals, specifically, Alpha strategies and Omega strategies. *Alpha* strategies promote change by activating approach forces while *Omega* strategies promote change by minimizing the avoidant forces. Table 6.7 and 6.8 adapt Knowles and Linn's work to sexual offender treatment.

Table 6.7
Alpha strategies

What	How
Make change more appealing →	Create strong, logical arguments that increase interest and justify and compel actions (Petty & Cacioppo, 1986). Remind offenders of the benefits of participating in treatment (e.g., increased social skills, better relationships, etc.) to increase approach forces.
Add incentives →	Provide incentives for compliance (e.g., advancement in phases or levels can spur motivation, and having specific criteria for graduation or completion provides clear and attainable goals.)
Emphasize consistency and commitment →	Point out patterns of cooperation and compliance to prompt offenders to continue with this course of action. Inconsistency is a threat to one's self-esteem (Dillard, 1991).
Provide consensus information →	People tend to use other people's behavior as a guide for their own behavior (M. Sherif & C. Sherif, 1956). If offenders see others cooperating, they will be more likely to cooperate. Have offenders who are completing the program speak to new members to demonstrate that other people are complying and succeeding.
Engage a norm of social reciprocity →	Be gracious and respectful to encourage reciprocation. Simple behaviors such as being polite, opening a door, making restroom keys easily accessible, or providing notepads for homework increase approach forces.

Table 6.8
Omega strategies

What	How
Sidestep resistance →	Redefine the interaction as not involving influence but rather as a consultancy.
Acknowledge resistance →	Resistance is often covert and hidden. Labeling resistance as what it is can defuse its power, rendering it less influential (Knowles & Linn, 2004). Beginning a session with a resistant offender by discussing resistance may diffuse it. Bringing it to the table will prevent acting it out.
Offer choices →	If someone is resistant to an idea, one strategy is to present them with an alternative. An alternative may satisfy the drive to resist and empower them to cooperate. Knowles and Linn (2004) use the example of providing a resistant child with such an alternative: "Do you want to brush your teeth first, or do you want to put on your pajamas first?" Offer an offender a choice of whether or not to participate. This allows the offender, without direct prompting, to evaluate the consequences of resistant behavior and, ideally, make a decision not to resist change.
Counter-argue resistance →	Make arguments that nonparticipation is self-defeating (e.g., "If you continue to hold back and resist participating, you are not going to change. You are going to stay the way you are. It seems that staying the way you are will lead to making more of the same mistakes that you have made in the past. On the other hand, participating in treatment could lead to changes that contribute to your happiness.").
Depersonalize the interaction →	Encourage a discussion on a topic that the offender is willing to talk about while avoiding sensitive topics. Also, encourage a discussion on sexual offenses in general, or a recent offense in the media, avoiding the need for personal disclosure too early.
Raise self-esteem →	Self-affirmation decreases resistance. Jacks and O'Brien (2004) point out that activities that build up efficacy and self-esteem make people less distrustful.

(adapted from Knowles and Linn, 2004)

Alpha and Omega Strategies in Action

Client: So what are you going to force me to talk about today? (Sigh) This is oppressive! It's like being in Nazi Germany or something. People invading my privacy, making me talk about stuff that I don't want to talk about. Can't we just talk about baseball?

Therapist: Hi, Frank. **(engage in a norm of social reciprocity—Alpha)** Well, I am not going to force you to talk about anything. We can work on that together. If you want to talk about baseball for a few moments we can. (pause) I see you have on an Angels hat. You said before that you were a fan. Did they win the other day? **(sidestep resistance—Omega)**

Client: (Long silence; shakes his head)

Therapist: I understand that you don't want to be here, but you do have a choice. **(offer choices—Omega)**

Client: I don't have any choices. If I do my own thing and just chill, I'll be going back to prison. It's my parole officer's choice that I am here; it's not mine. I don't need to change.

Therapist: I understand that it feels that way. But you really don't have to come. I've worked with some people who have chosen to finish their time in prison. I understand that you really don't want to do that—I don't think that many people would—but in truth, you do have a choice. **(offer choices—Omega)**

Client: (Shaking his head) My choice is that I just go back to my life and you leave me alone.

Therapist: What goes on in your life? Are you happy in it?

Client: That is a whole other story. My wife got a restraining order. I can't visit my nieces and nephews. My family won't talk to me. It's just a mess. But you're no help.

Therapist: It sounds like a mess. I suppose it's tough not having anyone to talk to. I guess you could choose not to talk to me, but it sounds like you want to talk to someone. Isn't this better than nothing? **(counter-argue resistance—Omega)**

Client: Okay, you got me. I want to talk to someone, but I don't want to come here, I don't want to see you, and I don't want to talk to you. If I start talking to you, I will end up being here forever. I know how it works. When people start talking to you, you make up reasons to keep us in the program. No one ever gets out.

Therapist: Well, that's not how it works. I can show you what it takes to complete the program. You have to go through certain steps and accomplish some of the goals that you talked about, but you can complete the program. **(add incentives—Alpha)** A lot of guys complete the program. You'll get to meet some of them when you start group. Before people complete they come to group and tell about their experiences here. **(provide consensus information—Alpha)**

Client: I don't want to talk about what some bitch said I did in front of other guys.

Therapist: I understand that. I think that's why you walked in here in a bad mood. Most of the guys that come here have trouble talking about their case. Some say that it's scary to make themselves vulnerable. But they get through it and realize that they are no different from anyone else in the room. Let's start with you telling me why it's hard to talk about it. **(acknowledging resistance—Omega)**

Client: If I do, will we ever get to talk about something that's positive?

Therapist: Sure, tell me something positive.

Client: Like what?

Therapist: Well, this is a sexual offender treatment program, so we do need to talk about your offense, and we need to talk about you as a person, but that doesn't mean that you can't direct the conversation sometimes too. In fact, you have done very well so far. You are cooperating and talking with me. I am actually learning something about you. If this is how it's going to be, I think we will eventually get to do some good work together. **(emphasize consistency and commitment–Alpha)** So you want to talk about something positive. What is something positive that you have accomplished? **(raise self-esteem–Omega)**

Client: Okay, I can talk about some stuff—like I am a good salesman. I can sell a hairpiece to a guy with a full head of hair. I also think that I could make a good husband if I had another chance. But I might not get it. I don't want my life to be this way forever. But I am not sure that you're really gonna help me. Maybe I should just forget it. Things are not going to change.

Therapist: From what you are telling me, it seems that your life has not been what you've wanted in a long time. It seems that if you continue to hold back, and resist participating, and refuse to talk to me, you are not going to change. You are just going to stay the way you are. It seems that staying the way you are means making more of the same mistakes that you have made in the past. **(counter-arguing resistance–Omega)**

Client: (Angrily) What if I don't want to change? What if I like the way that I am? It's all those people that I have to be with in this program, and in my neighborhood, that get me trippin'. They need to change. The only thing I need to change is to get out of this damn program.

Therapist: There are a lot of good reasons to change. You have been complaining about other people. Maybe if you make some changes in yourself, you can figure out how to stay away from them. It's also important to realize that nobody's perfect. Even you admitted you needed to figure out how you could meet some women. Perhaps you could change by improving your skills to meet women and developing happier and healthier relationships. You also said a few minutes ago that you were a good salesman. Maybe you could change by improving those skills in a positive direction. **(make change more appealing—Alpha)**

Client: Okay, okay, I got ya. But I am not going to talk about my offense.

Therapist: Well, that is going to be a problem, because if you choose to be in the program, you are going to need to talk about your offense and other things about yourself. The more that you refuse to participate in the program, the longer you are going to be here. **(offer choices—Omega)** If you can graduate through the first phase of this program, you are closer to completing. You should also know that after the first phase of this program, we focus a lot more on life issues such as developing relationships and exploring and developing your life after parole. **(add incentives—Alpha)**

Client: Man, I'm having a hard time just showing up now, and you want me to come every week like this. I don't think I can do it.

Therapist: I think that you can. After a rough start a few weeks ago, you've made all your appointments. You are already doing it. You've proved to me that you are capable. **(emphasize consistency and commitment—Alpha)**

Client: Thanks, Doc.

Therapist: Thank you **(engage in a norm of social reciprocity—Alpha)** for sticking it out this far. **(emphasize consistency and commitment—Alpha)**

Other Strategies

Motivational Interviewing

Motivational Interviewing (MI) is a method intended to create a collaborative and working alliance with psychotherapy patients (Rollnick & Miller, 1991, 1995, 2002). The relationship is additionally defined by a shared understanding of goals and tasks of therapy in addition to the working alliance. Many of the change agent's characteristics discussed previously must be employed if this method is to be effective. Change agents are encouraged to develop six global characteristics or skills. These are empathy, acceptance, egalitarianism, warmth, genuineness, and overall Motivational Interviewing spirit (Moyers, Miller, & Hendrickson, 2005).

Six Global Motivational Interviewing Characteristics

- Empathy: Convey an understanding of the offender's perspective.

- Acceptance: Show unconditional positive regard and respect for the offender.

- Egalitarianism: Provide support of offender's autonomy, choice, and responsibility.

- Warmth: Express care, compassion, and friendliness.

- Genuineness: Express openness, trustworthiness, and honesty.

- MI Spirit: Advise with permission, affirmation, emphasizing control, open questioning, reflecting, reframing, and providing support.

Patience

Although short on research, we have witnessed that many of the offenders who were the most resistant in the initial stages of change became the most complaint and invested in the change process. As described in the stages of change, model offenders usually enter the change process in the precontemplation or contemplation stages (Prochaska & DiClemente, 1992). They are not convinced that they have a problem or that they can change. In addition, most offenders will be resistant to a process they do not know or understand. Therefore resistance should be expected and even welcomed. Several meetings with an offender may be required in order for the frame to be developed. In some cases, 6 months to a year might be required to successfully engage an offender. In cases where offenders are highly resistant and unwilling to participate in the change process, a pretreatment phase with a specific time frame such as 6 months may be set to guide interventions and assess an offender's potential for change.

Validation

If the motivation for resistance can be seen for what it really is, self-preservation, the same forces can be used to facilitate change. Providing education and exploring resistance with offenders invites offenders into the frame. Validating and delving into the offenders' concerns can be profoundly beneficial. Additionally, ignoring obvious differences between the offender and change agent, such as racial, cultural, or gender differences, can lead to entrenched assumptions and attitudes that are difficult to overcome.

Change agents should also be cognizant that some offenders may have beliefs that dispute the efficacy of psychotherapy. For example, some offenders genuinely believe that their religious or spiritual practice is the only avenue of change for them. Instead of challenging these beliefs, validating and exploring differences can be beneficial. In some cases, resources that might facilitate offender change (such as increased social support) can be identified and utilized.

Non-Confrontational Interaction

There is no evidence that harsh confrontation is useful with any offender let alone resistant ones. Presenting psycho-educational materials, points of view, or engaging in explorative dialogue in a manner that does not increase anxiety or shame is recommended. Using basic social skills including respect, compassion, empathy, and active listening, as well as frequent check-ins regarding the offender's feelings about the topics being discussed, can go a long way in engaging and building rapport.

Another way to engage in explorative dialogue with offenders is the use of media or representational material. For example, factitious sexual offender cases that are similar to the offender's behavior or sexual offense can be useful in educating offenders regarding offense dynamics and are often less threatening and reduce resistance. Similarly, the use of current news articles or film is also a useful way to engage offenders.

Brake and Shannon (1997) also suggest taking a "one down" position that utilizes open-ended questioning techniques can enhance compliance. This approach is often referred to as the "Colombo" approach. Many resistant offenders are quick to engage in conflict. Letting the offender direct the conversation during the early stages of treatment often leaves little room for resistant tactics. This intervention could also be an opportunity to validate the offender's feelings regarding the restrictions of supervision or being mandated into treatment.

This is not to say that any confrontation is useless. Though currently and justly under much scrutiny, the use of confrontation, if not harsh or punitive can serve a purpose. Sexual offender treatment is usually time limited, requiring change agents to be directive (not harsh nor punitive) at times. As long as a sound working relationship has been established, the use of confrontation can assist in facilitating change. Roberts (2002), drawing on his work with borderline patients, points out that confrontation can provide the vehicle for bringing attention to discrepancies between what the offender desires and what is true. Additionally, confrontation coupled with education can bring to awareness unhealthy and maladaptive coping styles and behaviors. However, if employed in an unsupportive and uncaring manner, the therapeutic alliance will suffer. If confrontation is to be used at all, it should be in a respectful, non-attacking manner that is intended to provide insight and understanding.

Stimulating Attention

W. Marshall and L. Marshall (2005) expressed that the goal of sexual offender treatment is to get offenders to learn and understand, not to bore them. As with any learning and growing process, offenders must be present and attend to the issues at hand. Materials or methods that are uninteresting or tedious will not likely convince someone to change. Several tactics will engage offenders. Experiential exercises that oblige offenders to participate are recommended. If an offender is allowed to wither away in a corner, he will likely become more resistant and separated from the process. Experiential exercises that encourage non-threatening introspection and interaction can be key to developing lines of communication in both individual and group settings. (See *Challenging Experience* by John Bergman & Saul Hewish, 2003)

Humor can also be a useful tool to stimulate healthy attention if appropriate and devoid of sarcasm and cynicism. There is little doubt that joking with offenders involves many risks. Humor often misses its intention and aggravates hidden pains and insecurities. In addition, some resistant offenders may be waiting for an opportunity to create distance or criticize the therapists. However, humor is without a doubt a powerful tool in resolving intractable resistances (Cassell, 1974). In terms of psychotherapy, humor can reduce the perceived disparity between an offender and a therapist while at the same time making the therapy process a positive and memorable experience (Ellis, 1977).

Creativity

One of the most powerful tools, if not the most powerful tool, in facilitating change in resistant offenders is the change agent's ability to be human, know oneself, and pay attention to the dynamics of the interaction. There is an art to the work of changing offenders that has not yet been properly measured or articulated. The ability to be directive, genuine, empathic, patient, and goal oriented (W. Marshall & L. Marshall, 2005) is what really informs the work and engages offenders in the change process. For therapists, the ability to remain cognizant of the basic tenets of change and the psychotherapeutic process will provide valuable resources for future change. Relying on a blend of frequent consultation, well-thought-out treatment planning, experience, and, yes, instinct, can provide creative and effective interventions.

Table 6.9
Labeling and intervening with resistance in various change stages

Stage of Change	Resistance	Intervention
Stage One: Pre-contemplation	Refusal to participate or engage.	**Consciousness Raising** • Define the frame. • Provide education regarding resistance—"change is hard and scary." **Dramatic Relief** • Honor and validate feelings about supervision and treatment.
Stage Two: Contemplation	Distress or psychological discomfort arises as offenders acknowledge they have a problem. They may express a desire to maintain control over their lives as is, especially since they feel the criminal justice system is controlling them.	**Self-Reevaluation** • Discuss resistance and self-defeating behavior. • Outline overall goals. • Personalize goals and assert the benefits of changing.
Stage Three: Preparation	Fear and ambivalence about changing may arise. Up to this point, change has been mostly an intellectual endeavor. Actually changing is hard. Old, dysfunctional patterns look appealing because they are familiar.	**Self-Liberation** • Integrate learning from past failures and successes. • Remind the offender of the goals and adapt strategies to ensure compliance and attainability.
Stage Four: Action	The offender talks a good game but may have some difficulty with follow through.	**Reinforcement Management** • Provide consistent, structured support and encouragement. • Review accomplishments from previous stages. • Enforce consistency and commitment. • Provide rewards for successes.
Stage Five: Maintenance	Wanting to terminate too early. The offender believes that the work is done.	**Stimulus Control and Counter-Conditioning** • Provide education regarding relapse or reoffense potential. • Instill acceptance of the need for ongoing growth and change. • Redefine the treatment goals to keep the offender engaged. **Helping Relationships** • Encourage prosocial community supports and activities.

Stages of Change and Resistance

Resistance can arise at any point during the course of change. As discussed in chapter 4, the Transtheoretical model and its stages of change can be useful in identifying the appropriate intervention to address resistance. Table 6.9 offers examples of manifestations of resistance at each stage of change and suggested interventions.

The Good Lives Model and Resistance

Thus far we have discussed specific approaches and tactics necessary to work with resistant offenders. In addition to developing the frame and planning specific steps to offender change, we believe that in order to properly engage resistance, a particular tone, or theme, needs to be set with each offender. This is important because most offenders approach the change process with the perspective that "not much good can come from this if I am being forced to do it." Changing a tone of resistance and divisiveness to a tone of agreement and collaboration requires a belief in both an offender's potential to live a happy, harm-free life and his ability to participate in change. The Good Lives Approach (Ward & Marshall, 2004) is a comprehensive conceptual model that, we believe, lays a resistance-reducing framework for enhancing the partnership between change agent and offender.

Most sexual offender change models are risk-need models and view the enhancement of each offender only through the lens of risk reduction. The Good Lives Model (Ward, 2002), on the other hand, asserts that approaches to change must emphasize the enrichment of an offender's capabilities and strengths in addition to employing sound risk-reduction strategies. Instead of approaching the change process from a problem-focused or deficit-based perspective, the Good Lives Model attempts to address the etiological contributors of sexual offending by focusing on the attainment of basic "human goods" (characteristics, actions, state of affairs, experiences, and states of mind) that are essential for basic human functioning (Ward & Marshall, 2004; Marshall, Ward, & Mann, 2005). A lack of these "human goods" relates to the causal factors of sexual offending (Ward & Marshall).

The Good Lives Model identifies nine primary "human goods" for all of humankind: life (good health and optimal living), knowledge, excellence in work and play (including mastery experiences), excellence in agency (autonomy and self-directedness), inner peace (freedom from emotional turmoil and stress), relatedness and community (including intimate, romantic, and family relationships), spirituality (meaning and purpose in life), happiness, and creativity (Ward & Marshall, 2004). In many cases these goods have been unable to manifest in the offender's life, while as Ward (2002) points out, some offenders simply do not have the skills to attain these basic needs. Despite the importance that these life qualities offer for all of us, many change agents would probably acknowledge that their daily work activities with offenders are not focused on these concerns. It is therefore crucial that change agents remain cognizant of the fundamental assumption underlying the model that sexual offenders have the same human needs and aspirations as the rest of us.

Many offenders easily acknowledge the need for human goods, but they are stymied when it comes to attainment. The Good Lives Model provides insight into how these human goods can be acquired based on an offender's strengths, skills, and resources. In the manner that we have applied this model, the offender is encouraged to participate in treatment planning that utilizes the nine human goods. He must then identify internal conditions or personal skills and capabilities that will assist him in defining and living a meaningful life. The offender is then asked to identify external conditions (e.g., supports and resources) that can be utilized in implementing a good life (Ward & Marshall, 2004). The collaborative involvement with the offender is crucial because there is no single definition of what constitutes a good life. How the good life is defined is dependent upon each individual's strengths and desires. Therefore each plan must be individualized and specific to one's life circumstances and conditions.

Offenders need to focus on addressing specific risk factors (deviant sexual arousal, cognitive distortions, intimacy deficits, social and cultural factors, self-esteem, emotional regulation problems, etc.). However, long-term change likely includes a focus on human goods, and it's important to identify how these human goods relate to the risk factors in the offender's specific case. In addition, addressing non-criminogenic needs of offenders, such as anxiety, low self-esteem, and psychological distress promotes the change agent–offender alliance (Ward & Stewart, 2002). A change agent who acknowledges that an offender has issues and concerns beyond the specifics of his sexual offense can motivate an offender to adopt pro-social attitudes and participate in the whole process of change.

In terms of efficacy, the Good Lives Model is a relatively newer model and does not boast a significant amount of empirical support; however, Haaven and Coleman (2000) utilized this model in their work with developmentally delayed sexual offenders. In an effort to assist these offenders in constructing a personal identity, the authors worked out the development of two constructs—the "new me" and the "old me." The old me defines the person who committed the sexual offense and lived by the values, beliefs, and goals that generated the offending behavior (i.e., risk factors). The new me defines a person with a different set of goals that lead to a good life with objectives that are met in socially acceptable and personally fulfilling ways.

In our clinic, the Good Lives Model was applied to a weekly sexual offender therapy group of 10 sexual offenders with a wide range of offenses. Six of the offenders had multiple offenses. The Good Lives Model was applied by educating the offenders in regard to the nine human goods. Subsequently, each human good was the focus of discussion for three-week blocks. The homework, discussion, and introspection exercises revolved around applying the nine human goods to six basic questions:

1. In what way did my past approach to this human good contribute or not contribute to my sexual offense?

2. How does this human good apply to my life today?

3. How would I like this human good to be present in my life?

4. What internal or personal strengths do I possess that are going to help me attain my goal?

5. What external opportunities (social supports or resources) do I have access to that will help me attain my goal?

6. What are my biggest obstacles in attaining my goals?

The group responded favorably throughout. In fact, the group as a whole expressed gratitude for the model and its application. The greatest obstacle for the facilitators was redirecting participants to attend to their positive attributes because members tended to spend inordinate amounts of time on their deficits and obstacles. While processing this particular phenomenon, most of the group members expressed anxiety and fear of failing. One member said that setting positive goals "puts a lot of pressure on me to succeed. It's a tall order. I don't know if I know how to [succeed]." This member's comments were revealing. If we, as change agents, do not empower offenders to set and meet life goals, they will likely fail, or simply remain the same. In addition, our observation was that the resistance that many had previously exhibited toward the program (out of the frame) shifted to an intrapsychic resistance (in the frame) that prompted significant discussions (and revelations) in the group regarding shame, self-esteem, trust, and intimacy. It was also evident that the offenders' abilities to communicate with and utilize the facilitators greatly increased. Although anecdotal, we find this example hopeful in addressing specific risk factors, reducing resistance, and promoting optimism regarding longstanding offender change.

Engaging Resistance: An Exercise

Case Exercise

Part I: Andrew is a 35-year-old Caucasian male with a history of raping a 15-year-old disabled female. In addition, Andrew has a long history of reported but unadjudicated criminal conduct. He was referred to the sexual offender treatment program after serving an 8-year sentence for the rape. His participation in the program has been held up because his attorney continues to protest his parole requirement of participating in treatment. He attended his first session at the clinic dressed in a three-piece suit. He started by boasting to offenders in the waiting room that his family was extremely wealthy and never hesitated to get the best lawyers for him. "They won't keep me in this program long."

Once in the interview room, he was superficially pleasant and engaging. He initiated a conversation about the location of the clinic, which he feels is "in too unappealing of a neighborhood to force people to come into." As the session continued, Andrew apparently cooperated by answering basic questions and providing relevant personal information until he was asked to discuss his offense. "I am not going to talk about that. I didn't do it, so I have nothing to say." After several minutes of impasse, the therapist stated that if Andrew was going to be accepted into the program, he would need to talk about his offense. Andrew responded by stating, "I am here because my parole agent told me that I had to come here for this session, and after that, if you tell me that I don't have to come anymore, I won't have to come. So when are you going to tell me that I don't have to come?"

After being informed that there was no specific end time for the program (that it depended on his progress), Andrew became irate. He immediately sank into his chair and broke eye contact. He refused to talk unless a specific question was asked. Even then, several prompts were required to obtain adequate detail.

During the next couple of sessions, his eye contact remained poor. When he did make eye contact, he pursed his lips, shook his head, rolled his eyes, and sighed. On a couple of occasions, he stared intently at the change agent in a threatening manner. Throughout the sessions he made various comments such as: (sarcastically) "How are *you* going to help *me*?" and "I am not going to let you play head games with me for your own enjoyment." At the end of the third session, he became very angry and retracted his signed release. He declared that the change agent was not to talk to his parole officer. He left the room, slamming the door.

He called back within 30 minutes of leaving the session, apologized, and seemingly took responsibility for his misbehavior and requested another chance. He concluded by saying, "That little bitch is making this stuff up. She did everyone in the neighborhood, and she wants to get me into trouble."

Despite his apparent concession, Andrew showed up late to the next session and refused to talk. He sat silently staring out of the window. During the following three sessions, Andrew vacillated between relative compliance and resistance. For two sessions he focused on his fears of people finding out about his past and the difficulty of getting a job. In the next session, he was argumentative and condescending. He expressed that there was no way that he was going to get anything out of therapy because "you are just not as smart as I am. You haven't had the life that I have." He also stated that it was just impossible for him to open up to other people. Besides, he said that discussing his case would only lead to trouble. "I don't trust people working for the criminal justice system. You guys all talk. I signed the papers; I know. You talk to my parole agent. She's both a woman and a parole agent. I don't trust parole agents or women."

He concluded, "This just isn't going to work. Besides, I heard that if I win an appeal of my case, I will not have to register as a sexual offender. I'll put you and the rest of this mess behind me. Until then, I'm just going to play the game."

- Identify the motivations for Andrew's resistance.
- Identify resistance that is within the frame.
- Identify resistance that is out of the frame.
- Which strategies would you use to engage Andrew's resistance?
- If you were the change agent, what, if any, types of counter-resistance would you be experiencing?

Part II: Two years have passed since Andrew entered treatment. He has formed a working alliance with his therapist and identified personalized goals to work on. Specifically, Andrew made efforts to be less dependant upon his family. He maintained steady employment for 13 months and worked on developing empathy for others, learned that objectifying women has undermined his goal of establishing a relationship, and that many of his preconceptions about women were wrong.

Andrew also became a strong group member. He admitted his offense, as well as many previous allegations, and recently presented his offense chain to the group. He identified and articulated a number of cognitive distortions regarding his hostility toward women and his own sexual entitlement. He also admitted that he consistently maintained lies about his offense because "I thought I needed to 'deny to my death.'" He admitted that he struggles with feelings of entitlement, frustration, anger, resentment, and sporadic desires to use alcohol. He once stated that he hoped to stay in the program after he was released because the structure was helpful.

In a recent therapy session, Andrew expressed that he was developing feelings for a woman he met at work. They have only had lunch together with other coworkers, but he wants to ask her out for a private lunch. As he explored this situation he became angry and irate. "Who am I kidding? You would never encourage me to talk to a woman. You are probably right. I mean, once I tell her about my past, that will be it. She'll have nothing to do with me. Even if I tell her and she's willing to try it—I mean try it really slow—my probation officer will just come in and fuck it up."

During the following two sessions, Andrew began to question his participation in the program. "I can't believe that I am talking about this. I raped a girl over 10 years ago. I feel awful about it. I went to prison. I came here and did good work. When am I done? Isn't it possible that I'm done? Isn't it possible that at this point all I am doing is limiting myself from developing a normal life?"

He concluded by stating, "Look, I am off parole in 6 months. I think we should wrap it up early."

- Identify the motivations for Andrew's resistance.

- Identify resistance that is within the frame.

- Identify resistance that is out of the frame.

- Which strategies would you use to engage Andrew's resistance?

- If you were the change agent, what, if any, types of counter-resistance would you be experiencing?

Chapter Seven

A sage is skilled at helping people without excluding anyone.
—Lao Tzu

Partnerships for Change

On a daily basis, sexual offender change agents face numerous challenges from offenders they assist and from the "systems of change" they work within. These "partnerships for change" exist on many levels, and at times require change agents to consider multiple intended and unintended consequences as they make decisions. Although learning techniques to engage resistance with sexual offenders is valuable and has been the focal point of our discussion over the past few chapters, without systemic structures to support these processes and training to teach change agents how to navigate these systems, our efforts with sexual offenders are likely to be significantly less effective.

To illustrate the web of interactions and decision making that exists on a typical day for a change agent supervising sexual offenders, consider the following list of entries that might be found within a parole agent's file on a particular client:

6:30 am... checked with client's halfway house staff to see if client had met curfew the previous night. Staff reported that client got home 20 minutes past his curfew... client reported to staff that he had gotten off work late.

8:15 am... Talked with client's employer... verified that client had been asked to stay late at work because of staff shortages. Client was informed that he needed to communicate more effectively in the future with halfway house staff, as well as check in with parole about any changes to his schedule.

10 am... Touched base with client's treatment provider about client's upcoming polygraph test. Discussed issues of most concern that client would be tested around – specifically, client's attendance at strip clubs and viewing of pornography.

2 pm... Returned phone call from Department of Children and Family Services regarding a supervised visit with client's 15-year-old son. Referred to forensic evaluator's report for recommendations regarding these visits. Forensic evaluator suggests that these visits should initially be supervised. Evaluator reports that client's risk to offend teenage boys is low... client has no history of child abuse or history of offenses against children... victims were adult females. Client's testing revealed no sexual interest or arousal to children.

3 pm... Returned call from client's attorney, who is attempting to get conditions of probation modified. Recommended a meeting with client and his attorney to discuss whether this would be in the best interest of the client. Set meeting date for next week.

Since most sexual offenders eventually spend the majority of their lives residing in the community, the interactions and decision making depicted above are typical. Yet, without a clear understanding of one another's roles and responsibilities, any one of these interactions between the parole agent and other involved party could become problematic and drain significant time and resources from the parole agent's day. Additionally, without these types of informed interactions, the offender and those involved in his life could be at increased risk. As offenders reintegrate into society and begin to live under a structure of increased community accountability, it is crucial that change agents work together to develop goals that will allow the offender the highest likelihood for success in the community, while at the same time maximize efforts to protect victims, their families, and others who may be at risk for future victimization.

Resistance and Working Together

As discussed throughout the book, engaging resistance is a systemic process. Whenever resistance remains unresolved between two or more parties involved in the management of sexual offenders, including with the offender himself, goals of increased community safety and effective offender re-entry are at risk. International, national, and state organizations, both independently and federally funded, have been created in part to help the multiple stake holders, and their respective change agents, develop and maintain these crucial systems. For a list of these national organizations please consult Table 7.1. For professionals working as change agents within the field of sexual violence, becoming aware of and involved in these important groups and those that exist within their own states or local areas is highly recommended.

Table 7.1

Organizations that promote and support collaborative sexual offender management practices

- Association for the Treatment of Sexual Abusers - www.atsa.com

- Center for Sex Offender Management - www.csom.org

- Safer Society Foundation - www.safersociety.org

- International Association for the Treatment of Sexual Offenders - www.iatso.org

- American Probation and Parole Association - www.appa-net.org

- Bureau of Justice Assistance - www.ojp.usdoj.gov/BJA

- National Sexual Violence Resource Center - www.nsvrc.org

- Stop It Now! - www.stopitnow.org

Some state organizations, such as The California Coalition on Sexual Offending (CCOSO), have specific mission statements that address management principles that can help guide change agents and communities as they develop guidelines for community sentencing. CCOSO's vision includes the following statement: "...CCOSO and its chapters strengthen local and statewide agencies and professionals to enhance community safety." Their mission goes on to list the following specific goals:

- Increase awareness by educating and training the community and professional organizations whose purpose is to manage and treat sexual offenders.

- Provide and promote a network of professionals in the field of sexual offending.

- Provide feedback and recommendations regarding legislation and public policy.

- Provide information regarding management and treatment of sexual offenders to all interested parties.

- Develop and promote standards of care and best practices related to sexual offending.

- Promote research in offender and victim treatment and community management practices.

- Inform and influence media presentations on issues of sexual abuse.

- Mentor and encourage potential professionals to enter the field.

Unfortunately, policy makers often fail to consider groups like ATSA, CSOM, and other networks of experts as they work to create and promote legislation that helps and protects involved parties within sexual violence cases. Some organizations are even attacked when they try to present rational arguments for or against certain types of sexual offender legislation, with opponents labeling these groups as advocates or "special interest groups" that protect the rights of offenders. And while it is partially true that these organizations do have the offender's well-being in mind as they promote their agenda, their aim isn't to do it at the expense of victim and community safety. Professionals within these organizations should be commended, as they often work tirelessly to educate policy makers, judges, and other stake holders involved in sexual offender management. However, limited funding (most coming from membership dues and annual conference fees) limits the amount of impact any one group can make.

Within the United States, models have emerged over the past 10 years that help to promote the development and expansion of sexual offender management teams. Some states, with the help of the CSOM (and other funding sources), have received federal funds and specialized training through The Comprehensive Approaches to Sex Offender Management (CASOM) Discretionary Grant Program, a program under the United States Department of Justice's Office for Justice Programs. CSOM's explicit goal is to provide "funding to help jurisdictions effectively manage sexual offenders in the community by implementing new or enhancing existing programs. Programs need to increase public safety and reduce victimization." For more information about these funding opportunities, go to http://www.ojp.usdoj.gov/BJA/grant/casom.html.

Enhancing Collaboration

There are some inherently good reasons to collaborate. By definition collaboration involves information sharing, a willingness to allow others to influence our opinions, the right to be heard and respected, and the sharing of limited resources (space, money, etc.). The goal of collaboration is simple: to help one another meet goals that without the support and help of other parties would be more difficult to achieve. Implied in this definition is that the goals of collaborating parties are not of the competing nature, and that common goals are possible and desirable for all parties.

A **collaborative relationship** is a mutually beneficial and well-defined relationship entered into by two or more organizations to achieve common goals. The relationship includes a commitment to the following steps:

· A definition of mutual relationship and goals;

· A jointly developed structure and shared responsibility;

· Mutual authority and accountability for success; and

· A sharing of resources and rewards.

Exercise

Take a moment to consider the professionals with whom you work in treating sexual offenders:

- Does your relationship feel like a mutual one?

- Does the collaborative relationship have mutually developed goals?

- Does it feel like you have a shared authority with the other stakeholders, or does it feel like one dominates?

- How are goal successes and failures that take place with the clients shared?

- Which resources do you share well? Are there resource issues that cause conflict?

For a variety of unfortunate reasons, some potential collaborators, such as victim advocates, and the victim advocacy community in general, have not been as involved in sexual offender management efforts as have professionals from criminal justice and sexual offender specific treatment agencies. While a few advocates may ignore or frown upon management efforts that address sexual offender behavior, in the authors' experiences the victim advocacy community has rarely been invited into the conversation. When systems are, or become, unilateral with how they view their responsibilities, the unintended consequences are misunderstandings between stakeholders. However, in reality, supervision, treatment, and victim advocates can benefit from effective collaboration because their joint efforts facilitate the possibilities for safer, better informed communities and citizens; victims who have a voice in the sexual offender management process; and more successful offender reintegration into the community.

On a local level, collaboration can also assist stakeholders in achieving their own goals. For example, many victim advocate agencies would put "end sexual violence" at the top of their goal list. Without having an active voice in the discussion on the management of known sexual offenders, victim advocate perspectives could run the risk of being marginalized. Advocates can oftentimes present another angle to the discussion that an offender treatment provider could never offer. Likewise, offender treatment providers, who should have a good grasp of the research on risk prediction, can offer suggestions to victim advocates and treatment providers that may actually lead to increased safety measures.

For example, consider the case of 45-year-old male who raped a 24-year-old woman 10 years ago and recently was released from prison after a 7-year sentence. The offender in this case has one child, a 13-year-old boy. During the assessment phase of treatment, it is discovered that the offender also had sexual interest in teenage boys and had been masturbating to fantasies about boys while he was incarcerated. The boy in this case, an indirect victim of his father's sexual offense, really missed his father and asked the victim advocate to allow him to spend time alone with his father on weekends. While in some circumstances this request might be reasonable (i.e., for a rapist with no child victims or deviant interest in children), limited information sharing in this situation could produce a very high-risk situation.

In systems where collaboration is not valued, vulnerable parties' safety can be compromised, even though both stakeholders may believe they are doing everything necessary to protect potential victims. Questions arise from both victim advocate and offender treatment communities about why collaborative efforts are even necessary. In some jurisdictions, stereotyping (i.e., all sexual offenders are pedophiles and very dangerous) has increased tension between these two groups of professionals. Over the years, however, the question seems to be changing from "Why should we collaborate?" to "How do we collaborate with limited resources, time, specialized staff, and public pressure to protect our interests?" Some would argue that the various parties invested in the management of sexual offenders speak different languages and the problem is that no one has taken time to come up with clear translation.

Collaboration benefits all involved because the "job specialization (of each party) ...minimizes containment gaps that can be actively sought out by perpetrators for the sake of avoiding accountability measures... (while) cross training allows team members to appreciate and understand the functions of other team members." (CSOM, 2000). According to both CSOM and ATSA (2001), there are many benefits to collaborating when dealing with sexual offender community release:

> "Collaboration takes the form of intra-agency, interagency, and interdisciplinary teams made up of professionals who specialize in sexual offender cases. Teamwork tends to overcome the fragmentation that is often generated by the multi-disciplinary, layered nature of the criminal justice system. As teamwork improves, offender management gaps begin to disappear" (CSOM).

Further, "effective partnerships mean that the community can exercise early interventions in the offender's deviant lifestyle when the behaviors are not yet criminal in nature" (ATSA).

Broadening the scope of collaboration in sexual offender management cases requires a willingness of existing team members to reach out to those groups that can sometimes be challenging to engage. As was discussed in chapter 5, bringing together legal counsel from the prosecution, defense, and law enforcement personnel opens the discussion even further and promotes investment into the process for groups who have significant influence into the implementation of effective treatment and supervision practices. For example, if defense attorneys can understand how treatment and specialized conditions might benefit their client, reduce his risk, and help him through parole, they might be more likely to support mandated treatment.

Though the actual members of a successful sexual offender management teams may differ by jurisdiction, supervision officials (probation or parole) typically take the lead in these groups. They usually minimally consist of a specially trained supervising officer, treatment provider, and polygraph examiner. Other relevant individuals who may be included in the team are victim therapists, child welfare workers, family therapists, physicians, specialized law enforcement officers, and other individuals with involvement in the case at hand (i.e., landlords, defense and prosecuting attorneys, job supervisors, family and friends, courts and judges, and schools [ATSA, 2001]). Each jurisdiction should take an inventory of the different parties involved in the management of sexual offenders within their communities and find ways to include all parties in sexual offender management discussions.

Which Processes Increase Resistance Between Change Agents?

Agency and change agent resistance to collaboration may stem from numerous sources. For instance, many current mainstream management approaches offer little room for discussion about collaboration. For example, some agencies have concerns about protecting their funding and maintaining their community reputations, while individual professionals in an agency may feel collaboration could increase their workload. Some supervision and treatment professionals may lack accurate information and training on victim issues and victim advocacy, which leads to questions like, "Why do I need to collaborate with them?"

At the same time, some potentially valuable collaborators may just lack accurate information. For example, victim advocates may not be provided with research-based information and training on sexual offending behavior, adjudication, recidivism, and how local offenders are managed. D'Amora and Burns-Smith (1999) found that many agencies are reticent to collaborate because they fear new information or they fear secondary trauma among their agency's members. Unfortunately, few have explored the benefits of involving victim advocates in supervision or treatment efforts. This lack of victim advocate perspective may bring about feelings of cynicism regarding the efficacy of community management and a preference for incarceration. Advocates who do collaborate may risk peer disapproval or even hostility because they are viewed as offender sympathetic. These professionals may only be willing to address the issues within policy discussions rather than in day-to-day management protocols. Various supervision and treatment staff may find working with victims and their advocates uncomfortable because they hold misperceptions about both parties. That is, treatment staff may feel dealing with victims will make their work too victim-centered and hamper their ability to effectively treat offenders.

Several processes can lead to greater resistance among sexual offender management team members. Three of these processes will be discussed below and should be quite recognizable to readers.

1. **Fear of Strangers** occurs when there is an expressed reluctance to share information with those you aren't familiar with. This is a societal value that has intended and unintended consequences when taken to extremes. Parents teach their children this concept from the time they are old enough to comprehend the subject matter. Most helping professionals would agree that a certain amount of distrust about strangers is reasonable and expected. To inherently trust people with whom you have limited experience could lead to uncomfortable, and in some cases, unsafe situations. In the context of work settings, we are all somewhat leery of new people who enter our vocational environments. Discussions around the water cooler about what the new person is like are common and almost expected. Change agents are no different.

Change agents working with sexual offenders are often asked to share detailed information with other team members that may go against traditional patterns of interaction within their respective fields. Treatment providers are asked to offer feedback to probation officers on a regular basis and allow probation officers to weigh in on risk management decisions. Many traditional treatment providers hold strong to the value of client confidentiality that was drilled into their heads during graduate school and reinforced in most therapeutic environments. Many public defenders have the perspective that they have to protect their client's legal rights, regardless of the issue of community safety. Supervision agents may believe that they know best how to use information they discover in the field, and that asking for information from treatment providers may only contaminate their decision-making process.

Moreover, because of regular turnover that exists many times in treatment settings and probation departments, change agents are constantly asked to develop relationships with new team members. Problematic relationships with previous change agents often haunt new relationships and prevent trust from being easily established.

2. Another barrier to collaborative efforts could be best described as **Stockpiling**. This occurs when people resist sharing knowledge because they view information as a limited and valuable resource that, when shared, diminishes the amount of power they have in the relationship.

Treatment providers engaging in stockpiling behavior might be unwilling to train probation officers in the area of risk prediction. Despite how ludicrous it might seem, they might view their ability of risk prediction as "too scientific or clinical" for the probation officer to understand. Supervision agents who are unwilling to allow other types of change agents to go on ride-alongs or sit in on supervision discussions with the offender are another example of stockpiling behavior.

Information stockpiling exists for other reasons as well. Limited funding for projects leads some change agents to have concerns about their job security. They also worry that if they share information it could lead to more work and responsibility.

A significant downside to stockpiling behavior is that it leads to combative relationships among team members. Additionally, when information is locked away it fails to grow and improve. Change agents must remember that the knowledge of the group is always greater than the knowledge of any one person. Stockpiling discourages furthering group knowledge.

3. The final barrier to effective collaboration is called the "**Not Invented Here**" (Katz & Allen, 1982) barrier. This barrier becomes apparent whenever change agents avoid considering previously performed research or knowledge that was not originally developed within their group or institution. Though challenges do exist to fully keep up with the ever-growing body of research within the sexual offender management field, not attempting to seek and utilize accurate information could qualify as unethical. It would be similar to surgeons using an outdated surgical technique they invented, despite years of evidence that safer, less invasive techniques will produce better results.

Within teams of change agents, this barrier can prove quite problematic. For example, if an agency providing sexual offender treatment for decades had never updated their risk assessment protocols, they might still be using their own clinical opinion to report risk levels back to the court. An ever-growing body of research suggests that much more accurate methods of doing risk assessment are available—like actuarial and empirically derived, structured risk assessment tools. If that particular agency provides a gross underestimate of risk for a particular offender, which then influences a judge and supervision agent to have less restrictive conditions for that particular offender, potential victims could be at greater risk.

Signs that you might be working with change agents putting up this barrier include those who

- Are unwilling to stay current on developments in the field.

- Are not involved in state or national organizations known to disseminate updated information.

- Read research and claim, "That would never work here... the research isn't accurate."

- Are very private about their risk assessment and treatment strategies. For example, treatment providers should be quite willing to share treatment plans and the type of work their clients are completing in treatment.

Since all collaborative systems are imperfect and are constantly in flux, it is likely that every system experiences some version of these barriers from time to time. We believe there is value in naming the processes and discussing them with other team members. The information generated from these discussions can sometimes improve collaboration significantly and lead to more cohesive professional relationships.

Exercise

- Can you identify places within your work where "fear of strangers" is at play? What does your system do to welcome and integrate new members?

- Are there places within your collaborative network where "stockpiling" of information is occurring? What information do you possess that might be beneficial to other team members?

- Is your system resistant to information that was "not invented here"? Who is responsible within your system for keeping abreast of changes in the research and implementing changes based on new information?

Overcoming Collaboration Resistance

D'Amora and Burns-Smith (1999) suggest six factors required to produce a successful collaboration. They include a shared mission, a firm commitment from all members, trust (and mechanisms to build trust between collaborators), an appreciation for the different work styles and strategies of diverse disciplines, an openness and willingness to integrate new knowledge about sexual offenders into everyday practice, and most importantly, open and respectful communication.

Engaging resistance among system players must be a priority of any change agent working with sexual offenders. So how can this occur? CSOM (2000) provides the following recommendations on how to help this process along:

- Stress community management as vital to both victim and public safety, as all offenders eventually return to the community.

- Involve victim advocates in establishing community programs to potentially improve the quality of services to victims as well as offenders.

- Identify common interests, frustration, and goals among groups.

- Clarify the roles of each group and how they uniquely contribute to the prevention of future victimization.

- Share concerns and address misconceptions or unrealistic expectations.

- Ensure all groups are provided with up-to-date research findings regarding sexual offender management and victim assistance.

The need for coordinated efforts to manage the growing number of sexual offenders in the community has increased significantly over time. This chapter will review a few of the more comprehensive and widely accepted models of sexual offender management and overall theories of change that show promise with increasing collaboration among professionals and with sexual offenders.

The Containment Approach

Within several areas of the United States, the containment approach is the model of choice for managing sexual offenders in the community. In this model, agencies partner together so that case evaluation and risk assessment, sexual offender treatment, and intense community supervision take place in a coordinated fashion (English, 1998).

> "The Containment Approach is a particular method of individual case processing and case management of sex offenders in the criminal justice system. It rests upon the dual premise that sexual offenders are 100% responsible for the damage they inflict on others and that they must constantly and consistently be held accountable for their inappropriate thoughts and feelings as well as for their illegal behaviors." (English, Jones, Krauth, & Pullen, 1996)

The containment model is a case management strategy that aims to eliminate sexual reoffenses of known sexual offenders residing within communities. Using a case-by-case management strategy aimed at reducing specific opportunities for reoffense, the model holds sexual offenders continuously accountable for the damage caused by their sexually assaultive behavior.

The model initially used three mutually enhancing activities as its basis: criminal justice supervision, sexual offender specific treatment, and polygraph examinations. Over time, the model has been adapted to add additional components (victim advocates), which will be discussed later in this chapter. Overall, as English (1998) reports, the containment approach contains five critical components.

1. A Consistent Multi-Agency Community and Victim Safety Philosophy

2. A Coordinated, Multidisciplinary Action Strategy

3. Individualized Offender Case Management and Treatment

4. Consistent Public and Agency Policies

5. Quality-Control Procedures

Within each of these components, collaboration and conflict can occur in multiple places. Additionally, change agents have opportunities within each of these tenets to either engage or increase resistance with clients, other change agents, and the communities where they live and work. Readers are encouraged to examine more detailed descriptions of the containment model principles, which can be found in English's (1998) work. Each component will be discussed below, with particular attention paid to examples of where collaborations between and among change agents, offenders, and the community can and should occur within the tenet.

1. A Consistent Multi-Agency Community and Victim Safety Philosophy

Put simply, decisions about an offender's placement and activities within the community are made with the victim(s) or potential victim's safety in mind. To ensure that this goal is met, some teams begin any decision-making discussion by asking, "What's best for the victim?" This would include decisions made about community notification practices, which directly and indirectly impact the victims involved in a case. Without a change agent assigned to the task of understanding how these decisions will impact victims differently, additional harm could result. For example, when a sexual offender is released back into the community without the victim's being notified and given access to support services, this process could be devastating for him or her.

This tenet also implies that change agents across agencies must have a similar understanding of victim-related issues. Reactions to overwhelming psychological stressors such as sexual abuse are extremely complex and require unique responses in order to help victims with their recovery process. Briere and Spinazzola (2005) suggest that a one-size-fits-all approach to understanding victims is faulty. For example, an adult who grew up having a relatively healthy and normal childhood and not having any other type of ongoing psychological disorders will likely not have a severe traumatic reaction to certain events, such as having her purse stolen in a crowd of people. On the other hand, those individuals who have a history of traumatic experiences (early life trauma, enduring trauma, or frequent interpersonal trauma) may be more vulnerable to stress effects (Briere & Spinazzola).

Decisions about "what's best" for the victim need to be made with accurate information about the victim's current level of functioning and from multiple professional perspectives. Myths about victims must be dispelled with accurate information and within forums to process this new data. Change agents with expert knowledge in victim issues should find helpful ways to share this information with other less-informed change agents. One recommendation is to have containment team members take part in a brainstorming session about what common things they've heard other people say about rape victims, for example, and then use this information to dispel common myths.

Similarly, this issue also relates to how change agents communicate information and misinformation about sexual offending to the media. Change agents who make inaccurate statements about sexual offenders such as, "All these guys are really dangerous and we need to do everything possible to watch every move they make," may in some cases create unnecessary hysteria within communities and lead politicians to suggest legislation (i.e., some notification practices) that could actually endanger victims. For example, if notification practices make widely known the release from prison of a sexual offender whose victims are his children, ages 10 and 12, the consequences for those children could be far-reaching, and yet the increase in community safety could be negligible. In summary, change agents must be thoughtful in developing coordinated responses to the communities they serve, and to the past and potential victims they hope to protect.

2. A Coordinated, Multi-Disciplinary Action Stategy

This tenet requires that change agents understand their roles and how these roles intersect with other agencies. Furthermore, an effectively coordinated, multidisciplinary action plan defines the leadership model of the team and how decisions will be made. Some states have created specialized sexual offender management boards or teams that include appointed professionals from multiple disciplines. Before an offender can be released in these states, the case is reviewed by change agents representing the various disciplines who will be interacting with the offender once he reaches the community. The goal, of course, is for decisions about offenders to become more consistent and shared among the multiple stakeholders.

With more centralized decision making, offenders may have fewer places to manipulate the system. In order to be effective, however, action plans cannot only contain restrictive measures, but must also contain solutions to common barriers faced by offenders. Some re-entry challenges can quickly trigger offenders into maladaptive behaviors, which may lead to increased risk levels.

Coordinated action plans may actually reduce resistance when they intentionally provide direction, support, and structure to offenders' lives. The delivery of this direction, support, and structure by change agents can either work to engage or disengage clients in the change process. A change agent who doesn't help an offender learn skills to obtain employment, but rather just keeps telling the offender to "get a job," might be creating more harm than good. The best coordinated plans must provide measures that ensure community safety, while also imparting direction and support that gives the offender an opportunity to live productively within society.

3. Individualized Offender Case Management and Treatment

Within the containment model, this tenet relates to the triangle approach to effective community supervision. Each corner of the triangle represents a different change agent—supervision official, sexual-offender-trained polygraph examiner, and sexual offender treatment provider (English, 1998). Contained within the triangle is the sexual offender. Successful "triangles" work to create a high level of accountability for the offender. Frequent communication between these change agents should ideally result in a more contained offender. While community safety is the primary goal, a secondary goal is that the offender receives consistent messages and isn't left with any questions about the expectations from the containment team. Confusion and lack of information lead to unpredictable behavior in non-offending populations, and maybe even more so with offenders who sometimes lack structure and goals in their lives.

How a containment team handles disclosures, often of very personal and critical information, made by offenders during treatment, on polygraph exams, and in conversations with supervision should be viewed as one of the most crucial places in our interactions with offenders where change agents can influence resistance, for better or worse. For example, if an offender discloses another victim during his pre-polygraph interview, and is then heavily confronted by his therapist for "lying all this time," it will likely create more resistance and confusion in the offender. The change agent could use this as a learning opportunity to help the offender better understand why disclosure was so challenging, the characteristics of that particular offense behavior, etc. Additionally, sexual offender therapists aren't always aware of how the polygraph examiners that they send offenders to see actually practice. While most adhere to strict ethical standards and respect clients, some have been known to resort to unethical questioning practices that produce false positive results. After some unfortunate experiences with one polygraph examiner, a treatment provider discovered that the polygraph examiner tested one offender for over 3 hours because he "knew the guy was lying to me."

Within effective containment approaches, disclosures are viewed as opportunities to understand more about the offender's world and the limits and resources they need to effectively live in society. For example, once change agents become aware that a known rapist has child victims, in addition to adult victims, numerous efforts might be put into place that would reduce the client's access to children and interaction with potential fantasy material, while increasing treatment interventions addressing sexual interest in children. The offender may not always agree with the decisions made by the containment team. However, our experience is that when decisions are explained with a supportive, rational approach, rather than in a punitive, emotional manner, the offender is more likely to accept the plan and become willing to eventually work with, rather than against, the change agents.

Ethically, systems of change must also make very clear to an offender what disclosing certain types of information will mean. For example, if an offender makes a disclosure and then receives a response inconsistent with what he has been told previously, an increase in resistance will likely occur. Additionally, because this information will most likely leak back to the other offenders within his treatment group, one poor decision may increase the resistance of several offenders. For example, one offender was not told by his treatment provider that he could be prosecuted for disclosing specific information on his polygraph exam. When the specific information regarding an offense he committed over 20 years ago was disclosed to authorities by the polygraph examiner, the offender felt betrayed, which led to increased resistance with this particular offender and the rest of his group.

4. Consistent Public and Agency Policies

These agency and public policies set the guidelines for how systems will respond to some extremely complicated scenarios. For example, change agent teams should be able to answer the following questions:

- How will we make decisions about family reunification procedures? What needs to happen for this to be considered?

- Do we come down harder on offenders who are angrier and in more denial, or do we see that as part of the change process?

- Whom do we disclose the polygraph information to and what disclosures, if any, are reportable?

- What will we tell potential employers of the offender about his offense history?

- In what cases will we enact specialized supervision conditions? What measures will we use to make this decision?

- How will we address issues of secondary trauma and burn-out on our team? Will our agency help pay for therapy to help professionals who are suffering with this condition as a result of the work?

This list highlights many of the complex decisions that should be put into policy by agencies employing change agents who work with sexual offenders. Clear policies help offenders and change agents know the rules of interaction. When decisions about issues like family reunification become arbitrary, subjective decisions of one change agent in the offender's life, it can often set up an un-necessary conflictual interaction that increases resistance.

Change agents should be regularly informed about potential changes in legislation about sexual offenders and how this will impact their clients. Demonstrating a willingness to discuss these changes with offenders is critical. Some change agents make the mistake of embracing the attitude of, "Well, you did the crime, so don't complain about dealing with the consequences" or "You're just lucky to be out on the street." By utilizing motivational inter-viewing techniques, change agents can empathize with the impact policy changes have on an offender's life, while moving the offend-er toward solutions to the problem.

Concerns about family reunification are often a sticking point with some offenders. Instead of offering a "let's wait and see approach," containment teams should construct policies that guide their deci-sion-making process and are apparent to the offenders. Rather than stringing along an exclusive pedophile—with multiple child victims, on lifetime probation—about whether he will be allowed to return home to live with his children, ages 7 and 9, change agents should address the concern early in treatment and help the offender work through the reality that most exclusive pedophiles aren't placed in residences with children. Helping offenders sort out the reality of their lives as a registered sexual offender is a change agent's responsibility. While this reality may not always fit with the initial wants and needs of the offenders, it may help them begin to construct a picture of the options they do have in their lives.

Finally, agencies of change need consistent policies about how they will take care of each other when the work becomes overwhelming. The question, listed above, about secondary trauma experienced by change agents is meant to suggest that containment teams are strongly encouraged to address the reality and likelihood of this outcome for some change agents. Agencies of change should discuss this issue in new staff orientation and provide resources for all staff members. Supervisors should talk about the issue with staff from a perspective of "when this happens" instead of "if this happens." Appropriate debriefing measures should be employed when traumatic events occur, like client reoffenses or suicides. While more discussion about the topic of staff training is contained in chapter eight, we believe that discussing these issues within collaborative teams also helps to build cohesiveness among containment team members. For example, resources could be shared among containment team members to hire experts on trauma debriefing when necessary.

5. Quality-Control Procedures

These procedures range from ongoing case review sessions of current clients to post-mortem evaluations of cases that resulted in violations of supervision conditions, or in worst cases, a new sexual offense. Quality control also requires involving information technology professionals, within agencies, to develop databases where important data can be retrieved to help guide decision-making efforts. For example, if a containment team realizes that offenders who reside in the southwest portion of a particular town have failed drug tests at disproportionate levels to offenders who live in other areas of that town, then change agents might want to take that into consideration when placing a soon-to-be released offender with a known drug history in the community.

Creating quality-control measures also allows change agents to see what they are doing well! When working with a population that is much more recognized for negative reasons than positive ones, asking and answering questions that support the good work most change agents do on a regular basis is critical to professional well-being. An illustration of this point is to consider the known sexual recidivism rate of a caseload of sexual offenders on probation. We are likely to find that this number, in most cases, is quite low. Increases in this critical number should lead us to question what changes are taking place in our practices and/or among our offenders. Regardless, the data then allows change agents to evaluate their practices in a more informed manner. Additionally, data collection helps change agents develop measures of assessment that are more objective. While change agents should always pay attention to their emotional reactions as they work, making decisions based on these reactions is not always advisable or best for the offender and community. Objective data collection keeps change agents honest and allows them to step back from the difficult nature of the work.

> "Containment professionals can burn out, get soft, miss red flags, or become cynical and otherwise ineffective. Working together as a team is the first line of defense against these common phenomena." (English, 1998)

Quality-control measures can help to reduce resistance among containment team members over time because as data starts to drive practice more than personal opinions, personal biases reduce and professionalism increases. For example, while some disagreement remains over how much sexual offender treatment professionals should rely on empirically guided and actuarial risk assessment tools, hardly anyone asserts that we shouldn't use them at all. Some differences of opinion about measuring certain sexual offenders' risk (i.e., Internet offenders) remains; however, the increase in consistent data regarding child molesters' and rapists' risk potential has reduced some tension among change agents.

We also support the practice of showing offenders, themselves, some of the data from the sexual offender literature. In recent years, some sexual offender treatment programs have made it a regular practice to discuss dynamic risk factors with offenders. Additionally, other programs discuss the recidivism rates for men in the program and common factors among this group. One sexual offender group utilizes solution-focused group discussions as a way to provide valuable information for change agents to use as they reassess containment strategies. For example, an offender group told two change agents that the reason he believed certain clients were failing in treatment was related to the supervision in a group home. Upon further investigation, it was discovered that several staff members in this home were selling drugs to the offenders.

Success of the Containment Model

English (1998) reports that collaborations using the containment approach have produced several positive results. Parole and probation officers feel confident that the model has improved the likelihood that offenders, still active in their offense behavior patterns, will be detected committing maintenance behaviors, rather than offense behaviors. An improved understanding of their responsibilities and those of other containment team members has been reported by change agents working within this sexual offender management framework. In many ways this has led change agents from multiple disciplines to believe that they can provide and receive better information. Some teams have reported fewer conflicts because they are all working toward shared, explicit goals.

The Colorado Sex Offender Treatment Board, the first formal containment model in the United States, has been especially successful in creating multi-agency collaborations. The Colorado board issues specific guidelines for the evaluation, treatment, and monitoring of all released sexual offenders. Additionally, specialized law enforcement personnel, treatment providers from prisons, victim therapists, and others with primary involvement are welcomed into these discussions. These "strategies operate in circumstances of multi-agency collaboration, (with) explicit policies and consistent practices that combine case evaluation and risk assessment, sexual offender treatment, and intense community surveillance designed specifically to restrict offender's privacy and access to victims" (English, 1998, p. 219).

Case Example

Jim, a 35-year-old sexual offender, was released from prison about 2 years ago. His known offense history included sexually molesting his 14-year-old niece over the course a year. Upon his initial release, Jim was placed in individual therapy once a week, and onto the case load of a good probation officer. However, this officer had very little training on how to work with sexual offenders. Jim began a relationship with an age-appropriate woman who had children between the ages of 3 and 5. The probation officer allowed Jim to live with this woman because the children were much younger than his previous victim, and because Jim reported that his offense, while wrong, "was against a well-developed teenage girl, not a young child."

Two years into his probationary period, the probation department supervising Jim's case began using a containment approach. Jim's new probation officer was well-versed in sexual offender management strategies and recognized that Jim needed more specialized sexual offender treatment. Additionally, Jim was required to have a sexual history polygraph and then regular maintenance polygraphs every 6 months. The results of Jim's sexual history polygraph revealed that Jim had sexually molested several other children ranging in age from 5 to 15. It also revealed that Jim had started to engage in some grooming behaviors with one of the female children in the home where he currently resided.

Jim's treatment team immediately had Jim move out of the house and into a more structured halfway house environment where his daily behaviors could be more closely monitored. While no new charges were filed, Jim's probation conditions were tailored to meet his areas of risk. Additionally, Jim's treatment providers began to address his sexual deviance issues with children.

Jim was very angry with the team's decision and attempted to sabotage his own treatment and supervision. Jim also began the process of splitting, whereby he began telling his probation officers lies about what his treatment provider had said about the change in his probation conditions.

- How does your team handle changes of probation conditions with an offender? What steps do you use to reduce resistance when these additional conditions are added?

- How do you handle circumstances when offenders tell you information about another containment team member?

- What steps would you take, and who would you include in the process, of working through Jim's increasingly concerning behavior?

A Victim-Centered Approach to Sexual Offender Management

An outgrowth of the containment model, which has always recognized the victim perspective as case management plans are developed, victim-centered approaches of sexual offender management have even shifted the focus of change agents' collaborative efforts further toward recognizing the needs of the victim. Now, in addition to supervising offenders, systems are readily recognizing and addressing the needs of victims by including victim advocates on the collaborative teams. Connecticut was the first state to develop this type of collaborative triad existing among local probation departments, sexual offender treatment providers, and the victim advocacy community (D'Amora & Burns-Smith, 1999). Three jurisdictions within the state of Connecticut have utilized this model that places probation officers, victim advocates, and several experienced treatment providers in teams that meet on a regular basis. Team responsibilities include direct contact with the offender (such as treatment sessions, home visits, and treatment planning meetings) and families of the offender and victims, while also providing education to the community and others indirectly involved in the management of the sexual offender (i.e., halfway house staff). Probation officers and victim advocates participate in some treatment groups; however, the inclusion of probation officers in treatment groups has been reduced over time (D'Amora, May 26, personal communication). The decision to have non-treatment providers involved in actual therapy groups has not been without controversy. In fact, McGrath, Cumming, and Holt's (2002) national study of treatment providers found that while treatment providers find value in ongoing, in-depth dialogue with probation officers regarding shared clients, they also report a lack of consensus in practice and attitudes among treatment providers with regard to probation officers' facilitating, co-facilitating, and observing sexual offender treatment groups. This valuable study supports the need for more systemic research on how well our systems of change are actually working and how to improve areas where distrust or role confusion and disagreement may exist.

Within the more victim-inclusive model, an expectation similar to the containment model exists—that collaboration is essential and that no task is one person's responsibility. Tasks require an attitude of shared responsibility. For example, it is quite common in this model to have probation officers, therapists, and victim advocates involved in offender home and field visits. Hence, supervision is not just a probation officer's responsibility. Probation officers are often trained in risk assessment procedures and regularly weigh in on risk assessment evaluations, especially those assessments that monitor dynamic risk factors, where probation officers may have more detailed information to include in their assessment because of their contacts with offenders in the community. Victim advocates review offender files and may have contact with the victims to keep them updated on relevant issues. The system works with checks and balances—an effective system that requires monitoring from team members outside the system (i.e., a team member from another area in the state may come in and observe the process involved in their meetings), open communication, and a willingness to work through differences.

Victim-centered approaches are starting to take hold in other areas around the United States. These models, influenced heavily by the containment model, appear promising, yet require significant time and energy to keep the collaborative relationships effective. More research on the effectiveness of the more traditional containment model and the victim-centered containment model is greatly needed.

Collaborative Community Support Programs

Throughout much of our discussion in this chapter the focus has been on the collaborative relationships/partnerships among and between change agents and offenders. Another important group of partnerships, collaborations within the broader community (citizens, community organizations, churches, etc.), will be discussed in this section. Given the fact that sexual offenders will spend much more time in the presence of community members than with official change agents, it is critical that we discuss how we can utilize the resources community members can offer and direct their efforts in constructive ways.

Research suggests that most citizens support the notion that adult offenders should be provided with supervision and reintegration efforts (Sprott, 2003); however, "due to funding policies in many locales, support programs for ex-offenders (often innovative and grass roots) tend to disappear as quickly as they appear, sometimes leaving offenders disappointed and embittered" (Maruna, 2001). Sexual offender programs are in a unique position because many nonprofit agencies are "unable to risk the notoriety and possible liability associated with assisting high-risk and/or high-profile sexual offenders" released to the community (Cesaroni, 2001). Nevertheless, despite a lack of funding and the risks involved in supporting sexual offender treatment programs, two community-based, collaborative efforts between community members, agencies of change, and offenders continue today to enhance the more common systemic approaches to community release and supervision: Circles of Support and Accountability and chaperone programs.

Circles of Support and Accountability

In the early 1990's a project known as the Circles of Support and Accountability (or the Community Reintegration Project) was founded in Canada. Developed and implemented by the Mennonite community and other church organizations, the goal of this program was to promote community involvement in preventing further sexual offending behaviors among released sexual offenders. This model promotes the idea that communities must bear some responsibility for the reintegration of offenders back into communities. The project emphasizes the importance of offender re-entry back into the community and the need for rehabilitation. It acknowledges the humanity of both offenders and victims, and the value of helping offenders create a meaningful and accountable relationship with the communities in which they reside.

Rooted in restorative justice concepts, the Circles of Support and Accountability model aims to meet the needs of offenders, victims, and communities where offenders will reside. While the actual support circles are not designed as a replacement to traditional justice processes (therapy, supervision, victim advocacy), they should be considered as an alternative and complementary approach (Newell, 2005). Furthermore, they are not designed to resolve the past and/or mediate between actual victims and offenders. The support circles do, however, seek "to reconcile the offender with the wider community and often allows contact with community members who are survivors of sexual abuse" (Cesaroni, 2001).

A support circle begins when four to six community volunteers, frequently from local religious communities, agree to befriend a released sex offender. They provide advice and support, and agree to confront indicators of problematic behavior. While advanced education and expertise within the field of sexual offender management are not required, all volunteers are screened and trained extensively before joining a support circle. Certain communities in the U.K. and Canada identify offenders still in custody who have high levels of risk for sexual recidivism and high levels of need, but anticipated low levels of community support. These offenders are viewed as good candidates for a support circle and are matched with a circle upon release. Once matched, the offender and support circle members create a contract of commitment. The contract stresses the importance of openness and confidentiality. However, the offender recognizes that support circle members will remain in close contact with supervision and law enforcement personnel. Support circles meet on a regular basis, weekly in most cases, and less formal individual meetings between the sexual offender and circle members are frequent. The number of contacts may decrease over time, as the offender shows signs of positive adjustment within the community and risk for reoffense decreases (see www.ccjf.org/what/circles.html).

Support circles are appealing because many law enforcement and community supervision agencies are overwhelmed with their responsibility to manage high-risk offenders upon release. Change agents acknowledge that even with the best containment tactics in place (i.e., extensive parole conditions, registration, police monitoring, and unannounced social service contacts), socially isolated offenders, detached from and stigmatized by their community, can become lost and driven underground. British law enforcement officer Detective Chief Inspector Neale (2005) asserts that support circles can help supplement more traditional supervision and treatment networks, as they offer support and stability for a sexual offender, while at the same time demanding personal accountability. Since circle members maintain an open relationship with law enforcement personnel, precursory risk behaviors can be detected and responded to in a proactive manner, well before additional criminal behaviors are committed. This may lead to fewer revocations of community supervision and result in reduced prison costs, without sacrificing community safety (Neale, 2005).

"Many (offenders) lack social skills and must learn to initiate and sustain healthy and appropriate relationships" (Cesaroni, 2001, p. 89). The significant unmet social needs and serious loneliness that some sexual offenders experience upon their release from prison can interfere with an offender's reintegration process. One study of sexual offenders who participated in support circles found that volunteers helped them with both practical and emotional matters, and were crucial in teaching them to socialize more effectively (Cesaroni). Other factors that motivated offenders to participate in support circles included the desire to avoid police harassment or a media blitz and not having other social support. Volunteers from the same study reported that they felt the circles helped offenders become contributing members of the community. Volunteers participated in hopes that they could "break down fear and educate the community, ...as a form of reintegration or ...to free up police resources" (Cesaroni, p. 94).

Support circles offer an important bridge between the formal support and supervision of government agencies and the informal
support and chaperoning of friends and family members (as discussed in the next section on chaperones). Many released sexual
offenders are alienated from family and friends due to the nature
of their offense, the significant period of incarceration, or both, and
they return to communities that have little investment in them (Cesaroni, 2001). Since volunteers are not being paid to spend time
with offenders and because family pressures are not dictating or
informing the relationship, over time support circles may help to
provide offenders with a heightened sense of self-value. Offenders
may begin to believe that "they must see something good in me
for them to continue helping me."

The Circles of Support and Accountability model, however, has
some significant limitations. Realistically, implementing this
model on a large-scale basis would be very challenging. Finding
enough altruistic, responsible, and reliable circle members for the
thousands of sexual offenders released each year would be a large
undertaking. Most critical is the fact that not all sexual offenders
would desire the kind of active, intimate, frequent involvement that
support circles would provide and demand.

So what can change agents learn take from this model? While
implementing a support circle for each offender might not be possible, offenders do benefit from having additional support persons
in their lives. Change agents should not arbitrarily dismiss the support systems of offenders, even those that were in place prior to the
offender's arrest. Some initial skepticism of these support systems
is natural and maybe even healthy; however, change agents should
be open to the possibility that with appropriate education and
guidance these support systems could become valuable sources of
information and resources for additional community supervision.

While some change agents have had negative experiences with
faith communities, citing incidences of covering up pre-offense
and offense behaviors, some positive experiences also exist. For
example, a rapist who was involved in a support circle with several
elders in his church had his probation revoked when one of the

elders saw the offender entering a strip club and then immediately reported the violation to his probation officer. This support circle required significant time and resources from both the treatment provider and supervision officials; however, these efforts may have prevented another offense from occurring.

Chaperone Programs

Some systems responsible for managing sexual offenders in the community have come to appreciate the resources that can be gained when reaching out to the community at large, or the small community of a particular offender. Chaperone programs, sometimes known as Collateral Behavior Monitoring Programs, provide a structure to these efforts and have been employed in many jurisdictions that manage sexual offenders. For example, the county criminal justice system in Tarrant County, Texas (Phillips, 2003) operates a chaperone program as part of its approach to sexual offender management. This particular program is the result of collaboration between the Women's Center (a local victim's organization) and the sexual offender unit of the county's probation department.

Within most chaperone systems, the offender identifies a significant other whom he thinks would be appropriate to take on a chaperone role. Once identified and screened for appropriateness (if the person agrees to be a chaperone), candidates are trained to accompany and monitor their particular offender in some public places. Through multi-agency training, the chaperone is taught extensively about the dynamics of sexual offending behavior and specifically guided on how to recognize and respond to signs of relapse (CSOM, 2000).

One such program in Marion County, Oregon offers a 5-week training program designed for and presented to potential chaperones by a collaborative team of district attorneys, parole and probation officers, sexual offender treatment providers, victim advocates, and victim treatment providers. The potential chaperones are the friends, family, or employers of particular sexual offenders who are considered supportive of rehabilitation and community supervision efforts. This program also trains people about risk factors for sexual recidivism, stresses the value of specialized treatment and community supervision practices for sexual offenders, and demystifies the criminal justice system. Role-plays of common challenging situations help to prepare chaperones for everyday life situations they may encounter when in the community with the sexual offender.

Chaperone programs are not without their critics. Some supervision officials and treatment programs have eliminated these programs because of liability issues associated with "approving" a chaperone. These legitimate concerns are based on the assumption that a major lawsuit will ensue if an offender reoffends despite having an approved or certified chaperone. Critics cite instances of spouses covering up problematic behaviors because of mixed incentives. Turning in a spouse could lead to financial and additional legal problems, as well as potential investigations into their own lives. Additionally, there is controversy over who should pay for these programs. Some agencies require the offender to pay for these services, while others offer the service for free.

Despite these potential drawbacks, Selby (2002) advocates strongly for including chaperone programs in a comprehensive sexual offender treatment program, and believes that a change agent would be making a serious mistake if s/he didn't attempt to involve the offender's spouse. Since the majority of sexual offenses occur within the family or around those known to the offender, not including these members in the process could only reinforce the patterns that existed prior to and during the actual offense behavior. Additionally, by not involving spouses in the treatment process, we allow the offender the opportunity to shape the views that the non-offending spouse will hold about treatment and supervision practices. Selby goes on to state that by getting spouses involved in treatment, we are in a much better position "to confront offender deception in vivo and to educate and protect family members and friends from being manipulated."

Most proponents advocate a sensible, slow, intensive process that helps change agents develop a comprehensive understanding of the dynamics involved in the relationship between the offender and support person. Entrance into a chaperone program should not necessarily mean that the person will actually become an approved chaperone. Ideally, the actual chaperone contract is individualized for each support person and considers the strengths and limitations of the support person. For example, some chaperone contracts may allow the chaperone to attend church with the offender, but deem them inappropriate to serve as a monitor for home visits with children. Having an approved chaperone should never trump good sexual offender management principles. Decision making, with or without the presence of a chaperone, should be informed by empirically based risk assessment measures and other objective sources of information like polygraph testing and phallometric and/or visual-reaction measures.

While few would argue against having positive, responsible support persons involved in an offender's life, structuring these support mechanisms in ways that work in conjunction with, and not against, sexual offender management teams is the challenge. With limited resources, staff, and time, actual chaperone programs, which sometimes include family and couple therapy, are not always given a high priority. These types of interventions are not always appropriate or possible; however, we believe that in many cases chaperone-type interventions are quite useful at increasing community supervision, decreasing client resistance, and improving overall client well-being.

Questions to Consider:

- While a Circle of Support model may not be possible in your jurisdiction, how much contact do you have with significant others in the lives of sexual offenders? What types of questions do you ask them? What efforts do you make to educate them about the change process?

- Does our system of change encourage/discourage the involvement of significant others involved in the lives of offenders?

- What beliefs does your team have about spouses of sexual offenders? How do you discriminate between problematic spouses and those who might be helpful in the change and supervision process?

In conclusion, collaborations within systems that manage sexual offenders are filled with endless possibilities. Strong levels of support exist for collaborative efforts in the sexual offender management field; however, opinions differ regarding those who should be involved in these systems of change and how they should be coordinated. Regardless of which system you work within (or what role you play), we encourage you to consider your current partners for change, those you might be leaving out, and how you might improve your existing partnerships. Researchers are encouraged to continue studying these processes so that model programs can be replicated and improved.

Chapter Eight

Any change, any loss, does not make us victims. Others can shake you, surprise you, disappoint you, but they can't prevent you from acting, from taking the situation you're presented with and moving on. No matter where you are in life, not matter what your situation, you can always do something. You always have a choice and the choice can be power.
—BLAINE LEE, THE POWER PRINCIPLE

Administrative Issues

Change agents attempting to reduce resistance with sexual offenders face an enormous task. Without appropriate support structures, their attempts can turn futile and lead to feelings of hopelessness and helplessness. However, if agencies that employ change agents are able to create and maintain healthy work environments that promote personal and professional health, services can be offered in ways that minimize resistance.

Throughout our discussion thus far, we have provided strategies that individual change agents and change agent teams can employ to reduce resistance. This chapter will focus specifically on those factors that must to be addressed by administrators of agencies that employ supervision officials, therapists, victim advocates, and other involved change agents. Specifically, we will address the importance of effective staff selection processes; healthy agency cultures; frequent, relevant staff training; addressing staff safety needs; and helping change agents develop and maintain appropriate boundaries with offenders.

Staff Selection

Change occurs within a system that allows and encourages it. With the goal of engaging resistance in a population where resistance is common, relevant agencies must be cognizant of the influence of staff recruitment (Tellier & Serin, 2005). The factors that individual change agents bring to the work play a major role in changing the offender. Individual factors also influence the functioning of an organization that promotes change. Program administrators would therefore be wise to take the time to properly screen candidates regarding attitudes toward sexual offenders and offender change, team skills, experience, therapeutic skill levels, stress management skills, and legal and ethical matters.

Attitudes Toward Offender and Offender Change

Since motivational forces have been associated with the ability to change (Tellier & Serin, 2005; Prochaska & DiClemente, 1982), ideal change agents are those who are able to hold and instill optimism in regard to the change process. Conversely, change agents who have negative attitudes toward offenders, or ideologically maintain that facilitated personal change is impossible, are unlikely to play an effective role in change. Viewing treatment or supervision as nothing more than extended punishment will also likely inhibit offender change.

Staff attitudes are linked to positive and desirable work outcomes. Simourd (1997) found that favorable attitudes correlated with general job satisfaction, organizational commitment, and job performance. On the other hand, job dissatisfaction can have a profound impact on the functioning of an agency as a whole. As discussed previously, sexual offender clinics that do not maintain strong supportive team relationships experienced excessive inter-agency conflict, increased scrutiny of offender's motives, and co-worker hostility (English, 2005). It is therefore the responsibility of both the organization and individual staff to build an environment that fosters healthy attitudes toward offenders and offender change. This process begins with identifying and screening out individuals who do not believe offenders can change and/or have rigid pre-existing attitudes/agendas regarding offenders.

Team Skills

In addition to assessing potential staff for attitudes detrimental to the goal of offender change and program health, program managers must assess their ability to work as a team. The predisposition to collaboratively work in a team setting is a positive attribute.

Individuals who are reluctant to share ideas and receive or give feedback can potentially weigh heavily on a team that relies on support and collaboration. Similarly, potential team members must understand why the team approach is being implemented. Healthfield (2005) pointed out that successful team building requires members who want to be part of a team; are in agreement with the team's goals, principles, vision and values; and expect their skills and knowledge to develop while part of the team. Finally, potentially strong team members are excited and challenged by the opportunity to work with the team.

Strong team members work together to develop consistent program rules and policies. Failure to enforce program rules in a consistent way develops splitting (i.e., when offenders pit one staff member against another or pick favorites in order to facilitate acting out). Similarly, staff members are aware of each other's strengths and weaknesses and take steps to utilize these strengths and compensate for weaknesses. Some of the best teams are not those that boast having the highest education or the strongest reputations, but rather those that communicate well and work closely together.

Case Example 1

Mary recently received her clinical license to practice psychotherapy. After completing her fellowship at a correctional institution working with sexual offenders, she obtained a job in an outpatient offender clinic. Her experience working in a correctional institution was excellent, but this was her first time to work in an outpatient program.

She quickly found the groups in the clinic to be very different from the ones in the institution. Offenders participating in prison were punctual and generally compliant. In her new outpatient setting she found the offenders less friendly and more resistant. Group members wandered into the group late and tried to spend the entire session complaining about being mandated to treatment. After a few weeks of trying to get the group focused on the work, she decided to let them talk about whatever they wanted. She also decided to let offenders leave the group a little early. After a period of time, her offenders began telling her that she was the best staff member, and offenders not in her group vied to get her as a therapist.

Members in other groups, upon hearing about Mary's approach, became increasingly disruptive. Other therapists began to question Mary's approach. She was eventually asked whether or not she was enforcing the rules and working on sexual offender issues. Mary initially denied removing some of the rules and turning her sexual offender group into an open discussion group but eventually admitted her shift.

During a staff process meeting, Mary was able to articulate how stressed and overwhelmed she felt as a result of working with such a resistant population. As a team, they explored how Mary's feelings led her to manipulate the members into liking her. (Specifically, the group was allowed to avoid addressing issues related to sexual abuse, responsibility, accountability, and general self-regulation.) They discussed the impact on the clinic as well as the clients. Along with her colleagues, Mary was able to identify how the offenders were testing her and splitting her from the rest of the staff. They explored self-care skills, stress management, and offender resistance. The team then developed a plan to assist Mary in restoring order and consistency to the group.

Case Example 2

Darrell, a long-time probation officer, felt it was important to provide consistent and clear messages to offenders regarding acceptable and unacceptable behavior. The use of illegal substances, for instance, always resulted in a violation. He also made sure that his offenders were compliant with treatment recommendations. He regularly performed home visits to meet with offenders and their families. Offenders on his case load generally expressed that he was tough but a "straight shooter."

Nicole, a new probation officer, joined Darrell's unit. She made it known to offenders on her case load that the use of marijuana or alcohol (even if it was a condition of their probation not to drink) would not result in a violation. In return, they were not to give her a hard time and they would get a job. She was very active in the offenders' lives, providing referrals for vocational training, family services, and meal programs. Nicole also told her probationers that treatment was not that important. If they were mandated, they had to go, but they didn't really have to do the homework—just show up. "If you sign into the program, that's good enough for me."

Eventually, Darrell's offenders begin to label Darrell as a "hard ass" who didn't really care about them. "He just likes to pull power trips." Darrell's probationers began to loathe him.

Nicole and Darrell met to discuss the challenges that had arisen since they began working together. Darrell educated Nicole regarding the merits of treatment and the role that substances play in both sexual and non-sexual reoffense. Conversely, Nicole identified employment and family issues as major factors in reoffense. The two decided to develop a joint policy manual for consistent enforcement of the rules and to meet weekly to review cases and develop interventions.

Experience

Program administrators often covet seasoned and experienced staff members. Individuals who have had exposure to sexual offenders face-to-face have a sense of what to expect from the job in terms of both the benefits and pitfalls of working with this population. Individuals with extensive experience, from different agencies, can bring an abundance of know-how and varying perspectives that can potentially energize an organization that is at risk of being overly routine or subject to "groupthink." (Groupthink occurs when the group goals of cohesiveness, agreement, and unity become more important than considering alternatives.) On the other hand, experienced staff may also enter a new job unable or unwilling to learn new tasks or methods. The program administrator is therefore warned to evaluate flexibility as well as experience.

In addition, the literature presents conflicting results regarding the impact of extensive experience in working with sexual offenders. Specifically, one study suggested that some individuals with many years of experience with sexual offenders may develop negative attitudes toward offenders and rehabilitation as a whole (Jurik, 1985; Jurik & Winn, 1987). Another research project found that individuals working with sexual offenders for one year or less, or for 25 years or more, had the most positive attitudes toward offenders and rehabilitation (Lariviere & Robinson, 1996; Farkas, 1999). This contradiction suggests that program managers need to take the time to assess potential staff members individually.

Finally, verifying experience is crucial. It has been our experience that some applicants either distort or completely misrepresent previous work experiences. For example, one interviewee applying for a therapist position stated that she had extensive experience working at a sexual offender clinic only to concede during the interview that she did not actually work with offenders but with victims' families. We strongly encourage background checks to verify training and experience. The use of case vignettes is essential in identifying applicants' abilities to apply prior training and experience to the distinctive needs of a clinic.

Therapeutic Skill

Having years of experience working with sexual offenders does not always translate into skill. Despite the paucity of research, an informal survey of program managers by the authors suggested that individuals with extensive résumés did not always exhibit the skills commensurate to their reported experience. In some cases, clinicians who worked in relative isolation had very poor knowledge of diagnostic criteria, risk assessment, and current advancements in the field. As pointed out previously, interventions that are intentional and thought out are likely the most effective. In terms of treatment, McGrath, Hoke, and Vojtisek (1998) found that recidivism for sexual offenders who participated in sexual offender specific treatment was significantly lower than those who received non-specialized treatment or no treatment at all. Therefore the ideal, experienced sexual offender therapists should be able to articulate potential treatment plans and strategies that are goal oriented and specific to sexual offender treatment.

Additionally, staff members should be encouraged to be genuine, bring new interventions and theoretical perspectives to the team, and be familiar with current best practices.[1] Similarly, probation and parole officers would be best served if they had a comprehensive understanding of effective sexual offender management practices. This may include a thorough knowledge of best treatment practices as they are often in a position to administer group treatment and/or approve and monitor sexual offender treatment programs. Finally, writing skills, verbal skills, coping skills, stress management skills, and a fundamental knowledge of ethical and legal matters as they relate to sexual offenders are important. Program managers are encouraged to utilize case vignettes and extensive questioning regarding theoretical perspectives and knowledge related to sexual offender treatment and management.

Agency Culture

The field of sexual offender assessment, treatment, and management has changed dramatically during the past 30 years. Many of the practices employed have been a process of trial and error and eventual redevelopment. One psychologist equated the sexual offender treatment practices with cancer research of the late 1960's and early 1970's when many of the practices initially used resulted in poor success rates but have been revolutionized over and over again with increasing success. The practice of sexual offender treatment and management will likely undergo many transformations with ideally increasing success.

Agencies need to assure that the culture of their organization maintains a proactive stance that keeps in stride with the current practices regarding the management and treatment of sexual offenders. Promoting a culture that values and monitors research

---

[1] For example, the current research suggests that change agents administering therapy are most effective when cognitive-behavioral practices are utilized (Marshall, Jones, Ward, Johnston, & Barbaree, 1991; McGrath et al., 1998).

development, treatment, and assessment efficacy, as well as ongoing collaboration with professionals from a variety of fields, will increase competence and help overcome potential blocks to offender change. Such collaboration will help prevent falling into a rigid practice of utilizing outdated approaches, recklessly shifting focus based on any new idea, or operating from a "seat-of-the-pants" approach that employs interventions that are not well thought out and are based on the whim of the change agent.

An agency that minimizes resistance and counter-resistance takes steps to prioritize its goals and apply strategies to meet those goals. The primary goal is public safety. Attaining this goal requires clear expectations regarding agency roles and functions. This includes developing mission statements and maintaining staff members that value and commit to the agency's perspective and the overall objective of the field.

Only through interdisciplinary communication can awareness of the field as a whole be obtained. "Professionals in the treatment, victim advocacy, and criminal justice fields have struggled with the enormous scope of sexual violence for years. Each of these systems has worked to develop more effective approaches to address the individual and societal issues involved" (D'Amora & Burns-Smith, 1999). Identifying individuals and organizations in the community that are invested in offender change can bring valuable perspectives that enhance program culture. In short, agency culture is enhanced when it emphasizes collaboration, competence, and commitment.

Staff Training

The beliefs held by mental health professionals have been found to greatly affect the nature and quality of services afforded to offenders (Ward et al., 1996) and the amount of interprofessional collaboration on sexual offense cases (Finkelhor et al., 1984). Beliefs also impact how well treatment efforts work with sexual offender populations (Fedoroff & Moran, 1997; Hogue, 1993) because believing an intervention will succeed is a key tenet underlying its actual ability to succeed. Further, being exposed to consistently negative judgments and stereotypical beliefs based on criminal history can turn a staff member's expectations into a self-fulfilling prophecy (Lott & Saxon, 2002)—that is, encourage recidivism, solely because it is expected. As a result, Epps (1993) suggested that those who work with sexual offenders must not only be aware of their biases toward their clients but must also remain realistic about the nature of sexual offending. Additionally, Radley (2001) concluded that it is important to assess not only the attitudes that staff hold toward sexual offenders, but also to determine their ability to model appropriate attitudes to others and about themselves.

Staff Safety

We can all probably recall a time when we felt uncomfortable prior to some type of performance. This may have occurred prior to our first speech in college or for colleagues, or maybe it was just the first day on a new job. Even experienced therapists talk about feeling a certain level of anxiety each time they meet a new client. For most, a certain amount of anxiety helps us as we work with others.

However, when anxiety turns to fear and uneasiness, job performance is affected. For individuals working in mental health and criminal justice systems, this fear can have significant effects on both personal and professional well-being. One factor that increases fear and reduces feelings of safety is client violence toward mental health professionals. Within the mental health profession, we know that workplace violence toward mental health professionals is common and that this behavior does not just occur in restrictive settings. Bernstein's (1981) study measuring assaultive behaviors against California psychotherapists discovered that 26% of assaults occurred in community-based settings. The other 74% took place in more restrictive settings, like hospitals or prisons, which continue to see an escalation in violence toward mental health and medical professionals.

Guy, Brown, and Poelstra's (1990) research should raise significant concern for the future of the mental health field, especially within more restrictive settings. They found that 46% of all assaults involved students or trainees, although the incidence of assault decreased steadily as years of experience increased. One can only wonder whether fewer graduate students and qualified professionals will seek employment opportunities in higher-risk settings if these rates continue to rise. Interestingly enough, Kleespies (1998) concluded that, although medical training programs may not be perfect, medical students are being better prepared for emergencies than are students in the mental health disciplines.

While it should be acknowledged that violent behavior and client resistance can never be totally avoided, we do believe that change agents can benefit from receiving appropriate training on how to handle challenging situations that could lead to verbal and physical altercations with clients. Additionally, it is critical that program administrators make safety planning a regular part of their training agenda with both new and experienced change agents. Personal skills training and environmental analysis and modifications are critical to helping change agents feel safe. We believe that change agents who feel safe and prepared to work with challenging and potentially violent clients will work more effectively with client resistance.

Programs should develop a model to evaluate how well they are addressing the safety needs of their staff. Gately and Stabb (2005) offered specific program development training recommendations for trainees working with potentially violent clients. These same recommendations could serve as a model for any agency working with the offender population:

1. TRAINING STAFF ON APPROPRIATE ASSESSMENT OF RISK POTENTIAL

   Change agents, new and experienced, need adequate training on how to accurately determine an offender's risk potential. Without these specific skills, change agents begin to make generalizations about clients possibly on both ends of the spectrum (i.e., low risk versus high risk). While most clients probably do pose a low risk of violence potential, change agents should be able to more accurately assess and then act when confronted with a client who actually does pose serious risk. McNiel (1998) asserted that mental health professionals should "know the truth about the base rates for violence among their clients." Change agents should be kept abreast on the current research relating to the population with whom they are working and not allow media-driven stereotypes to influence their risk assessment and possible emotional stance toward offenders.

2. PREVENTION APPRECIATION

Despite its acknowledged importance, prevention training is often not discussed and implemented within mental health settings. Issues such as agency safety policies and plans, personal safety, and workplace safety are often created in haste and rarely given significant time during staff training. While many agencies require training in crisis management and office safety at the onset of employment, ongoing training is rare. Training change agents about how to work with violence-prone offenders, creating office conditions that reduce stress for offenders, and safety planning for the office environment should be addressed on a regular basis.

Since many probation offices and mental health environments utilize office space that was not originally designed for their current purpose with offenders, program administrators are often challenged by the office environments they are given to use. Barriers to creating healthy and safe office environments include program financial strain and problems finding office space that is conducive to working with sexual offenders. The fact that contracts for sexual offender work often change can result in an unfortunate attitude of unwillingness among some program administrators to invest significant amounts of capital into office improvements.

Prevention planning should also address situational variables that can fuel client frustration. Change agents who use an unstructured appointment schedule often leave offenders waiting for long periods—during which they may spend time complaining with other offenders. Office spaces with small or no waiting rooms and offices with high levels of noise should be addressed. Finally, office layout and the need for security alarms, bathroom security, and security cameras should be addressed in all programs that work with violent offenders. One program that failed to take adequate measures eventually found out that drug deals were regularly taking place in their bathrooms and that some potentially dangerous clients were hiding out in unused treatment rooms.

Gately and Stabb's (2005) study indicated that these simple safety issues are not being adequately covered in psychology training programs, which suggests that the change agents of tomorrow may not be prepared to address these concerns. This oversight brings into question whether programs and training sites are aware of the guidelines the Occupational Safety and Health Organization (2004) created for the health care and social service industries, which were intended to eliminate or reduce worker exposure to conditions that could lead to death or injury from violence. OSHA offers guidelines for workplace safety that include management commitment and employee involvement, workplace analysis, hazard prevention and control, and safety and health training.

3. MODEL FOR EVALUATING AGGRESSIVE BEHAVIOR WITH CLIENTS

    Kaplan and Wheeler (1983) suggested that potentially violent situations with offenders move through different phases. Each phase of a violent episode (triggering, escalation, crisis, recovery, and post-crisis depression) manifests distinct behaviors and offers unique challenges. By incorporating models like this into initial and ongoing training with change agents, program administrators can help employees evaluate an episode with more specificity and promote a more deliberate intervention plan.

    Another model for evaluating and responding to aggressive behavior is offered by Hunt (1993), who studied different types of aggressive patterns. These patterns include over-aroused aggression, impulsive aggression, affective aggression, predatory aggression, and instrumental aggression. Although Hunt acknowledged clients may not clearly demonstrate one of these exact patterns of aggression, he asserted that having an awareness of this framework can help clinicians feel more aware and competent when faced with and helping to prevent a potentially violent situation from intensifying. For example, if a client is sensitive to over-arousal, it might be important to keep encounters simple and calm. Likewise, if a client tends to experience exaggerated responses to small offenses, clinicians may need to spend more time to build and maintain rapport and limit confrontation (Gately & Stabb, 2005).

4.   VERBAL AND BEHAVIORAL INTERVENTION STRATEGIES

Training on specific intervention strategies that can be used during each phase of a violent episode is crucial in reducing the actual number of incidents that eventually turn physically violent. Intense emotions can interfere with the offender's ability to process information. Change agents who have guidance on when to shift the focus from verbal approaches to actual safety maneuvers could help in maintaining personal safety. Verbal strategies, such as empathic statements or distraction, are often all that is needed to de-escalate a situation.

Caraulia and Steiger (1997) suggested that by just acknowledging the concerns of an anxious client, change agents often reduce the risk of violent behavior. They asserted that a supportive response can be as simple as a word of reassurance, a smile, or a willingness to listen. They offer several strategies for effective listening that can help de-escalate a situation: Avoid being judgmental, give your undivided attention, focus on feelings, use silence, and use restatement—many of the same strategies involved in the motivational interviewing techniques discussed in chapter 4.

When verbal interventions have limited impact with the escalating offender, change agents need strategies for removing themselves and others from dangers associated with the crisis stage. Some defensive strategies, such as how to exit a room in the safest way, defensive body positioning, and nonviolent strategies for breaking free from a client's grip, can help increase clinician confidence and decrease anxiety and fear. These strategies are best learned through interactive practice programs, and should not be limited to reading, online education, and group lectures. Kiely and Pankhurst (1998) found that training was often limited to control and restraint techniques, while Gately and Stabb (2005) found restraint and defensive techniques to be the topic least attended to by training programs. Research on this topic with sexual offender specific treatment and supervision programs is nonexistent.

5. POST-CRISIS STRATEGIES

Inevitably crises will occur, some of which will lead to a physical or strong verbal confrontation, possibly in the form of a verbal threat from a client. Programs must have a plan for helping change agents who have experienced these events. Intervention strategies for the recovery phase or the post-crisis depression phase of a violent incident are important. Common errors committed by program administrators and change agents involve both the client and the change agent. We should be careful not to rush clients through a crisis situation. When adrenaline levels are elevated, it is crucial that enough time passes for a client to relax both emotionally and physiologically. Change agents may do an effective job of reducing the initial phase of the crisis for a offender but then push the offender too quickly back into the stressful situation that produced the event. Elevated levels of adrenaline can make the offender more vulnerable to misinterpretation of his/her environment, which can lead to a return to crisis behavior (Kaplan & Wheeler, 1983).

Change agents need to give themselves time to deal with the effects of a crisis. Education in post-crisis care can reduce much of the negative impact that both offender and victims can suffer from a violent encounter. Although a common recommendation is that post-crisis care should include a debriefing opportunity for both the offender and the clinician (Caraulia & Steiger, 1997), some controversy currently exists about the effectiveness of such interventions (Jacobs, Horne-Moyer, & Jones, 2004).

Debriefing may be especially important to consider for a sexual offender whose first attempt to reintegrate back into the community fails. For example, some offenders manifest resistance to treatment and supervision by behaving inappropriately with a treatment provider or supervision agent. These behaviors can sometimes lead to an offender's having his probation or parole revoked and being returned to prison for a short period of time. When this offender is released again, it might be helpful if some type of debriefing can occur between the offender and the change agent who was involved in the initial problematic episode. Although each case should be evaluated individually for appropriateness, this type of clarifying session could be helpful in reducing further resistance with the client and reducing anxiety and fear in the change agent who was threatened.

In conclusion, programs that treat sexual offenders should strongly consider how well they prepare their employees, both clinical and administrative, for working with resistance and offenders. Recommendations include creating a committee for workplace safety that includes all levels of employees. Staff training on these topics should be ongoing and may require agencies to hire experts outside the agency to perform more in-depth training. Additionally, it should not be assumed that more seasoned change agents will be safer than novices. Finally, program administrators and more experienced change agents should model how to process these challenging events. Programs should require de-briefing groups in which all change agents are required to participate.

Professional Boundaries

Closely related to staff safety concerns are issues of maintaining professional boundaries with clients. Throughout our discussion about sexual offender specific issues, we have addressed several ethical concerns (limits of confidentiality, duty to report types of abuse, program expectations, etc.) and their relevance to creating an effective therapeutic frame within an integrated, multi-systemic containment model. In this section, we will discuss professional boundary violations, which are related to numerous legal and ethical regulations in most professional disciplines (psychologists, social workers, probation officers, correction officials, attorneys, etc.), as they are significantly related to change agent, client, and overall systemic resistance. Not only can failing to follow ethical and legal mandates result in significant professional liability problems, but such errors in judgment can also be devastating for the actual change agent-client working relationship, as well as the professional relationship between and among other change agents.

Most change agents would consider it quite obvious that many sexual offenders have maligned relationship patterns. Considerable time in treatment and supervision are devoted to correcting these relationship patterns, many of which were directly or indirectly related to their offense behavior. Many change agents would also recognize that these same patterns are also at work in how sexual offenders try to relate to them and other change agents. Yet, too often, unexplored and unchallenged maladaptive dynamics within the relationships change agents have with offenders can lead to blurred boundaries. These errors often result in increased resistance as well as significant animosity and distrust among change agents and clients alike.

Therapists receive some instruction about appropriate boundaries and how to handle potential dual relationships with clients in their graduate studies courses. Usually at least one course is devoted to legal and ethical concerns and attempts to help new therapists learn how to avoid multiple relationships with clients. It has been our experience, however, that these discussions do not take place often enough once clinicians begin full-time clinical practice, even within forensic settings, where one would expect these discussions to occur more often. We start, therefore, by reviewing some pertinent professional, ethical guidelines, with the American Psychological Association's (APA, 2002) Ethical Principles of Psychologists and Codes of Conduct as our example.

The APA's first ethical principle concerns the issues of Beneficence and Nonmaleficence. This principle states that psychologists

> "should strive to benefit those with whom they work and take care to do no harm.... Because psychologists' scientific and professional judgments and actions may affect the lives of others, they are alert to and guard against personal, financial, social, organizational, or political factors that might lead to misuse of their influence." (APA, 2002, p. 3)

Additional APA codes provide clear direction for psychologists as they define what are and are not appropriate behaviors with clients. These codes include clear expectations about sexual relationships with current clients: They should never exist.

Forensic psychologists adhere to guidelines set forth by the American Psychology Law Society (APLS), which is Division 41 of the APA. With respect to the issue of multiple relationships, section 6.03 of the Specialty Guidelines for Forensic Psychology states:

> Forensic practitioners are vigilant in recognizing the potential conflicts of interest and threats to objectivity inherent in multiple relationships with attorneys, judges, parties, examinees, patients, and other participants to a legal proceeding. Forensic practitioners recognize that some personal and professional relationships may interfere with their ability to practice in a competent and objective manner and they seek to minimize any detrimental effects by avoiding involvement in such matters whenever feasible or limiting their assistance in a manner that is consistent with professional obligations. (APLS, 2006, p. 10)

These APLS guidelines explicitly direct forensic psychologists to work to avoid behaviors that could jeopardize objectivity in their work duties, including their relationships with other change agents. Although intended for forensic psychologists, we would argue that these same principles should apply to anyone working as a change agent with sexual offenders, and that multiple relationships with offenders should be avoided at all costs.

While ethical codes are important and should guide clinical practice, change agents need concrete ways to consider the appropriateness of their relationships with offenders. To guide helping professionals in making decisions about suitable relationships with clients, Schoener (1997) discussed what is known as the zone of helpfulness. On one end of the zone of helpfulness spectrum is the cold, aloof, and indifferent therapist, while on the other end rests the over-involved, intrusive therapist. To maximize their helping capabilities, therapists should attempt to create a client-therapist relationship that falls in the middle of this spectrum. Although client progress could be thwarted at either extreme, over-involved, intrusive therapists put themselves in serious danger of violating ethical codes and damaging their clients. For example, clients report that they feel uncomfortable when therapists disclose too much information. While the authors recognize that client-therapist relationships are more multi-dimensional in nature than this linear model suggests, it does offer a starting point for our conversation.

One of the most significant and damaging behaviors contained within the over-involved end of the spectrum occurs when sexual contact between therapists and current clients takes place. Most change agents would strongly agree that sexual contact with clients is harmful and should be avoided; however, inappropriate behaviors, including sexual ones, do occur between change agents and offenders. There is a dearth of literature on boundary violations, including sexual ones, between change agents and sexual offenders; however, given several incidences that the authors have witnessed over the years, and the overall incidence of sexual relationships between therapists and clients, it is fair to assume that problematic relationships occur far too often. Because professional decision making becomes skewed in these relationships, community and change agent safety are compromised when they occur.

We recognize that it would probably be a rare occasion for therapists, probation officers, attorneys, and other change agents to wake up one morning and announce to the world that they have decided to have sexual contact with offenders under their care. Furthermore, what change agent would actually admit to it? However, much like the offenders we supervise, these behaviors typically occur after a series of successive approximations. Personal disclosures lead to more advanced behaviors, which can lead to poor decision making on the part of the change agent. Manipulative offenders can easily spot change agent weaknesses or vulnerabilities. It is the change agent's job, with the help of colleagues and supervisors, to identify those areas where s/he is most vulnerable.

Case Example

One change agent who took great pride in the type of clothing she wore often received extensive compliments from certain offenders. When it came time for case discussions about these offenders, she would minimize problems these "complimentary" offenders were having and was less inclined to interpret their behaviors as risky. Additionally, she would tend to have more involved discussions with these offenders before and after group. They would start to talk about where they shop for clothes, what their favorite brands were, and what kinds of clothes she would wear out at night when she went dancing. One offender would then comment on how he used to go to similar clubs and attempt to solicit sympathy from the change agent with statements like, "Isn't it too bad I'm not allowed to go to those places anymore." This same offender noticed that she came into group each week with coffee from a well-known coffee chain. He asked if she wanted to meet for coffee sometime.

This change agent finally came to realize, with the help of her supervisor, how some of her behaviors contributed to the "coffee proposal." Although this behavior may seem like a long way from having a sexual relationship with an offender, it can be seen as one step toward the erosion of boundaries. As professional boundaries disintegrate, the likelihood that other transgressions will continue, without an intervention, increases. Research on therapists who had admitted to sexual violations with clients found that the therapists admitted to nonsexual boundary violations prior to the sexual behavior (Lamb, Catanzaro, & Moorman 2003). Whether these violations consisted of disclosing personal information or crying in front of an offender after a fight with a significant other, these therapists, when looking back, could acknowledge these behaviors were one step on the way to the actual sexual transgression.

So who is most vulnerable? Are you vulnerable? Research (Lamb et al., 2003) exists regarding characteristics that put therapists at risk for becoming vulnerable to sexual transgressions with patients. When asked about what they believed to be contributing life factors to the development of these inappropriate relationships, Lamb and colleagues identified two significant types of contributing factors. See Table 8.1 for a list of precursors to inappropriate sexual relationships with clients, as identified by therapists who had actually committed a sexual boundary violation.

Within our change agent teams, it is critical that we are not only attuned to vulnerabilities and struggles of the offenders we work with, but also of our colleagues. Inevitably, all change agents at different points in their lives will experience one or more of these factors, especially type one items.

Table 8.1
Precursors to inappropriate sexual relationships with clients

Type One - Factors related to dissatisfaction in therapists' personal lives

- Relationship problems
- New job
- Employment problems
- Financial troubles
- Feeling lonely
- Insecurity
- Birth of a child
- Loss of a parent

Type Two - Actual activities or interactions related to the client

- Increase in social interactions that led to increased familiarity
- Ongoing contact with the client after therapy ended
- Fantasizing about the person
- Continued therapy even though client had already met treatment goals or was no longer benefiting from treatment

(Lamb et al., 2003)

Effective supervisors should take significant steps with the change agents they supervise to identify over-involvement well before it reaches the point of a sexual boundary violation. In order to do so, supervisors must be aware of a change agent's style of relating with offenders so that they can clearly identify areas of psychological and relational vulnerability. They should have a strong sense of each change agent's case load and the relationship issues between the offenders and change agent. For example, a lead probation officer or clinical director should regularly ask change agents under their supervision specific questions regarding the offenders they are working with:

- Are you making progress? Are you struggling? How do you explain these results?

- With whom are you having a difficult relationship, and how are you responding to that relationship?

- Whom do you have positive feelings toward, and how are these feelings manifested in the change agent-offender relationship?

- Who do you talk about often, and who do you rarely talk about?

- Do you advocate for one offender more than others?

- Do you have a disproportionate number of case contacts with certain offenders?

- Do you seem to require more or less (e.g., drug or polygraph testing) from certain offenders?

- Are there offenders to whom you feel more comfortable self-disclosing?

Although not a comprehensive list of questions or an empirically proven way to catch all potential or existing boundary violations, these questions could give administrators a sense about the type of offender(s) individual change agents might be most vulnerable to and which ones they need more supervision around. We believe that change agents at all stages of their career should be asked to consider these questions on a regular basis.

Related to the question of therapist self-disclosure noted above is the amount of self-disclosure helping professionals do with clients. This is another important factor related to the more over-involved end of the spectrum. Schoener (1997) reported that excessive self-disclosure is the single most common precursor to therapist-client sex and includes many of the following behaviors:

- Revealing personal needs or problems;

- Disclosing personal information during sessions on a regular basis, rather than on a rare basis;

- Divulging personal information not clearly connected to session content or necessarily supportive of client's needs;

- Taking up more session time with therapist self-disclosures than with client disclosures; and

- Continuing to disclose despite negative or romanticized feedback from the client.

Some of these self-disclosure issues are straightforward, while others are more subtle. There probably isn't a change agent in the profession who hasn't had a bad day on the job and revealed frustration to clients in one way or another. However, there are appropriate and inappropriate ways to disclose personal information. For example, acknowledging personal emotions on an infrequent basis may serve as healthy modeling for offenders, and could be helpful as a change agent attempts to teach offenders how to communicate feelings without being abusive. On the other hand, when change agents reveal emotions regularly, followed by extensive self-disclosure such as "I'm so frustrated with my husband... he never cares about my feelings.... I feel much better when I'm at work," the professional relationship could be negatively impacted.

Perhaps not all boundary violations will lead to actual sexual behaviors between change agents and their clients. However, if these factors can lead to sexual transgressions, they can also lead to other problematic decision making short of sexual behavior, but potentially very serious/dangerous when it comes to managing sexual offenders in the community. Consider the following examples:

Example 1

One change agent, Mike, could really relate to Jake, one of the offenders he was supervising. Jake grew up in the same part of town that Mike did, went to the same high school, and actually shared some of the same friends. Conversations between Jake and Mike quickly went from discussions about adherence to probation conditions to "how hot Marcie was in high school and still is today." Mike knew that Jake had a drug problem in addition to his history of rape behavior. However, Mike knew that Jake was having financial problems and didn't want to make him take time off of work to go do a drug test. Jake's treatment provider began commenting to Mike that he was concerned about whether Jake was using drugs again, but Mike didn't seem to listen. Finally, after 3 weeks of missing group treatment, and no action from Mike, Jake's treatment provider called Mike's supervisor, Charlene. Charlene immediately ordered Jake into the office for a drug test, which he failed by testing positive to crystal methamphetamine and marijuana. It was also discovered that Jake had been out of work for several weeks and had been robbing homes in the area to support his drug problem.

Example 2

Stephanie, a sexual offender therapist, found George, a multi-victim child molester, to have many qualities in common with her recently deceased father. George presented as kind and caring, always came to group prepared, and contributed positively when Stephanie called on him. Stephanie would spend extra time after group with George. When George kept forgetting to set up his polygraph exam with the agency polygraph examiner, she didn't report it to the probation officer right away. Weeks went by, and when the probation officer stopped by George's home, she found significant amounts of child pornography on his computer. George had also been chatting with adolescent girls using an online messaging service. When confronted, George blamed Stephanie for not helping him with his fantasy problem and demanding that he take his polygraph. The probation officer was angry with Stephanie for not holding George accountable.

In both of these examples, professional nonsexual boundary issues negatively influenced the change agent-offender relationship, as well as relationships between different change agents. Higher-risk behaviors were not identified earlier because Mike and Stephanie allowed their professional relationships to be influenced by personal factors. Future client and systemic resistance is a likely result of both outcomes.

We challenge all change agents to evaluate the boundaries that exist within their relationships with offenders, be open to questions from colleagues and supervisors around these issues, and recognize that these concerns may manifest themselves at different points in their career, especially during and after difficult, critical life events. Change agents should be informed by supervisors that professional boundary issues, sexual or nonsexual, will emerge at some point in time over the course of their career in working with offenders, and that part of the job is to anticipate and do everything possible to prevent these from occurring. Agencies should develop policies on how they will help change agents resolve these issues, when appropriate, with support and counseling if detected early in the process and before any significant amount of harm is done. Finally, agencies need clear policies of how they will respond to more problematic boundary violations that should include language from professional codes related to the particular change agent's profession.

Conclusion

Throughout this chapter, we have addressed numerous factors that are rarely included in the discussion of how to effectively reduce sexual offender resistance. Many of the suggestions we have made regarding staff training and increased supervision require additional resources that, at first glance, some agency administrators will deem impossible to provide. We assert that not considering issues of appropriate staff selection, staff training, staff safety, and quality supervision can lead to increased numbers of inappropriate change agent hires, change agents who feel unsafe and unprepared, and change agents who make poor decisions about their personal and professional behavior with offenders. Effective change agent systems must engage these challenges and recognize that any one of these important issues, if not addressed, could directly and indirectly affect our attempts to work effectively with offenders and protect our communities.

Chapter Nine

He that will not apply new remedies must expect new evils; for time is the greatest innovator.

–Francis Bacon, Essays, II, On Innovation

Conclusion: Change in Motion

Throughout the book, we have explored the idea of resistance in hopes of better understanding the many factors that lead sexual offenders to resist change agents' efforts. This exploration for "new remedies" that will ensure fewer "new evils" has allowed us to appreciate more the difficult nature of the work facing change agents working daily with sexual offenders, and a different vantage point from which to understand the world in which sexual offenders dwell within society. Furthermore, this effort has highlighted for us why creating partnerships for change is challenging and requires constant attention if we hope to help offenders, while at the same time keeping society properly informed and our communities safe.

The past several decades within the field of sexual offender management and treatment have seen some noteworthy accomplishments. The dedication of change agent professionals from various disciplines—clinicians, academics, criminal justice personnel, policy officials, etc.—to juggle some very challenging, and sometimes conflicting, goals deserves significant recognition. Despite these efforts and successes, change agents working with sexual offenders also know that with every victory comes another challenge to tackle.

In efforts to reduce resistance with sexual offenders, we believe effective practices do exist. In a field that many times emphasizes what isn't working, and in which many aspects are challenged regarding their usefulness, change agents should be recognized for the progress they have made in recent years. Listed below are a few of the areas to be recognized.

Individualized Case Planning

Both supervision and treatment professionals have made strides to better recognize that all sexual offenders are not the same. Many change agents are making efforts to set up supervision plans that keep the community safe, while not unnecessarily blocking the offenders' access to necessary goods—jobs, appropriate relationships, etc. Treatment providers are utilizing program models based on research, specifically dynamic risk factor research, which directs clinicians to spend treatment time on those factors that are most relevant to individual offenders. Furthermore, clinicians are using techniques, such as motivational interviewing, to decrease resistance and to improve cooperation with offenders. This is significant progress from the days when all offenders were given the same conditions of supervision, asked to complete the same homework assignments, and confronted heavily when they veered from the path of perceived cooperation. Overall, change agents are beginning to recognize that sexual offenders are a diverse group of individuals and that we can increase the likelihood that these individuals will respond positively to our interventions if we consider and respond thoughtfully to the various types of resistance they present.

Change Agent Community Involvement

Never before has it been more important for change agents to be involved in educating their communities and having a voice in public policy creation. Change agents and organizations such as ATSA and CSOM have made commitments to help change agents learn how to better advocate for best practice efforts. We have heard and witnessed countless stories of change agents meeting with community members, attending public forums, providing lectures at universities, and putting in immeasurable time writing briefs to government policy makers. Change agents recognize that their work doesn't begin and end within the parameters of their daily job description.

CSOM (2001) presented several recommendations to reduce unintended consequence for offenders reintegrating into society. Regular community education efforts, appropriate risk assessment procedures (which then lead to only necessary community notification practices), and vigilante warnings are just a few of the recommendations suggested. Change agents from across the country have influenced the creation of fair and just community policies, which hopefully increase community safety and reduce barriers for offenders attempting to make positive strides in their lives. These individual and collaborative efforts don't always receive the recognition they deserve, which speaks even further to the dedication and concern of professionals working with sexual offenders.

Integrating Victim Perspectives with Policy and Treatment Programs

While creating policies to protect past and potential future victims may not seem like a novel concept, how this occurs has changed over time. Collaborative efforts have begun across the United States that include victim advocate professionals working within change agent teams. These efforts allow for individualized case planning in cases of incest and provide another unique perspective in developing supervision and treatment plans. More importantly, these efforts have brought together two groups of professionals (i.e., victim and offender), who have sometimes been wary of one another. Myths about certain change agents being "offender apologists" while others serve as "offender haters" are broken down when these two groups learn to work together cooperatively toward common goals. Cross-discipline education efforts also help providers on both sides of the issue learn more about how to integrate one another's research findings into everyday practice efforts.

Other areas of significant progress that have required collaborative efforts and could be explored at length include research-informed risk assessment procedures, the differentiation of adult from juvenile sexual offenders (and sexually reactive children), and the improvement of case management and supervision techniques used by correctional and treatment professionals. Furthermore, the advancement of cognitive-behavioral research and the re-emergence of behavioral therapies, both quite capable of leading to quantifiable results, is promising. Despite the many challenges we face in the future, the field of sexual offender management has made and continues to make changes that are informed by history and research.

Redefining Resistance

Change is hampered by the delay of intervention, especially with sexual offenders. We assert that messages and support for change do not have to be delayed until the first psychological/treatment intervention. Change can begin and resistance can be reduced by the first interaction with the criminal justice system. Although many would argue this is an unrealistic goal, we believe that at least approaching this goal is worthwhile. Consider it a harm-reduction approach to sexual offender resistance!

Redefining resistance begins with redefining our goals as change agents. If our daily interactions with sexual offenders work toward goals of continued pathologizing, finding shortcomings, and further ostracizing them, we'll probably achieve these results and end up with individuals who may be worse off than when they were offending. If we seek to understand the nature of their resistance, work toward keeping offenders within the therapeutic/reintegration "frame," and are careful not to spend too much time "feeding the resistance," then we might just start moving these men and women along the path of change. Motivational interviewing techniques emphasize the importance of the change agent's developing interventions that meet the offenders where they are in their change process, not forcing the offender to a place where he isn't ready to reside. For many change agents, this process is exhilarating—the thing that keeps the work interesting and challenging—while for others, it leads to frustration, anger, and burnout.

In order to engage resistance, change agents should be open to the possible reasons that change is difficult. We can begin to relate to the process of the offenders we work with when we step back and understand ourselves better (how we ourselves change—or don't) and how the systems we work within impact our beliefs and influence our dilemmas. Redefining resistance is understood best when we start to recognize that resistance isn't good or bad, within one or the other, something that begins and ends, or a state within a relationship that should be avoided at all costs. Instead, resistance is a paradox of sorts. For example, if we are able to see that a person believes something is worth fighting for or holding onto, regardless of how dysfunctional it might seem, at least it shows us he is passionate about something and could possibly be passionate about something else—something better. Maybe we should focus more on the offender who doesn't seem to care at all—not even enough to resist or fight for what he believes to be true.

We have explored many explanations for resistance throughout this book. We hope that readers walk away open to the idea that sexual offenders who present as hostile, display low motivation, are uncooperative, disclose little about the offense initially, and show little responsibility for their crimes are not necessarily untreatable. Instead, such behaviors may be due to a variety of factors within the offender, change agent, society, criminal justice systems, or interactions between these players. Resistance is an unintended consequence of an imperfect system of change. Once we accept this limitation, change can begin to occur. Famous football coach Woody Hayes may have said it best: "Paralyze resistance with persistence."

Balancing Traditionally Conflicting Philosophies

Change agents approaching today's challenges with sexual offenders must consider several approaches that have traditionally been considered mutually exclusive. It is our opinion that in order to facilitate change one must consider the values and limitations of each philosophy before blindly accepting or rejecting them (or construing them as polar opposites). Each philosophy can provide change agents with practical questions to consider as they engage in their daily work with sexual offenders.

To Punish or to Rehabilitate

Most change agents would probably agree that some form of both punishment and rehabilitation is necessary in helping sexual offenders. Where change agents from various disciplines (i.e., treatment, supervision, law enforcement, corrections, victim advocates, attorneys) disagree is the degree to which each is important. Change agents form their respective positions about these constructs from their personal experiences, professional affiliations, expected job outcomes, need for income, and the views of family, friends, and society. Effective change agents are aware of how these factors enter into professional decision making on both a personal and team level. Well-functioning teams recognize how highly publicized cases impact not only their clients, but also the decision making that occurs surrounding these episodes. For example, when an offender in the community reoffends, change agent teams should be cautious not to overreact, without sufficient reason, to the behavior of other offenders they supervise or treat. That is, placing an offender back in prison for being 10 minutes late to group because his bus was late probably wouldn't be an appropriate response to a man who had been compliant for the past 18 months.

Change agents also have to balance their desire to treat offenders as individuals within the reality that decisions they make will influence other offenders' behaviors. For example, if change agents allow certain behaviors to go unpunished or address them inconsistently, other offenders might become unclear as to what is expected of them. Change agents need to consider their own personal reactions to and relationships with individual offenders and continually question how these impact their decision making. As with any population, some will evoke positive responses, while others will evoke negative ones. Change agents should be aware of how these attitudes influence decisions to punish or "give the offender another chance," viewing certain misbehaviors as part of the change process.

Maybe, the most important part of this discussion involves change agents accepting the reality that whatever decisions they make, have intended and unintended consequences. Ideally, our interventions hit the mark and produce an intended response. Nevertheless, change agents should come to expect that even the most well-executed intervention or decision about an offender comes with mixed outcomes. Effective change agent teams are able to openly discuss and anticipate both realities and consider them prior to, during, and after these decisions are made.

Collaborative Versus Adversarial (Uncooperative) Relationships

In discussing these different philosophies, we are addressing not only the relationship among and between different change agents, but also between change agents and offenders. Huxham (1996) defined collaboration as the exchange of information, the altering of activities, the sharing of resources, and the enhancement of the capacity of another for the mutual benefit of all and to achieve a common purpose. To create collaborative relationships with change agents and offenders alike, all parties must own the piece they play in creating resistance. For example, treatment providers must recognize the biases they bring when negotiating treatment contracts and attempting to influence the decision making of supervision officials. If several offenders who are treated by private agencies or providers are placed back into custody for probation violations, the practice will experience financial repurcussions. While providers want to be objectively supportive of the supervision process, decisions may be influenced by other financial motivations. Decisions made for the wrong reasons lead to mistrust and a lack of cooperation among potentially collaborative forces.

CSOM (2000) offers some key descriptors of adversarial and collaborative relationships. Supervisors of change agent teams would benefit from reviewing these different ends of the pendulum and taking time to better understand how teams can move from more entrenched adversarial positions to collaborative responses. Noncollaboration may give offenders more opportunity to reoffend, whereas collaboration's ultimate goal is public safety (as collaboration, in the form of fast, effective communication, may result in early intervention to deviancy prior to reoffense). Efforts to achieve collaboration and cooperation among change agents will also model healthy, nonadversarial relationships for offenders. Some change agents may need more coaching and support from supervisors, as they may not innately have the skills to be collaborative team members.

For improved collaboration with offenders, we have discussed numerous ways of how to engage and work with offenders to create change. The critical aspects of these strategies include under-

	Table 9.1 Traits of adversarial and collaborative (uncoopertive) approaches	
Collaborative Approaches	• Parties positioned as joint problem solvers	
	• Issues identified before positions crystallize	
	• Joint search used to determine facts	
	• Face-to-face discussions encouraged among all	
	• Workable options sought	
	• Field of options broadened	
	• Outcome must be satisfactory to all parties	
	• Trust and positive relationships promoted	
Adversarial Responses	• Rules position parties as adversaries	
	• Face-to-face contact restricted among contending parties	
	• Seeking to win arguments	
	• All-or-nothing approach to resolution of issues	
	• Narrowing options quickly	
	• Characterized by suspicion and high emotion	
	• Parties often dissatisfied with outcome	
	• Often fosters bitterness and long-term distrust	

standing the different types of denial and resistance, the function of these beliefs and behaviors, and utilizing effective strategies to counteract resistance. Marshall et al. (2005) spoke to this point by addressing ways to work positively with sexual offenders. Instilling hope, enhancing self-esteem, emphasizing approach goals, and working collaboratively are offered in their recommendations for sexual offender therapists. We believe these goals should extend to all members of the change agent system.

In summary, creating collaborative relationships among and between change agents and offenders requires constant attention and consideration. D'Amora and Burns-Smith (1999) eloquently noted:

Professionals in the treatment, victim advocacy, and criminal justice fields have struggled with the enormous scope of sexual violence for years. Each of these systems has worked to develop more effective approaches to address the individual and societal issues involved. A variety of successes have been achieved in each of these fields, including better treatment outcomes, changing social views, and more successful prosecution and accountability. At the same time, we have not been able to eliminate the problem. Despite our best efforts, sexual violence remains a pervasive societal problem, and, when the system responds inadequately to offender behavior, victims can be further hurt by system-induced trauma.

Social Rejection Versus Reintegration

The final conflict to address may well be the most difficult to resolve. One reality discussed throughout has been the challenge of reintegrating offenders into a society that for some understandable, as well as other misinformed and irrational reasons, doesn't want them. As we've come to discover, social exclusion has long-term effects on both physical and psychological aspects of normal individuals. For example, research findings suggest that excluded individuals may be at increased risk for aggressive behavior, decreased levels of cooperation and helping others, decreased meaningful thought, distorted time perception, and increased levels of self-destructive behavior. As we exclude offenders from society at large, we risk doing more damage to them, potentially elevating their risk level by exposing them to adversarial conditions.

Legislation regarding community notification impacts both those offenders attempting to reintegrate into society and community safety. As has been discussed previously in this book, as well as by other authors (Hogue, 1993), even though some people may hold positive and/or hopeful attitudes about transitioning criminal offenders from prison into the community, these attitudes tend to evaporate when it comes to sexual offenders. Instead of hope, sexual offenders tend to elicit stronger and more negative emotions. This is evidenced by the fact that sexual offenders are subject to more strict and aggressive legislation than even the most violent of criminal offenders. For example, as Prentky, Lee, Knight, and Cerce (1997) asserted, sexual offenders are most often the focus of proceedings for commitments to segregated prison units or mental health facilities, and are the subject of an immoderate number of ad hoc discretionary and dispositional decisions.

Even though sexual offenders are the subject of an inordinate amount of legislative actions, there is little evidence that these actions actually reduce sexual offending or recidivism. Zevitz and Farkas (2000) asserted, "Despite the extensive attention and public support that notification laws have generated, empirical research on their impact is nearly nonexistent" (p. 10). Although the research is scant, one study that we were able find by Schram and Milloy (1995) found that the arrest rates between offenders subject to community notification and a group of offenders with no notification were similar. The only difference noted by these researchers was that those in the notification group were rearrested twice as quickly after reoffense than those in the matched no-notification group. It should be stressed that the overall reoffense rate was essentially the same.

Notification laws have clear consequences. Younglove and Vitello (2003) point out that "notifying neighbors about the presence of a registered sexual offender very often results not in (the) sense of safety and well-being (intended consequence), but rather just the opposite—panic and vigilantism" (p. 32). Zevitz and Farkas (2000) found in their research that various parole agents reported numerous problems with finding residences for released sexual offenders. Zevitz and Farkas also noted that some people who have "agreed to house the sex offender received death threats and decided not to house him." In countless other examples a media blitz has crippled heartfelt attempts to provide housing that would provide both security to the offenders and increased safety to the community by allowing effective monitoring and collaboration.

In some cases, the lack of the community's willingness to engage this problem may actually increase risk. For example, in one California city several offenders were removed from their home with less than 12 hours' notice because a day care opened up near their home. As a result of the inability to find new places to live, most lost their jobs, and some were moved to jurtsidications where they had no social support and where treatment was unavailable. One offender who was relocated 50 miles from his previous residence contacted his therapist requesting phone support due to the stress of losing his residence, his job, and his support network. He was also fearful that he might be violated because he was mandated into treatment by the courts and treatment was not available in his new location. This type of poor community planning contributes to increased risk of recidivism by preventing offenders from stabilizing the dynamic variables known to contribute to reoffense.

Community notification is intended to increase community safety (or at least a sense of safety), but one common and rarely acknowledged consequence is the harassment of sexual offenders. Incidences of such harassment are being tracked in various states. In 1995, Oregon reported that 10% of the 237 sexual offenders in the community notification program had experienced harassment. In contrast, in 1996, New Jersey reported only five recorded instances of physical or verbal assaults against publicized sexual offenders, and Washington state reported only 33 instances, out of a total 942 notifications (Lieb, Quinsey, & Berliner, 1998). Regardless of how low the rates of reported harassment appear, such incidents are likely underreported (as discussed by Lieb et al., 1998). In addition, offenders believe that they will not receive protection from law enforcement agencies. They also fear drawing more attention to themselves. As a result, Zevitz and Farkas (2000) opined "the basic dilemma associated with community notification is balancing the public's right to be informed with the need to successfully reintegrate offenders into the community" (p. 8). Offenders who are forced underground are less likely to cooperate with management and treatment interventions. An accurate appraisal regarding whether or not the community is safer with notification also needs to be occur.

Offenders are already fighting an uphill battle when they return to the community. Current legislation tightens the reins on almost all sexual offenders' lives, and usually does so with little or no discernment regarding the actual risk levels of specific sexual offenders. There may be a small number of released sexual offenders for whom reintegration back into mainstream life should never have been recommended. We must, however, strive to find ways to safely integrate the majority of sexual offenders back into society. As change agents, we must work collaboratively with the public and media to provide better education regarding the dangers of fear-driven solutions.

Changing Ourselves

Our discussion has come full circle. By now, readers should have a greater appreciation for the complexity of the change process. In many ways our work with offenders is similar to other kinds of relationships we have in our lives. With friends, hopefully we consider their feelings and circumstances before rushing to judgments about a bad day they might be having. We unconditionally love our children and take time to carefully consider who they can play with, what foods they should eat, and how much help they will need with their schoolwork regardless of how they are acting on any given day.

We contend that each person who interacts with an offender makes a considerable impression on him that will inevitably either move the offender toward compliance and change or toward resistance and deviance. We can be empathic, motivational, and responsible supervisors of change or we can be negative, non-empathic, careless decision makers who don't consider the importance of everyday decisions in our work with these offenders. Most of us struggle somewhere in the middle on the many difficult issues we face. Our work is challenging, and surrendering to this notion helps the successful change agent move forward after making mistakes and stand humbly in success.

We can each recall times when people have asked if we get tired of working with the same old problems and same kind of people. The response given sometime surprises people: "Every case is different, every guy is unique, and that's what makes this work challenging and rewarding." If change agents are tired of their work and see all sexual offenders as the same, then we would argue that it's time for supervisors to step in and help those change agents explore their responses. Some readers might be surprised that we don't recommend a job change or the more drastic response of firing a buned-out individual. However, we must remember that the change process recommended with offenders is quite similar to the process that occurs within the change agent and among systemic partners.

One of famous sociologist Margaret Mead's most famous quotes is "Never doubt that a small group of thoughtful, concerned citizens can change the world. Indeed it is the only thing that ever has." Our concern for each other as professionals and offenders alike will be a major part of the impetus for ensuring maximum progress for offenders and our development and health as change agents.

We have included the Change Agent Inventory (see Appendix A) with this text to help change agents better understand where they are personally and professionally in their work with sexual offenders. This tool can be used individually or within staff discussions or supervision periods. There are no right or wrong answers. Mainly we include it because, in writing this book, we found it personally helpful to explore many of the areas we've included within the inventory as a way of clarifying how the work has impacted us, our coworkers, and our relationships with sexual offenders. For some professionals this will be the first time you've answered these questions, and more experienced change agents might recognize changes in how you respond now to these questions versus how you would have responded in your early days within the profession.

Resistance is normal, healthy, and not just for offenders. Engaging resistance creates potential for growth within the sexual offender, change agent, society, and our systems of care. John F. Kennedy once said, "Change is the law of life, and those who look only to the past or present are certain to miss the future." We owe it to the pioneers within our field to continue to challenge the process and look for new solutions to the significant problems of sexual abuse that still continue to damage the lives of many.

Change Agent Inventory

As change agents we must be willing to evaluate, understand, and sometimes change approaches and strategies in order to maximize our ability to facilitate change in sexual offenders. A proper evaluation begins with an investigation into our own beliefs and thinking patterns as they relate to sexual offending and sexual offenders. The following inventory is meant to be a private, self-administered exploration into the motivations, attitudes, and beliefs that influence us as change agents. The goal of this process is to illuminate the strengths that contribute to effective sexual offender change and management and at the same time highlight the obstacles that exist within change agents. In addition to facilitating personal insight and introspection, many of the questions in this inventory are intended to promote understanding of the offenders with whom we work.

Please take time to consider the following questions in depth. Write your answers in the space provided and review them at a later time. Remember this is for your own use. You may choose to keep your responses to yourself or share them with someone else (a therapist, colleague, etc). In either case, the choice is entirely yours. It is important to note, however, that the more honest you are, the more likely you are to benefit from this exercise.

PART 1: Being Evaluated

1. How do you feel about being asked to answer questions intended to evaluate the practices that you employ as well as your current beliefs and attitudes regarding sexual offenders?

_____

_____

_____

2. How would you answer the above question differently if you were going to share your answers with someone else? Why?

_____

_____

_____

_____

3. What are your thoughts about intensifying the focus on the role change agents play in offender change?

_____

_____

_____

_____

4. As a change agent, what might be revealed during this assessment that you would not want others to know? Why?

_____

_____

_____

_____

PART 2: Starting the Work

1. Did you choose to work with sexual offenders or were you assigned to this population?

_____

2. In what way did choosing or being assigned to work with sexual offenders influence the way that you initially worked with them?

_____

_____

_____

_____

3. What **beliefs or thoughts** influenced your decision to do this work?

_____

_____

_____

_____

4. What **feelings or emotional** influences informed your decision to work with this population?

_____

_____

_____

_____

5. When you first started working with sexual offenders, what **fears or concerns** did you have about working with this population?

_____

_____

_____

_____

a. What were the origins of these concerns or fears (e.g., per-
    sonal experiences, attitudes of family and friends, attitudes
    of colleagues, etc.) regarding working with sexual offenders?

    _____

    _____

    _____

    _____

b. What concerns do you currently have regarding working
    with sexual offenders?

    _____

    _____

    _____

    _____

c. Are your current concerns different from when you started
    the work? Why are they different?

    _____

    _____

    _____

    _____

6. When you first started working with sexual offenders, how did you explain or describe your work to your family and/or friends?

_____

_____

_____

_____

   a. Did you hold back information from anyone regarding your work? Why?

_____

_____

_____

_____

   b. What reaction did your friends and family have about your working with sexual offenders?

_____

_____

_____

_____

   c. How did these reactions influence you?

_____

_____

_____

7. Please write your **current** job duties as they relate to sexual
    offender change or management.

    _____

    _____

    _____

    _____

    a. How has your perception of your job duties changed since
        you began working with sexual offenders?

        _____

        _____

        _____

        _____

PART 3: Beliefs and Attitudes About Sexual Offenders

1. When you think of sexual offenders, what automatic or reflexive
    thoughts come to mind?

    _____

    _____

    _____

    _____

2. Before working with sexual offenders, what personal experiences did you, or someone close to you, have with sexual abuse and victimization? In what way did this experience influence your beliefs or attitudes about offenders?

_____

_____

_____

_____

3. Since you started working with sexual offenders, what personal experiences have you, or someone close to you, had with sexual abuse and victimization? In what way has this experience influenced your beliefs or attitudes about offenders?

_____

_____

_____

_____

4. Aside from sexual victimization, what personal experiences have shaped your attitudes and beliefs about sexual offending?

_____

_____

_____

5. If someone close to you were to be sexually victimized, in what way would your attitude toward sexual offenders change?

_____

_____

_____

_____

6. In what way does the news media or popular media (e.g., talk shows, TV dramas, etc.) influence your attitudes, beliefs, or behaviors toward sexual offenders as people?

_____

_____

_____

_____

7. In what way do your family and friends influence your beliefs and attitudes regarding sexual offenders?

_____

_____

_____

_____

8. Please write down your most negative experience while interacting with a sexual offender.

_____

_____

_____

_____

a. In what way did this experience influence your feelings, beliefs, and attitudes about offenders?

_____

_____

_____

_____

9. Please write down your most positive experience while interacting with a sexual offender.

_____

_____

_____

_____

a. In what way did this experience influence your feelings, beliefs, and attitudes about offenders?

_____

_____

_____

_____

PART 4: Beliefs and Attitudes About the Offender Change Process

1. What automatic thoughts, beliefs, and views do you hold about sexual offenders' ability to change?

_____

_____

_____

_____

    a. What informs your current beliefs and attitudes regarding offender change (e.g., personal experiences, research, colleagues, the media, etc.)?

       _____

       _____

       _____

       _____

2. How can you tell if an offender is at high risk to reoffend? What methods might you use to assess risk?

_____

_____

_____

_____

a. Can you reasonably support your assessment methods or opinion to another colleague?

_____

_____

_____

_____

3. Do you believe that sexual offenders can change or their risk of reoffense be reduced? How? Why?

_____

_____

_____

_____

a. What informs your current beliefs and attitudes (e.g., personal experiences, research, colleagues, the media, etc.) regarding a sexual offender's risk level changing?

_____

_____

_____

4. What methods do you use to affect change in sexual offenders?

_____

_____

_____

a. Can you reasonably support your methods or opinions to another colleague?

_____

_____

_____

_____

5. How can you tell if an offender is done with treatment?

_____

_____

_____

_____

a. Can you reasonably support your opinion to other colleagues?

_____

_____

_____

_____

6. What beliefs and attitudes do you hold that might promote change among sexual offenders?

_____

_____

_____

_____

7. What beliefs and attitudes do you hold that might inhibit change among sexual offenders?

_____

_____

_____

_____

8. What are your views on punishment and change?

_____

_____

_____

_____

9. In what way does the news media or popular media (e.g., talk shows, TV dramas, etc.) influence your attitudes, beliefs, or behaviors toward sexual offender change?

_____

_____

_____

_____

PART 5: Being a Change Agent

1. The causes of sexual offending are multifactorial. There are also numerous facets to sexual offender management. Effective change agents are aware of advancements in the field. How confident are you in your knowledge of current practices of sexual offender management? Please rate, on a scale of 1 to 5, your current knowledge level in each of the following fields/areas.

   Scale
   1— I have no knowledge about this field/area of sexual offender management.
   2— I know that this field/area exists and have very cursory information about its utility in sexual offender management.
   3— I have a basic knowledge of this field/area of sexual offender management and could use a refresher.
   4— I have more than a good understanding of this area of sexual offender management, but my information might not be current.
   5— I am current and knowledgeable about this field/area of sexual offender management.

   _____ Existing laws regarding sexual offenders in the community

   _____ Laws regarding sexual crimes

   _____ Victim perspectives on sexual offending

   _____ The impact of sexual crimes on victims

   _____ Sentencing practices

   _____ Issues offenders face transitioning from prison into the community

   _____ Sexual offender treatment

   _____ Sexual offender risk assessment

   _____ Sexual offender management practices in the community

   _____ Current sexual mores

   _____ Healthy sexuality

a. After completing the survey, do you feel comfortable with your current level of knowledge in each of the above areas?

_____

b. If you scored less than 5 on any of the above questions, we suggest you take steps to increase your expertise in those areas. The most effective way is to develop a plan, identify experts in the field, and collaborate with them. Please complete the following exercise to assist you in increasing your knowledge and maximize collaboration.

Existing laws regarding sexual offenders in the community

Plan:_____

Contact:_____Phone#:_____

Laws regarding sexual crimes

Plan:_____

Contact:_____Phone#:_____

Victim perspectives on sexual offending

Plan:_____

Contact:_____Phone#:_____

The impact of sexual crimes on victims

Plan:_____

Contact:_____Phone#:_____

Sentencing practices

Plan:_____

Contact:_____Phone#:_____

Issues offenders face transitioning from prison into the community

Plan:_____

Contact:_____Phone#:_____

Sexual offender treatment

Plan:_____

Contact:_____Phone#:_____

Sexual offender risk assessment

Plan:_____

Contact:_____Phone#:_____

Sexual offender management practices in the community

Plan:_____

Contact:_____Phone#:_____

Current sexual mores

Plan:_____

Contact:_____Phone#:_____

Healthy sexuality

Plan:_____

Contact:_____Phone#:_____

2. Collaboration is a crucial part of effective sexual offender management and change. What efforts have you made to collaborate with other professionals in your field or in a related field?

_____

_____

_____

_____

    a. Are there colleagues, professionals, or agencies (both in your specific field of work or a field related to offender management) with whom you consistently approach for information? Why?

_____

_____

_____

_____

    b. Are there colleagues, professionals, or agencies (both in your specific field of work or a field related to offender management) whom you avoid? Why?

_____

_____

_____

_____

3. Please review your job description listed in part 2. In what ways do you currently adhere or diverge from these job duties?

_____

_____

_____

_____

_____

   a. What is the purpose of each of these job duties?

   _____

   _____

   _____

   _____

   b. In what ways do these duties facilitate or inhibit offender change?

   _____

   _____

   _____

   _____

4. If necessary, do you have the power to change or alter your job duties to be a more effective change agent?

_____

a. What are the obstacles to making change in your job duties?

_____

_____

_____

_____

b. What strategies would be needed to institute change? (e.g., policy, legislative, etc.)

_____

_____

_____

_____

5. How are differences of opinion resolved between you and your colleagues? Please provide an example of a successfully resolved difference of opinion regarding sexual offender treatment or management and a failed difference.

_____

_____

_____

_____

_____

_____

a. Please write down the steps that led to each outcome.

Successful Resolution: _____

_____

_____

_____

Failed Resolution: _____

_____

_____

_____

6. There is little doubt that some of the strategies used in the past to manage sexual offenders have been ineffective. In order to keep up with change and effective sexual offender management, individuals and agencies need to constantly perform maintenance on their methods. Maintenance may include consulting with others in the field, remaining current with research and best practices, and performing ongoing evaluations of program efficacy. However, some individuals and agencies have difficulty recognizing the need for change, and/or believe that they lack the resources, ability, or willingness to change. In order to facilitate change it is important to assess where you (or your agency) are in terms of changing. Based on the Transtheoretical Model of Change (chapter 4), at what stage are you and/or your organization?

Please check:

_____ Stage 1: Precontemplation (Not believing that change is necessary or believing that there is no room for improvement).

_____ Stage 2: Contemplation (Believing that change or improvement might be useful but not believing that it is essential or possible. There might be some fear that change would be too painful or disruptive to the functioning of the organization).

_____ Stage 3: Preparation (There is more serious acknowledgment that change or improvement is necessary, as well as discussion and planning regarding how change and improvement might take place. Only sporadic attempts to change are made.)

_____ Stage 4: Action (Strategies are employed to make changes and increase effectiveness.)

_____ Stage 5: Maintenance (Strategies are employed to make changes and increase effectiveness. There are ongoing efforts to evaluate effectiveness and improvement.)

a. Please write, in detail, why you chose the stage that you did for yourself or your agency.

_____

_____

_____

_____

b. What strategies or interventions are needed to move to the next stage and/or facilitate ongoing maintenance?

_____

_____

_____

_____

PART 6: Continuing to Do the Work

Remaining effective as a change agent requires that you have an understanding of the meaning and purpose of the work that you do. Meaning and purpose assist us in remaining motivated and healthy. It is therefore important to regularly assess the reasons why you choose to continue working as a change agent. Some common motivations to work as a change agent with sexual offenders include: 1) playing a role in a very difficult and important social issue, 2) a healthy curiosity, 3) a connection to colleagues, 4) the satisfaction of addressing an issue that few others are willing to take on, and 5) the satisfaction of providing protection to an innumerable number of potential victims. (Clarke, 2005; English, 2005). This is clearly not an exhaustive list. What might you add?

1.   List 10 personal motivations for working with sexual offenders.

   1.

   2.

   3.

   4.

   5.

   6.

   7.

   8.

   9.

   10.

2. What are your strengths as a change agent?

_____

_____

_____

_____

3. What areas do you need to work on to improve your effectiveness as a change agent?

_____

_____

_____

_____

4. In order to maintain an enduring perspective that promotes prosocial change in offenders, change agents must engage in an ongoing process of self-care. This includes constantly attending to the influence of the work on one's professional and personal life. The influence could be either positive, negative, or both.

    Please indicate how your life has been affected by being a sexual offender change agent in the following areas:

    a. Emotional Life:

_____

_____

    b. Introspection and Thought Content:

_____

_____

c. General Trust:

_____

_____

d. Intimacy:

_____

_____

e. Sexual Attitudes or Activities:

_____

_____

f. Friendship:

_____

_____

g. Solo Activities/Hobbies:

_____

_____

h. Work Relationships:

_____

_____

i.   Physical Health:

_____

_____

j.   Happiness:

_____

_____

k.   General Mental Health:

_____

_____

l.   The Care of Your Family:

_____

_____

m. Issues Related to Personal Safety:

_____

_____

n.   Substance Use:

_____

_____

o. Attitudes Toward Children:

_____

_____

p. Attitudes Toward Adults:

_____

_____

q. Attitudes Toward the Opposite Gender:

_____

_____

r. Attitudes Toward the Prison System:

_____

_____

s. Attitudes Toward Mental Health Professionals:

_____

_____

t. Attitudes Toward Lawyers:

_____

_____

u. Attitudes Toward Governmental Policies:

_____

_____

v. Attitudes Toward the Media:

_____

_____

w. Your Long-Term Goals in Life:

_____

_____

x. Spiritual Practices:

_____

_____

y. People In Authority Roles (e.g.., teachers, police, coaches, judges, priest, etc.)

_____

_____

z. Other:

_____

_____

5. Effective change agents feel acknowledged and supported in
    their work. Is your supervisor, or a respected colleague, avail-
    able to you to discuss your thoughts, beliefs, and perceptions
    regarding the impact of working with sexual offenders?

    _____

    _____

    _____

    _____

    _____

    _____

    a. Do you feel that your supervisor and colleagues under-
        stand and support your role as change agent? Indicate the
        ways you feel supported as well as the ways that you are
        not supported.

        Feel Supported: _____

        _____

        _____

        _____

        Feel Unsupported: _____

        _____

        _____

PART 7: Additional Self-Exploration

1. How do you define the phrase "healthy sexuality"?

_____

_____

_____

_____

2. In the following section, can you describe your **most healthy** sexual thought, urge, and behavior during the past year?

> ### Examples of Sexual Thoughts, Urges, Behaviors, and Fantasies
>
> **Sexual Thoughts:** Definition: *Cognitions that include beliefs, opinions, and judgments related to sexual content.*
> For example, "For a split second when I was at work, a thought flashed through my mind: Oral sex seems so common and nonchalant among teenagers these days. What would it have been like if it was common when I was a teenager?"
>
> **Sexual Urges:** Definition: *Sexual drives or impulses that compel behaviors.*
> For example, "I was sitting in a meeting today and I felt aroused; I had a strong urge to leave the meeting and call my partner."
>
> **Sexual Behaviors:** Definition: *Physical actions that relate to, or include, sexual activity.*
> For example, "After my partner and I woke up on Sunday morning, we lay in bed and talked about our plans for the day. We started kissing each other passionately, and then we had sex."
>
> **Sexual Fantasies:** Definition: *Visual images or desires that reflect sexual interests.*
> For example, "During my class yesterday, I started daydreaming about the incredible sex I used to have with my girlfriend 5 years ago. I started to long for that to happen again."

a. Most Healthy Sexual Thought: _____

_____

_____

b. Most Healthy Sexual Urge: _____

_____

_____

c. Most Healthy Sexual Behavior: _____

_____

_____

3. In the following sections, can you describe your **least healthy** sexual thought, urge, and behavior during the past year?

a. Least Healthy Sexual Thought: _____

_____

_____

b. Least Healthy Sexual Urge: _____

_____

_____

c. Least Healthy Sexual Behavior: _____

_____

_____

4. How do your answers about your sexual thoughts, urges, and behaviors influence your work as a sexual offender change agent?

_____

_____

_____

_____

5. Is there life outside of your work? Please list 10 interests, hobbies, or activities that you engage in that are **NOT** related to sexual offender change or management.

Activity	Frequency	
	x per week	x per month
1.		
2.		
3.		
4.		
5.		
6.		
7.		
8.		
9.		
10.		

6. What are your long-term plans in terms of working with sexual offenders?

_____

_____

_____

_____

7. What are your long-term goals in life?

_____

_____

_____

_____

8. Are your long-term goals as a sexual offender change agent and your long-term life goals compatible?

_____

_____

_____

_____

PART 8: Summary

1. What was your over all experience of this inventory?

_____

_____

_____

_____

_____

_____

_____

_____

_____

2. What would you add?

_____

_____

_____

_____

_____

_____

_____

_____

_____

_____

References

Abel, G., Jordan, A., & Hand, C. (May, 2001). Classification models of child molesters utilizing the Abel Assessment for child sexual abuse interest. *Child Abuse & Neglect, 25*, 703-718.

Abel, G., Mittelman, M., Becker, J., Rathner, J., & Rouleau, J. (1988). Predicting child molesters' response to treatment. In R. Prentky & V. Quinsey (Eds.), *Annals of the New York Academy of Science* (pp. 223-235). New York: New York Academy of Science.

Addison, R. (Summer, 1977). The racially different patient in individual and group psychotherapy. *Journal of Contemporary Psychotherapy, 9(1)*, 39-40.

Ahlmeyer, S., Heil, P., McKee, B., & English, K. (2000). The impact of polygraphy on admissions of victims and offenses in adult sexual offenders. *Sexual Abuse: A Journal of Research and Treatment, 12(2)*, 123-138.

Ajzen, I. (1988). *Attitudes, personality, and behavior* (pp. xiv, 175). Home-wood, IL: Dorsey Press.

Ajzen I. (1991). The theory of planned behavior. *Organizational Behavior and Human Decision Processes, 50*, 179-211

Allen, B., & Brekke, K. (1996). Transference and counter-transference in treating incarcerated sex offenders. *Journal of Offender Rehabilitation, 23*, 99-109.

Allen, H., & Simonsen, C. (1995). *Corrections in America: An introduction* (7th ed.). Clifford Hills, NJ. Prentice Hall.

American Psychiatric Association. (2002). *The diagnostic and statistical manual of mental disorders (DSM-IV-Tr)*. Washington, DC: Author.

American Psychological Association. (APA). (2002). *The principles of psychologists and code of conduct*. Retrieved June 9, 2006 from http://www.apa.org/ethics/code2002.pdf

American Psychology Law Society, APA Division 41. (2006). *Specialty guidelines for forensic psychology*. Second official draft, released Jan. 11, 2006. Retrieved June 9, 2006 from http://www.ap-ls.org/links/SGFP%20January%202006.pdf .

Andrews, D., & Bonta, J. (1995). The Level of Service Inventory–Revised. Toronto, Ontario, Canada: Multi-Health Systems.

Andrews, D., & Bonta, J. (2003). *The psychology of criminal conduct* (3rd ed.). Cincinnati, OH: Anderson.

Arkowitz, H. (2002). Toward an interrogative perspective on resistance to change. *Journal of Clincial Psychology, 58,* 219-227.

Asch, S. (1940). Studies in the principles of judgments and attitudes: II. Determination of judgments by group and by ego standards. *Journal of Social Psychology, 12,* 433-465.

Association for the Treatment of Sexual Abusers. (ATSA). (2000, March 11). *The effective legal management of juvenile sex offenders.* Retrieved from http://www.atsa.com/ppjuvenile.html

Association for the Treatment of Sexual Abusers. (2004). *ATSA practice standards and guidelines for the evaluation, treatment and management of adult male sexual abusers* (p. 20). Retrieved from http://atsa.com/pubSoT.html# ATSA. Beaverton, OR.

Attorney General of the State of California. (2004). *Report to the legislature on the California sex offender information and Megan's Law.* Retrieved September 30, 2005 from http://ag.ca.gov/megan/pdf/megan_leg_rpto4.pdf .

Baron, R., & Byrne, D. (1991). *Social psychology: Understanding human interaction* (6th ed.). Boston, MA: Allen & Bacon.

Baumeister, R., Dewall C., Ciarocco N., & Twenge, J. (2005). Social exclusion impairs self-regulation. *Journal of Personality and Social Psychology. 88(4),* 589-604.

Baumeister, R., Twenge, J., & Nuss, C. (2002). Effects of social exclusion on cognitive processes: Anticipated aloneness reduces intelligent thought. *Journal of Personality and Social Psychology, 83,* 817-827.

Baumeister, R., & Scher, S. (1988). Self-defeating behavior patterns among normal individuals: Review and analysis of common self-destructive tendencies. *Psychological Bulletin, 104,* 3-22.

Becker, H. (1963). *Outsiders: Studies in the sociology of deviance* (p.95). New York: The Free Press.

Beech, A., Erikson, M., Friendship, C., & Ditchfield, J. (2001). *A six-year follow-up of men going through probation-based sex offender treatment programmes (Findings #144).* London, U.K.

Beech, A., Fisher, D., & Thornton, D. (2003). Risk assessment of sex offenders. *Professional Psychology: Research and Practice, 34(4),* 339-352.

Berger, P., & Luckmann, T. (1966). *The social construction of reality*. New York: Anchor Books.

Berliner, L. (1998). Sex offenders: Policy and practice. *Northwestern University Law Review, 92,* 1203-1229.

Bernstein, H. (1981). Survey of threats and assaults directed toward psychotherapists. *American Journal of Psychotherapy, 25(4),* 542-549.

Blanchard, G. (1998). *The difficult connection: The therapeutic relationship in sex offender treatment*. Brandon, VT: Safer Society Press.

Bodenhausen, G. (1988). Stereotypic biases in social decision making and memory: Testing process models of stereotype use. *Journal of Personality and Social Psychology, 55,* 726-737.

Boechler, S. (1998, June). *Sex offenders as others: The distancing of offenders, the benefits and the impact*. Paper presented at the 59th annual convention of the Canadian Psychological Association, Edmonton, Alberta.

Brake, S., & Shannon, D. (1997). Using pretreatment to increase admission in sex offenders. In B. Schwartz & H. Cellini (Eds.), *The sex offender: New insights, treatment innovations and legal developments* (vol II, pp. 5-16). Kingston, NJ: Civic Research Institute.

Brehm, J. (1966). *A theory of psychological reactance*. New York: Academic Press.

Briere, J. & Spinazzola J. (2005). Phenomenology and psychological assessment of complex posttraumatic states. *Journal of Traumatic Stress, 18(5),* 401-412.

Browne, K., Foreman, L., & Middleton, D. (1998, November-December). Predicting treatment drop-out in sex offenders. *Child Abuse Review, Vol 7(6). Special issue: Working with sex offenders*. pp. 402-419.

Brownell, K., Marlatt, G., Lichtenstein, E., & Wilson, E. (1986). Understanding and preventing relapse. *American Psychologist, 41,* 765-782.

Bruschke, J., & Loges, W. (2004). *Free press vs. fair trials: Examining publicity's role in trial outcomes* (p. 189). Mahwah, NJ:Lawrence Erlbaum Associates.

Buckley, K., Winkel, R., & Leary, M. (2004). Reactions to acceptance and rejection: Effects of level and sequence of relational evaluation. *Journal of Experimental Social Psychology, 40,* 14-28.

Bumby, K. (1996). Assessing the cognitive distortions of child molesters and rapists: Development and validation of the MOLEST and RAPE scales. *Sexual Abuse: A Journal of Research and Treatment, 8*, 37–54.

Butcher, J., Dahlstrom,W., Graham, J., Tellegen, A., & Kaemmer, B. (1989). *Minnesota Multiphasic Personality Inventory–2 (MMPI-2): Manual for administration and scoring.* Minneapolis: University of Minnesota Press.

Cacioppo, J., Hawkley, L., & Berntson, G. (2003). The anatomy of loneliness. *Current Directions in Psychological Science, 12*, 71-74.

California Coalition on Sexual Offending (CCOSO). (2002). *Guidelines for Outpatient Treatment of Adult Sexual Offenders © California Coalition on Sexual Offending (CCOSO)*, June 13, 2002. Retrieved from http://ccoso.org/papers/adulttreatment.pdf

California Current Population Survey. (2005). State of California, Department of Finance California Current Population Survey, (2005) California Current Population Survey. Report: March 2004. Sacramento, California. Retrieved from http://www.dof.ca.gov/HTML/DEMOGRAP/Reports/CPS/CPS_Extended_3-04.pdf

Cameron, J., Pierce, W., & So, S. (2004, Fall). Rewards, task difficulty, and intrinsic motivation: A test of learned industriousness theory. *Alberta Journal of Educational Research, 50(3)*, 317-320.

Campbell, T. (1994, December). Mental health law: Institutionalised discrimination. *Australian and New Zealand Journal of Psychiatry, 28(4)*, 554-559.

Caraulia, A., & Steiger, L. (1997). *Nonviolent crisis intervention.* Brookfield, WI: CPI Publishing.

Carone, S., & LaFleur, N. (2000, April). The effect of adolescent sex offender abuse history on counselor attitudes. *Journal of Addictions & Offender Counseling, 20(2)*, 56, 3 charts.

Carver, C., & Scheier, M. (1982). Control theory: A useful conceptual framework for personality-social, clinical and health psychology. *Psychological Bulletin, 92*, 111-135.

Cassell, J. (1974). The function of humor in the counseling process. *Rehabilitation Counseling Bulletin, 17*, 240-245.

Center for Sexual Offender Management. (2002, August). *Myths and facts about sex offenders.* Washington, DC: Author.

Cesaroni, C. (2001). Releasing sex offenders into the community through "circles of support"–A means of reintegrating "the worst of the worst." *Journal of Offender Rehabilitation, 34,* 85-98.

Clarke, J. (2005). *Impact issues for treatment providers.* ATSA 24th Annual Research and Treatment Conference. Salt Lake City, UT. November 16-19, 2005.

Clarke, J., & Roger, D. (2005, In preparation). *The construction and validation of a new scale to assess the impact on treatment providers working therapeutically with sexual offenders.* Presented at ATSA 24th Annual Research and Treatment Conference. Salt Lake City, UT. November 16-19, 2005.

Cohen, S. (2001). *States of denial: Knowing about atrocities and suffering* (p. 5 & 21). Cambridge, UK: Polity. Malden, MA: Blackwell.

Connell, J., Kubisch, A., Schorr, L., & Weiss, C. (Eds.). (1995). *New approaches to evaluating community initiatives: vol 1. Concepts, methods, and contexts.* New York: Aspen Institute.

Craig, L. (2005, May). The impact of training on attitudes toward sex offenders. *Journal of Sexual Aggression, 11(2),* 197-207.

Cullari, S. (1996). *Treatment resistance.* Needham, MA:Allyn & Bacon.

Cullen, F., Clark, G., Cullen, J., & Mathers, R. (1985, September). Attribution, salience, and attitudes toward criminal sanctioning. *Criminal Justice and Behavior, 12(3),* 305-331.

D'Amora, D. & Burns-Smith, G. (1999). Partnering in response to sexual violence: How offender treatment and victim advocacy can work together in response to sexual violence. *Sexual Abuse: A Journal of Research and Treatment, 11,* 293-304.

Danner, A. (2001). Constructing a hierarchy of crimes in international criminal law sentencing. *Virginia Law Review, 87,* 415.

Dewhurst, A., & Nielsen, K. (1999). A resiliency-based approach to working with sexual offenders. *Sexual Addiction & Compulsivity, 6(4),* 271-279.

DiClemente, C. (2005). The transtheoretical approach: Crossing traditional boundaries of therapy. *Journal of Addictions Nursing, 16(1-2), 5-12. Special issue: Contributions of the Transtheoretical Model: 1984-2004.* [Original Journal Article: Prochaska, J., & DiClemente, C. (1984). Homewood, IL: Dow Jones-Irwin.]

DiClemente, C., Connors, G., & Donovan, D. (2001). *Substance abuse treatment and the stages of change: Selecting and planning interventions*. New York: Guilford Press.

Dolan, B. & Coid, J. (1993). *Psychopathic and anti-social personality disorders: Treatment and research issues*. London, UK: Gaskell.

Dollard, J., & Miller, N. (2004). In E. Knowles & J. Linn, *Resistance and persuasion* (p.119). Mahwah, NJ: Lawrence Erlbaum Associates.

Drapeau, M., Korner, A., & Brunet, L. (2004). When the goals of the therapist and patients clash: A study of pedophiles in treatment. *Journal of Offender Rehabilitation, 38*, 69-80.

Edmunds, S. (1988). *Impact: Working with sexual abusers*. Brandon, VT: Safer Society Press.

Edmunds, S. (1997). The personal impact of working with sex offenders. In S. Edmunds (Ed.), *Impact: Working with sexual abusers* (pp. 11-29). Brandon, VT: Safer Society Press.

Elbogen, E., Patry, M., & Scalora, M. (2003). The impact of community notification laws on sex offender treatment attitudes. *International Journal of Law & Psychiatry, 26*, 207-219.

Ellerby, L. (1998). *Providing clinical services to sex offenders: Burnout, compassion fatigue and moderating variables* (Unpublished Doctoral Dissertation, University of Manitoba, 1998). Dissertation Abstracts International Section B: The Sciences & Engineering. 1999 May Vol. 59 (10 – B) 5575 cited by Clarke, J. (2005). Impact Issues for Treatment Providers. ATSA 24th Annual Research and Treatment Conference. Salt Lake City, UT: November 16-19, 2005.

Ellis, A. (1977). Fun as psychotherapy. In A. Ellis & R. Grieger, *Handbook of rational-emotive therapy* (p. 262-270). New York: Springer.

Emerson, S. (1988). Female student counselors and child sexual abuse: Theirs and their clients'. *Counselor Education and Supervision, 28*, 15-21

English, K. (1998). The containment approach: An aggressive strategy for the community management of adult sex offenders. *Psychology, Public Policy and Law, 4*, 218-235.

English, K. (2005). *Managing job impact: Research findings and recommendations*. ATSA 24th Annual Research and Treatment Conference. Salt Lake City, UT. November 17, 2005.

English, K., Jones L., Krauth B., & Pullen S. (1996). *A model process: A containment approach* (pp. 1-46). Washington, DC: U.S. Department of Justice Washington.

Ennis, L. & Horne, S. (2003). Prediciting psychological distress in sex offender therapist. *Sexual Abuse: A Journal of Research and Treatment, 15*, 149-157.

Epps, K. (1993). A survey of experience, training and working practices among staff working with adolescent sex offenders in secure units. In N. Clark & G. Stephenson (Eds.), *Sexual offenders: Context, assessment and treatment* (pp. 19-26). Leicester, UK: The British Psychological Society.

Farkas, M. (1999). Correctional officer attitudes toward inmates and working with inmates in a "get tough" era. *Journal of Criminal Justice, 27*, 495-506.

Fedoroff, J. & Moran, B. (1997). Myths and misconceptions about sex offenders. *Canadian Journal of Human Sexuality, 6*, 263-176.

Fenster, A. (1996). Group therapy as an effective treatment modality for people of color. *International Journal of Group Psychotherapy, 46*, 399-416.

Fernandez, Y. & Serran, B., (2002) Characteristics of an effective sex offedner therapist. In B. Schwartz & H. Cellini (Eds.), *The sex offender: New insights, treatment innovations and legal developments* (Vol. IV, p. 91). Kingston, NJ: Civic Research Institute.

Ferrell, J. (1998). Criminalising popular culture. In F. Bailey & D. Hale (Eds.), *Popular culture, crime and justice* (p. 71–84), Boston, MA: Northeastern University Press.

Filkins, J. (1997, January). The interactive effects of crime prototype and criminal stereotype on juridical decisions. Dissertation Abstracts International: Section B: *The Sciences and Engineering*, 57(7-B), 4780.

Finkelhor, D., Gomez-Schwartz, G. & Horowitz, J. (1984). Professionals' responses. In D. Finkelhor (Ed.), *Child sexual abuse: New theory and research* (pp. 200-215). New York: Free Press.

Frenkel-Brunswik, E., (1954). Social Tensions and the Inhibitions of Thought. *Social Problems, 2*, 75.

Freud, S. (1895). Project for a scientific psychology (p. 269-270). In *Standard edition of the complete psychological works of Sigmund Freud*. London: Hogarth Press.

Freud, S. (1900). *The interpretation of dreams* (p.72 & 517). London: Hogarth Press.

Freud, S. (1953). (J. Strachey, ed. and trans.) *Standard edition of the complete psychological works of Sigmund Freud.* VII, London, UK: Hogarth Press.

Furby, L., Weinrott, M., & Blackshaw, L. (1989). Sex offender recidivism: A review. *Psychological Bulletin, 00332909,* January 1, 1989, Vol. 105, Issue 1

Gabor T. (1994). *Everybody does it! Crime by the public.* Toronto: University of Toronto Press.

Garfinkel, H. (1956, March) *The American Journal of Sociology, 61(5),* 420-424.

Gately, L. & Stabb, S. (2005). Psychology students' training in the management of potentially violent clients. *Professional Psychology: Research and Practice, 36,* 681-687.

Gendreau, P., Little, T., & Goggin, C. (1996). A meta-analysis of the predictors of adult recidivism: What works! *Criminology, 34,* 575-607.

Gershoff, E. (2002). Corporal punishment by parents and associated child behaviors and experiences: A meta-analytic and theoretical review. *Psychological Bulletin, 128,* 539-579.

Gerstley, L. , McLellan, A., Alterman, A., Woody, G., Luborsky, L., & Prout, M. (1989). Ability to form an alliance with the therapist: A possible marker of prognosis for patients with antisocial personality disorder. *American Journal of Psychiatry, 146,* 508-512

Goldstein, A. (2001). *Reducing resistance: Methods for enhancing openness to change.* Champagne, IL: Research Press Publications.

Gottfredson, M., & Hirschi, T. (1990). *A general theory of crime.* Stanford, CA: Stanford University Press.

Greenson, R. (1967). The working alliance and the transference neurosis. *Psychoanalysis Quaterly, 34,* 155-181.

Gross, S., Jacoby, K., Matheson, D., Montgomery, N., & Patil, S. (2004). *Exonerations in the Untied States, 1989 through 2003: Executive summary.* A brief posted on the International Justice Project at http://www.internationaljusticeproject.org/ and http://www.law.umich.edu/newsandinfo/exonerations-in-us.pdf

Grubin, D., & Wingate, S. (1996) Sexual offense recidivism: Prediction versus understanding. *Criminal Behaviour and Mental Health, 6,* 349-359. Whurr Publishers Ltd.

Guy, J., Brown, C., & Poelstra, P. (1990). Who gets attacked? A national survey of patient violence directed at psychologists in clinical practice. *Professional Psychology: Research and Practice, 21,* 493-495.

Haaven, J., & Coleman, E. (2000). Treatment of the developmentally disabled sex offender. In D. Laws, S. Hudson, & T. Ward (Eds.) *Remaking relapse prevention with sex offenders: A sourcebook* (pp. 369-388). Thousand Oaks, CA: Sage.

Haley, J. (1973). *Uncommon therapy: The psychiatric techniques of Milton H. Erickson, M.D.* (p. 313). Oxford, England: W. W. Norton.

Hall, S., Critchley, C., Jefferson, T., Clarke, J., & Roberts, B. (1978). *Policing the crisis.* London: Macmillan.

Hanson, R. (2000). *The effectiveness of treatment for sexual offenders: Report of the Association for the Treatment of Sexual Abusers Collaborative Data Research Committee.* Presentation at the Association for the Treatment of Sexual Abusers 19th Annual Research and Treatment Conference, San Diego, CA.

Hanson, R., & Bussière, M. (1998). Predicting Relapse: A meta-analysis of sexual offender recidivism studies. *Journal of Consulting and Clinical Psychology,* Edited by the American Psychological Association, 66(2), 348-362.

Hanson, R., & Harris, A. (2000, February). Where should we intervene?: Dynamic predictors of sexual assault recidivism. *Criminal Justice & Behavior, 27(1),* 6-35.

Hanson, R., Morton-Bourgon, K. (2004). Predictors of sexual recidivism: An updated meta-analysis 2004-02 , Public Safety and Emergency Preparedness Canada, Public Works and Government Services Canada Cat. No.: PS3-1/2004-2E- ISBN: 0-662-36397-3

Hanson, R. & Slater, S. (1993). Reactions to motivational accounts of child molesters. *Journal of Child Sexual Abuse, 2,* 43-59.

Hare, R. (1991). *The Psychopathy Checklist—Revised manual.* Toronto, Ontario, Canada: Multi-Health Systems.

Harré, R. (1980). *Social being: A theory for social psychology.* Totowa, NJ: Littlefield, Adams & Co.

Healthfield, S. (2005). *Building successful work teams.* Retrieved from
http://humanresources.about.com/mbiopage.htm

Heidegger, M. (1971). *On the way to language.* San Francisco, CA: Harper
Row.

Henry, W., Strupp, H., Schacht, T., & Gaston, L. (1994). Psychodynamic
approaches. In A. Bergin & S. Garfield (Eds.), *Handbook of psychotherapy and behavior change* (4th ed., pp. 467–508). New York: Wiley.

Hess, A. & Weiner, I. (1999). *The handbook of forensic psychology (2nd ed).*
New York: Wiley.

Hindman, J., & Peters, J. (2001). Polygraph testing leads to better understanding adult and juvenile sex offenders. *Federal Probation, 65(3),* 8-15.

Hogue, T. (1993). Attitudes towards prisoners and sexual offenders. In N.
Clark & G. Stephenson (Eds.), *Sexual offenders: Context, assessment
and treatment* (pp. 27-32). Leicester, UK: The British Psychological
Society.

Hogue, T. (1995). Training multi-disciplinary teams to work with sex offenders. *Psychology, Crime and Law, 1,* 227-235.

Horowitz, L., Krasnoperova, E., Tatar, D., Hansen, M., Person, E., Galvin,
K., & Nelson, K. (2001). The way to console may depend on the goal:
Experimental studies of social support. *Journal of Experimental Social
Psychology, 37.*

Horvath, A. (2000). The therapeutic relationship: From transference to
alliance. *Journal of Clinical Psychology, 56,* 163-173.

Hudson, S., & Ward, T. (1997). Intimacy, loneliness, and attachment in
sexual offenders. *Journal of Interpersonal Violence, 12,* 323-339.

Hunt, R. (1993). Neurological patterns of aggression. *Journal of Emotional
and Behavioral Problems, 2,* 14–20.

Huot, S. (2002, October). *Recidivism, recidivism, recidivism! An update of
several Minnesota recidivism studies.* Paper presented at the 21st annual meeting of the Association for the Treatment of Sexual Abusers,
Montréal, QC.

Huxham, C. (Ed.) (1996). *Creating collaborative advantage.* London, UK:
Sage.

Imhoff & Associates. (1998). Youth on trial: Defending a juvenile sex offender. *Los Angeles Daily Journal, 111(79),* Friday, April 4, 1998. Re-
printed on http://www.molestationattorney.com/pages/defending.
asp

Ireland, J. (2004). Nature, extent, and causes of bullying among personality-disordered patients in a high-security hospital. *Aggressive Behavior, 30(3)*, 229-242.

Jacobs, J., Horne-Moyer, L., & Jones, R. (2004). The effectiveness of critical incident stress debriefing with primary and secondary trauma victims. *International Journal of Emergency Mental Health, 6*, 5-14.

Janis, I., & Mann, L. (1977). *Decision making: A psychological analysis of conflict, choice and commitment.* New York: Free Press.

Jenkins, P. (1998). *Moral panic: Changing concepts of the child molester in modern America* (p. 120). New Haven, CT: Yale University Press.

Jurik, N. (1985). Individual and organizational determinants of correctional officer attitudes toward inmates. *Criminology, 23*, 523-539.

Jurik, N., & Winn, R. (1987). Describing correctional security dropouts and rejects: An individual or organizational profile? *Criminal Justice and Behavior, 14(1)*, 5-25.

Kahn, M. (1995). *The tao of conversation.* San Luis Obispo, CA: New Harbinger Publishing.

Kaplan, S., & Wheeler, E. (1983). Survival skills for working with potentially violent clients. *Social Casework, 64*, 339-346.

Katz, R., & Allen, T. (1982). Investigating the Not Invented Here (NIH) Syndrome: a look at the performance, tenure and communication patterns of 50 R&D project groups. *R&D Management. 12*, 7-19.

Kaufman, A., & Kaufman, N. (1994). *Kaufman Functional Academic Skills Test (K-FAST).* AGS Publishing, 4201 Woodland Road, Circle Pines, MN 55014

Kear-Colwell, J., & Pollock, P. (1997, March). Motivation or confrontation: Which approach to the child sex offender? *Criminal Justice and Behavior, 24(1)*, 20-33.

Kibel, H. (1972). International conflicts as resistance in group psychotherapy. *American Journal of Psychotherapy, 26*, 555-562

Kiely, J., & Pankhurst, H. (1998). Violence faced by staff in a learning disability service. *Disability and Rehabilitation, 20*, 81–89.

Kiernan, R., Mueller, J., Langston, J., & van Dyke, C. (1987). The Neurobehavioral Cognitive Status Examination: A brief but differentiated approach to cognitive assessment. *Annals of Internal Medicine 107*, 481-485. Cognistat (Neurobehavioral Cognitive Status Examination). Available through PAR. www.parinc.com

King, L. (2005). *Public opinion & the judicial system: How does public opinion legitimately influence the course of justice?* Institute Of Justice Studies. Retrieved August, 2005 from http://www.justice.net.au/publications/Mc_book/public.pdf.

Kleespies, P. (1998). *Emergencies in mental health practice: Evaluation and management.* New York: Guilford Press.

Knowles, E. & Linn, J. (2004). *Resistance and persuasion* (pp. 235-257). Mahwah, NJ: Lawrence Erlbaum Associates, Publishers.

Kokish, R., Levenson, J., & Blasingame, G. (2005, April). Post-conviction sex offender polygraph examination: Client reported perceptions of utility and accuracy. *Sexual Abuse: A Journal of Research and Treatment, 17(2)*, 211-221.

Kottler, J. (1992). *Compassionate therapy: Working with difficult clients* (p. 13). San Francisco, CA: Jossey-Bass.

Kottler, J. (1994). Working with difficult group members. *Journal for Specialists Group Work, 19*, 3-10.

Kottler, J., Sexton, T., & Whiston, S. (1994). *The heart of healing: Relationships in therapy.* San Francisco, CA: Jossey-Bass.

Kottler, J. & Uhlemann, M. (1994). Working with difficult clients: A neglected area of study. *Canadian Journal of Counseling, 28*, 5-12.

Krosnik, J. & Petty, R. (1995). *Attitude strength: Anticedants and consequences.* Mahwah, NJ: Erlbaum.

Lamb, D., Catanzaro, S., & Moorman, A. (2003). Psychologists reflect on their sexual relationships with clients, supervisees, and students: Occurrence, impact, rationales, and collegial intervention. *Professional Psychology: Research and Practice, 34*, 102-107.

Langs, R. (1981). *Resistances and interventions: The nature of therapeutic work.* New York: Jason Aronson Publishers.

Lariviére, M. & Robinson, D. (1996). *Attitudes of federal correctional officers towards offenders.* Research (Report No-44). Research and Statistics Branch. Correctional Service of Canada.

Lea, S., Auburn, T., & Kibblewhite, K. (1999). Working with sex offenders: The perceptions and experiences of professionals and paraprofessionals. *International Journal of Offender Therapy & Comparative Criminology, 43*, 103-119.

Lemert, E. (1951). *Social pathology: Systematic approaches to the study of sociopathic behavior* (p. 75). New York: McGraw Hill.

Lerman, H. (1988). The psychoanlytic legacy: From when we came (p. 37-54). In L. Walker, *Child sexual absue*. New York: Springer.

Levy, R. (1997). The transtheoretical model of change: An application to bulimia nervosa. *Psychotherapy: Theory, Research, Practice, and Training, 34*, 278-285.

Lieb, R. & Matson, S. (1998, Sept). *Sexual predetor commitment laws in the United States: 1998 update*. Washington State Institute for Public Policy.

Lieb, R., Quinsey, V., & Berliner, L. (1998). Sexual predators and social policy. *Crime and Justice, 23*, 43.

Lilienfeld, S., Van Volkenburg, C., Larnz, C., & Akiskal, H. (1986). The relationship of histrionic personality disorder to antisocial personality and somatization disorders. *American Journal of Psychiatry, 143*, 718-722.

Locke, E., Shaw, K., & Saari, L. (1981, July). Goal setting and task performance: 1969-1980. *Psychological Bulletin, 90(1)*, 125-152.

Long, C., (2002, January). The impact of motivation on sexual offenders' progress in treatment. Dissertation Abstracts International Section A: *Humanities and Social Sciences, 63(6-A)*, 2146.

Looman, J., Abracen, J., & Nicholaichuk, T. (2000). Recidivism among treated sexual offenders and matched controls: Data from the Regional Treatment Centre (Ontario). *Journal of Interpersona Violence, 15*, 279-290.

Lott, B. & Saxon, S. (2002). The influence of ethnicity, social class, and context on judgments about U.S. women. *The Journal of Social Psychology, 142*, 481-499.

Lynch, J. (1979). *The broken heart: The medical consequences of loneliness*. New York, NY: Basic Books.

Maletzky, B. (1991). *Treating the sexual offender*. Newbury Park, CA: Sage.

Maletzky, B. & Steinhauser, C. (1998). The Portland sexual abuse clinic. In W. Marshall, Y. Fernandez, S. Hudson, & T. Ward (Eds.), *Sourcebook of treatment programs of sexual offenders* (pp. 105-116). New York: Plenum Press.

Manning, P. (1998). Media loops. In F. Bailey & D. Hale (Eds), *Popular culture, crime and justice* (p. 25-39). Belmont: Wadsworth

Marques, J., Day, D., Wiederanders, M., & Nelson, C. (2002, October). *Main effects and beyond: New findings from California's Sex Offender Treatment & Evaluation Project (SOTEP)*. Paper presented at the 21st annual conference of the ATSA, Montreal, QC.

Marques, J., Wiederanders, M., & Day, D. (2005, January). Effects of a relapse prevention program on sexual recidivism: Final results from California's Sex Offender Treatment and Evaluation Project (SOTEP). *Sexual Abuse: Journal of Research and Treatment, 17(1)*, 79-107.

Marshall, L., & Marshall, W. (2005, November). A motivational preparatory program for sexual offenders: Description and outcome. Presented at the 24th Annual Treatment and Research Conference of the Association for the Treatment of Sexual Abusers, November 16-19 2005. Salt Lake City, UT.

Marshall, W. (1993). The role of attachment, intimacy, and loneliness in the etiology and maintenance of sexual offending. *Sexual and Marital Therapy, 8,* 109-121.

Marshall, W., Fernandez, Y., Serran, G., Mulloy, R., Thornton, D., Mann, R., & Anderson, D. (2003). Process variables in the treatment of sexual offenders: A review of the relevant literature. *Aggression and Violent Behavior 8 (2)*, 205-234.

Marshall, W., Jones, R., Ward, T., Johnston, P. & Barbaree, H. (1991). Treatment outcome with sex offenders. *Clinical Psychology Review, 11,* 465-485.

Marshall, W. & Marshall, L. (2005, November). *Motivational and thera-peutic processes in the treatment of sexual offenders.* ATSA 24th Annual Research and Treatment Conference. Salt Lake City: Nov 16-19, 2005.

Marshall, W., Thornton, D., Marshall, L., Fernandez, Y., & Mann, R. (2001). Treatment of sexual offenders who are in categorical denial: A pilot project. *Sexual Abuse: A Journal of Research and Treatment, 13,* 205-215.

Marshall, W., Ward, T., & Mann, R. (2005, September). Working positively with sexual offenders: Maximizing the effectiveness of treatment. *Journal of Interpersonal Violence, 20(9),* 1096-1114.

Maruna, S. (2001). *Making good: How ex-convicts reform and rebuild their lives.* Washington, DC: American Psychological Association.

McConnaughy, E., Prochaska, J., & Velicer, W. (1983). Stages of change in psychotherapy: Measurement and sample profiles. *Psychotherapy: Theory, Research, and Practice, 20,* 368-375.

McGowan, M. (2003). *Who is the predator? How law enforcement, mental health (forensic and non-forensic), and the general public stereotype sex offenders.* Unpublished doctoral dissertation. California School of Professional Psychology/Alliant International University, Fresno, CA.

McGrath, R., Cumming, G., & Holt, J. (2002, January). Collaboration among sex offender treatment providers and probation and parole officers: The beliefs and behaviors of treatment providers. *Sexual Abuse: A Journal of Research and Treatment, 14(1)*, 49-65.

McGrath, R., Cumming, G., Livingston, J., & Hoke, S. (2003). Outcome of a treatment program for adult sex offenders: From prison to community. *Journal of Interpersonal Violence, 18*, 3-17.

McGrath, R., Hoke, S., & Vojtisek, J. (1998). Cognitive-behavioral treatment of sex offenders: A treatment comparison and long-term follow-up study. *Criminal Justice and Behavior, 25 (2)*, 203-225

McNiel, D. (1998). Empirically based clinical evaluation and management of the potentially violent patient (pp. 95-116). In P. Kleespies (Ed.), *Emergencies in mental health practice: Evaluation and management.* New York: Guilford Press.

Melamed, Y., & Szor, H. (1999, September). The therapist and the patient: Coping with noncompliance. *Comprehensive Psychiatry, 40(5)*, 391-395.

Merton, R. (1968). *Social theory and social structure. (2nd ed)*. New York: The Free Press.

Messer, S. (2002). A psychodynamic perspective on resistance in psychotherapy: Viva la resistance. *Journal of Clinical Psychology, 58*, 157-163.

Milam, J., Sussman, S., Ritt-Olsen, A., & Clyde, W. (2000). Perceived invulnerably and cigarette smoking among adolescents. *Addictive Behaviors, 25*, 71-80.

Miller, W. (1985). Motivation for treatment. *Psychological Bulletin, 98*, 84-107.

Millon, T. (1987). *Manual for the MCMI-II, 2nd edition*. Minneapolis, MN: National Computer Systems

Mischel, W. (1996). From good intentions to willpower. In P. Gollwitzer & J. Bargh (Eds.), *The psychology of action* (pp. 197–218). New York, NY: Guilford Press.

Moyers, T., Miller, W., & Hendrickson, S. (2005, August). How does motivational interviewing work? Therapist interpersonal skill predicts client involvement within motivational interviewing sessions. *Journal of Consulting and Clinical Psychology, 73(4)*, 590-598.

Murphy, C., & Baxter, V. (1997). Motivating batterers to change in the treatment context. *Journal of Interpersonal Violence, 12(4)*, 607-619.

Myers, D. (1992). *The pursuit of happiness*. New York: Morrow.

Myers, P. (2000). Reconsidering communicative psychoanalysis. *International Journal of Psychotherapy, 5(3)*, 203-18.

Neale, S. (2005, June). *A police perspective*. Retrieved October 15, 2005 from www.quaker.org.uk.

New, C. (2003). A chain of consequences: An information processing model of pretrial prejudgment. Dissertation Abstracts International: Section B: *The Sciences and Engineering, 64(5-B)*, 2443.

Newell, T. (2005, June). *Foreword*. Retrieved October 15, 2005 from www.quaker.org.uk.

Newman, C. (2002). A cognitive perspective on resistance n psychotherapy. *Journal of Clinical Psychology, 58*, 165-174.

Nicholaichuk, T., Gordon, A., Gu, D., & Wong, S. (2000). Outcome of an institutional sexual offender treatment program: A comparison between treated and matched untreated offenders. *Sexual Abuse: A Journal of Research and Treatment, 12*, 139-153.

Nichols, H., & Molinder, I. (1984). *The Multiphasic Sex Inventory Manual.* (Available from Nichols and Molinder, 437 Bowes Drive, Tacoma, WA 98466).

Nigg, J. (2001). Is ADHD a disinhibitory disorder? *Psychological Bulletin, 127*, 571-598.

Northey, W. (1999, August). The use of coercion in the treatment of incarcerated juveniles adjudicated on sexual offenses: Consequences and implications. *Child & Adolescent Social Work Journal, 16(4)*, 259-275.

Occupational Safety and Health Organization. (2004). *Preventing workplace violence for health care & social service workers*. Retrieved January 15, 2006 from http://www.osha.gov/Publications/osha3148.pdf

Ogloff, J., Wong, S., & Greenwood, A. (1990, Spring). Treating criminal psychopaths in a therapeutic community program. *Behavioral Sciences and the Law, 8(2)*, 181-190.

Oldham, J., Skodol, A., Kellman, H., Hyler, S., Rosnick, L., & Davies, M. (1992). Diagnosis of DSM-III-R personality disorders by two structured interviews: Patterns of comorbidity. *American Journal of Psychiatry, 149*, 213-220.

Parke, R. (2002). Punishment revisited—science, values, and the right question: Comment on Gershoff. *Psychological Bulletin, 128*, 596-601.

Paulhaus, D. (1991). Measurement and control of response bias. In J. Robinson, P. Shaver, & L. Wrightsman, *Measures of personality and social psychological attitudes: Volume 1 of measures of social psychological attitudes*. San Diego, CA: Academic Press.

Pawson, R. (2000, July). *Does Megan's Law work? A theory-driven systematic review*. ESRC UK Centre for Evidence Based Policy and Practice. Queen Mary, University of London, UK.

Petrunik, M. (2003). The hare and the tortoise: Dangerousness and sex offender policy in the United States and Canada. *Canadian Journal of Criminology and Criminal Justice, 45(1)*.

Phillips, S. (2003, October). *Research overview: Sex offender treatment approaches and programs*. New Mexico Sentencing Commission. Retrieved January 1, 2005 from www.nmsc.state.nm.us.

Polermo, G. (2005, December). Prisonization and sexual offenders: A compounded problem. *International Journal of Offender Therapy and Comparative Criminology, 49(6)*, 611-613.

Pope, K., & Feldman-Summers, S. (1992). National survey of psychologists' sexual and physical abuse history and their evaluation of training and competence in these areas. *Professional Psychology: Research and Practice, 23(5)*, 353-361.

Preston, D. (2000). *Addressing treatment resistance in corrections* (p. 47). In Compendium 2000 on Effective Correctional Programming.

Prentky, R., Lee, A., Knight, R. & Cerce, D. (1997). Recidivism rates among child molesters and rapists: A methodological analysis. *Law and Human Behavior, 21*, 635-659.

Prochaska, J. (1991). Prescribing to the stage and level of phobic patients. *Psychotherapy: Theory, Research, Practice, Training, 28*, 463-468.

Prochaska, J. & DiClemente, C. (1982). Transtheoretical therapy: Towards a more integrative model of change. *Psychotherapy: Theory, Research and Practice, 19*, 276-288.

Prochaska, J. & DiClemente, C. (1992). The transtheoretical approach. In J. Norcross, & M. Goldfried (Eds.), *Handbook of psychotherapy integration*. New York: Basic Books.

Prochaska, J., DiClemente, C., & Norcross, J. (1992, September). In search of how people change: Applications to addictive behaviors. *American Psychologist, 47(9)*, 1102-1114.

Prochaska, J. & Norcross, J. (2001). Stages of change. *Psychotherapy: Theory, Research, Practice, Training, 38,* 443-448.

Prochaska, J., & Velicer, W. (1997). The transtheoretical model of health behavior change. *American Journal of Health Promotion, 12(1),* 38-48.

Radley, L. (2001, July). Attitudes towards sex offenders. *Forensic Update, 66.*

Rainn.org (2006). Retrieved from http://www.rainn.org/statistics/index.html?PHPSESSID=fa26e5b26dbboffef3cbbdbfe46ed892

Reiner, R. (2002). Media made criminality: The representation of crime in the mass media. In M. Maguire et al. (Eds.), *The Oxford handbook of criminology.* Oxford: Oxford University Press.

Reitan, R. & Wolfson, D. (1992). *The Halstead–Reitan Neuropsychological Test Battery: Theory and clinical interpretation (2nd ed.).* Tucson, AZ: Neuropsychology Press

Reynolds, M. (1999). *Crime and punishment in America: 1999.* National Center for Policy Analysis, Policy Backgrounder No.229. Retrieved from http://www.ncpa.org/studies/s229/s229.html

Rice, M., & Harris, G. (2003). The size and sign of treatment effects in sex offender therapy. In R. Prentky, E. Janus, & M. Seto (Eds.), *Sexually coercive behavior: Understanding and management* (pp. 428–440). New York: Annals of the New York Academy of Sciences.

Rice, M., Harris, G., & Cormier, C. (1992). An evaluation of a maximum-security therapeutic community for psychopaths and other mentally disordered offenders. *Law and Human Behavior, 16,* 399-412.

Roberts, D. (2002, January). Shorter term treatment of Borderline Personality Disorder: A developmental, self-, and object relations approach. *Psychoanalytic Psychology, 07369735, 17(1).*

Roberts, J. & White, N. (1986). Public estimates of recidivism rates: Consequences of a criminal stereotype. *Canadian Journal of Criminology, 28,* 229-241.

Robinson, P. (2001). *Punishing dangerousness: Cloaking preventative detention as criminal justice* (p. 132). University of Pennsylvania Law School, Scholarship at Penn Law. Hosted by The Berkeley Electronic Press.

Roger, D. (1995). Emotion control, coping strategies, and adaptive behavior. In C. Spielberger, I. Sarason, J. Brebner, E. Greenglass, & P. Laungani, *Stress and emotion: Anxiety, anger, and curiosity* (pp. 255-264). Philadelphia, PA: Taylor & Francis.

Rogers, C. (1951). *Client-centered therapy.* Boston: Houghton Mifflin.

Rogers, R., Bagby, R. & Dickens, S. (1998). *Structured Interview of Reported Symptoms (SIRS)*.

Rollnick, S., & Miller, W. (1991). *Motivational interviewing: Preparing people to change addictive behavior* (p. 348). New York: Guilford Press.

Rollnick, S., & Miller, W. (1995). What is motivational interviewing? *Behavioural and Cognitive Psychotherapy, 23(4)*, 325-334.

Rollnick, S., & Miller, W. (2002). *Motivational interviewing: Preparing people for change (2nd ed.)*, p. 428. New York: Guilford Press.

Ross, L. (1977). The intuitive psychologist and his shortcomings: Distortions in the attribution process. In L. Berkowitz (Ed.), *Advances in experimental social psychology* (Vol. 10). New York: Academic Press.

Rossi, J., Redding, C., Snow, M., Fava, J., Rossi, S., Velicer, W., Prochaska, J. & Diclemente, C. (1989). *Smoking habit strength during maintenance: A termination stage for smoking cessation?* Paper presented at the 97th annual meeting of the American Psychological Association.

Salvendy, J. (1999). Ethnocultural considerations in group psychotherapy. *International J. Group Psychotherapy 49(4)*, 429-464.

Schall v. Martin (1984). In A. Hess, & I. Weiner (1999), *The handbook of forensic psychology (2nd ed.)*, p. 756. Hoboken, NJ: John Wiley & Sons.

Schlank, A., & Shaw, T. (1997). Using pretreatment to increase admission in sex offenders. In B. Schwartz & H. Cellini (Eds.), *The sex offender: New insights, treatment innovations and legal developments* (Vol. II, pp. 5-1 – 5-16). Kingston, NJ: Civic Research Institute.

Schneider, S., & Wright, R. (2001, June). The FoSOD: A measurement tool for reconceptualizing the role of denial in child molesters. *Journal of Interpersonal Violence, 16(6)*, 545-564.

Schneider, S., & Wright, R. (2004, January). Understanding denial in sexual offenders: A review of cognitive and motivational processes to avoid responsibility. *Trauma, Violence, & Abuse, 5(1)*, 3-20.

Schoener, R. (1997). *Boundaries in professional relationships*. Presented to the Norwegian Psychological Association in Oslo, Norway 3-4, September 1997. Retrieved from http://www.advocateweb.org/HOPE/boundariesinrelationships.asp

Schram, D., & Milloy, C. (1995). *Community notification: A study of offender characteristics and recidivism*. Washington State Institute for Public Policy, 1995 October. #95-10-1101. Retrieved from http://www.wsipp.wa.gov/rptfiles/chrrec.pdf

Schwartz, B. (1988). *A practioner's guide to treating the incarcerated male sex offender: Breaking the cycle of sexual abuse.* Washington, DC: Department of Justice, National Institute of Corrections.

Scott, K. & Wolfe, D. (2003). Readiness to change as a predictor of outcome in batterer treatment. *Journal of Consulting and Clinical Psychology, 71(5),* 879-889.

Seager, J., Jellicoe, D., & Dhaliwal, G. (2004, October). Refusers, dropouts, and completers: Measuring sex offender treatment efficacy. *International Journal of Offender Therapy and Comparative Criminology, 48(5),* 600-612.

Seidman, B., Marshall, W., Hudson, S., & Robertson, P. (1994). An examination of intimacy and loneliness in sex offenders. *Journal of Interpersonal Violence, 9,* 518-534.

Selby, T. (2002). We need spouses!!! *Arizona ATSA Communicator, 5 (1).* Retrieved on June 9, 2006 from http://www.azatsa.org/old_newsletters/Mar2002.html

Severson, M. (1992, September). Redefining the boundaries of mental health services: A holistic approach to inmate mental health. *Federal Probation, 56(3),* 57-63.

Shelby, R., Stoddart, R, & Taylor, K. (2001). Factors contributing to levels of burnout among sex offender treatment providers. *Journal of Interpersonal Violence, 16,* 1205-1217.

Shelton, J., & Ackerman, J. (1974). *Homework in counseling and psychotherapy.* Springfield IL: Charles C. Thomas.

Simourd, L. (1997). *Staff attitudes towards inmates and correctional work: An exploration of the attitude-work outcome relationship.* Unpublished Doctoral dissertation. Carleton University: Ottawa, ON.

Singer, J. (1997). *Message in a bottle: Stories of men and addiction.* New York: Free Press.

Skeem, J., Monahan, J., & Mulvey, E. (2002). Psychopathy, treatment involvement, and subsequent violence among civil psychiatric patients. *Law and Human Behavior, 26,* 577-603.

Smith, K., Subich, L., & Kalodner, C. (1995, January). The transtheoretical model's stages and processes of change and their relation to premature termination. *Journal of Counseling Psychology, 42(1),* 34-39.

Smith, R. (2004). Understanding the influence of others: Changing evaluations of messages or messages under evaluation? Dissertation Abstracts International Section A: *Humanities & Social Sciences, 64(8-A)*, 2706.

Sprott, J. (2003). Are members of the public tough on crime?: The dimensions of public punitiveness. *Canadian Journal of Criminology and Criminal Justice. 45(2)*, 243-257.

Stalans, L. (1993). Citizens' crime stereotypes, biased recall, and punishment preferences in abstract cases: The educative role of interpersonal sources. *Law and Human Behavior, 17*, 451-470.

State of California, Department of Finance California Current Population Survey. (2004, March). *California Current Population Survey Report.* Sacramento, CA.

Steele, C. & Aronson, J. (1995, November). Stereotype threat and the intellectual test performance of African Americans. *Journal of Personality and Social Psychology, 69(5)*, 797-811.

Strean, H. (1985). *Psychoanalytic approaches to the resistant and difficult patient.* Bingington, NY: Haworth Press.

Tellier, C. & Serin, R. (2005). *The role of staff in effective program delivery.* Retrieved from http://www.csc-scc.gc.ca/text/rsrch/compendium/2000/chap_21_e.shtml

Tierney, D. & McCabe, M. (2002). Motivation for behavior change in sex offenders: A review of the literature. *Clinical Psychology Review, 22*, 113-129.

Tittle, C. (1995). *Control balance: Toward a general theory of deviance.* Boulder, CO: Westview.

Tombaugh, T. (1996). *TOMM: The Test of Memory Malingering (TOMM).* North Tonawanda, NY: Multi-Health Systems Inc.

Turkat D., & Meyer, V. (1982). The behavior analytic approach. In P. Wachtel (Ed.), *Resistance: Psyhcodynamic and behavioral approaches.* New York: Plenum.

Twenge, J., Baumeister, R., Tice, D., & Stucke, T. (2001). If you can't join them, beat them: Effects of social exclusion on aggressive behavior. *Journal of Personality and Social Psychology, 81*, 1058-1069.

Twenge, J., Catanese, K., & Baumeister, R. (2002). Social exclusion causes self-defeating behavior. *Journal of Personality and Social Psychology, 83*, 606-615.

Twenge, J., Catanese, K., & Baumeister, R. (2003). Social exclusion and the deconstructed state: Time perception, meaninglessness, lethargy, lack of emotion, and self-awareness. *Journal of Personality and Social Psychology, 85,* 409-423.

Twenge, J., Ciarocco, N., Cuervo, D., & Baumeister, R. (2003). *Social exclusion reduces prosocial behavior.* Unpublished manuscript.

Vohs, K., & Schmeichel, B. (2003). Self-regulation and the extended now: Controlling the self alters the subjective experience of time. *Journal of Personality and Social Psychology, 85,* 217–230.

Ward, T. (2002). Good lives and the rehabilitation of sex offenders: Promises and problems. *Aggression and Violent Behavior, 7,* 513-528.

Ward, T., Connolly, M., & McCormack, J. (1996). Social workers' attributions for sexual offending against children. *Journal of Child Sexual Abuse, 5(3),* 39-56.

Ward, T., Keenan, T., & Hudson, S. (2000). Understanding cognitive, affective, and intimacy deficits in sexual offenders: A developmental perspective. *Aggression and Violent Behavior, 5,* 41–62.

Ward, T., & Marshall, W. (2004, August). Good lives, aetiology and the rehabilitation of sex offenders: A bridging theory. *Journal of Sexual Aggression, 10(2), Special Issue: Treatment & Treatability* 153.

Ward, T., & Stewart, C. (2002). Good lives and the rehabilitation of sexual offenders. In T. Ward, D. Laws, & S. Hudson (Eds.), *Sexual deviance: Issues and controversies.* Thousand Oaks, CA: Sage.

Watzlawick, P., Weakland, J., & Fisch, R. (1974). *Change: Principles of problem formation and problem resolution* (p. 172). Oxford, England: W. W. Norton.

Wechsler, D. (1997). *Wechsler Adult Intelligence Scale—III.* New York: Psychological Corporation.

Weekes, J., Pelletier, G., & Beaudette, D. (1995). Correctional officers: How do they perceive sex offenders? *International Journal of Offender Therapy and Comparative Criminology, 39,* 55-61.

Widiger, T. & Corbit, E. (1997). Comorbidity of antisocial personality disorder with other personality disorders. In D. Stoff, J. Brieling & J. Masser (Eds.), *Handbook of antisocal behavior.* New York: Wiley.

Wierzbicki, M. & Pekarik, G. (1993). A meta-analysis of psychotherapy dropout. *Professional Psychology: Research and Practice, 24,* 190-195.

Wilkinson, G. (1993). *The Wide Range Achievement Test: 3. Administration Manual.* Wide Range, Wilmington, DE.

Williams, K. (2001). *Ostracism: The power of silence.* New York: Guilford Press.

Winograd, T., & Flores, F. (1987). Understanding computers and cognition: A new foundation for design. In J. Ford, L. Ford, & R. McNamara, Resistance and the background conversations of change. *Journal of Organizational Change Management, 15(2)*, 105-121.

Younglove, J. & Vitello, C. (2003). Community notification provisions of "Megan's Law" from a therapeutic jurisprudence perspective: A case study. *American Journal of Forensic Psychology, 21*, 25-38.

Zevitz, R. & Farkas, M. (2000). The impact of sex-offender community notification on parole/probation in Wisconsin. *International Journal of Offender Therapy and Comparative Criminology, 44*, 8-21.

Zgoba, K., Sager, W., & Witt, P. (2003). Evaluation of New Jersey's sex offender treatment program at the Adult Diagnostic and Treatment Center: Preliminary results. *Journal of Psychiatry and Law, 31*, 133–164.

Author Biographies

CHARLES A. FLINTON is a clinical and forensic psychologist who specializes in the assessment and treatment of violent and sexual offenders. He is co-chair of the San Francisco Sexual Offender Management Alliance, a multidisciplinary collaborative that investigates effective ways to manage and reduce sexual violence in the community. He is director of Sharper Future-Bay Area, a forensic mental health clinic that provides intensive research-based assessment and treatment services to manage, contain, and reduce anti-social, violent, and sexually abusive behavior. Dr. Flinton also maintains a private practice that focuses on the assessment and treatment of adults who have been victims of crime. He provides psychological assessments and expert testimony.

ROBERT SCHOLZ is a licensed Marriage and Family Therapist, who has extensive experience in assessing and treating sexually-reactive children, adolescent and adult sex offenders and victims of sexual abuse. Robert works at Pepperdine University's Student Counseling Center, and also serves as an adjunct faculty member in Pepperdine's Graduate School of Education and Psychology. In addition he continues to help agencies develop effective program models for managing sexual offenders in the community, and creates and conducts trainings nationally for professionals in the fields of mental health, higher education, and law enforcement.